Volunteer Vacations

Volunteer Vacations

Ninth Edition

Short-Term Adventures That Will Benefit You and Others

Bill McMillon, Doug Cutchins, and Anne Geissinger

CHICAGO
REVIEW
PRESS

Library of Congress Cataloging-in-Publication Data
McMillon, Bill, 1942–
    Volunteer vacations : short-term adventures that will benefit you and others / Bill McMillon, Doug Cutchins, and Anne Geissinger.—9th ed.
        p. cm.
    Includes bibliographical references and index.
    ISBN 1-55652-582-6
    1. Voluntarism—Directories. 2. Associations, institutions, etc.—Directories. 3. Vacations—Directories. I. Cutchins, Doug. II. Geissinger, Anne. III. Title.
    HN49.V64M35   2006
    302′.14—dc22   2005017925

Many of the personal vignettes included in this edition were provided courtesy of the sponsoring organizations and permissions are their responsibility.

The authors have made every effort to ensure that all the listing information is correct and current at the time of publication.

Cover and interior design: Rattray Design

Cover Photos: © Photo Disc, Inc.

For Emma and Bea

Contents

Foreword

Ed Asner

IT'S BEEN SAID that "man would rather spend himself for a cause than live idly in prosperity." I'm sure upon uttering that axiom in a group, you'd see everyone nodding wisely—agreeing that hard work for a cause is preferable to the good life unfulfilled. It's a noble thought during a philosophical discussion. When everyone's in accord on that point, pull out some airline tickets to Perryville, Arkansas, and ask who's willing to give up their Bermuda vacation in order to work with livestock. Any takers?

It's a hard sell. Public service is an antiquity in today's society. In the thirties the Civilian Conservation Corps instilled in the minds of young men and women the notion that national service is an obligation, indeed, a privilege: putting something back into the country in exchange for all the benefits derived from living in a free and democratic society. It was a wonderful setup and one that should have been perpetuated.

Since that time, however, our country's military bent has made national service an anathema—national service has come to mean the draft, the military, risk of life and limb on some foreign shore. Some states, to supplement low budget allocations, use public service as punishment for misdemeanors. In Oregon, for instance, DWI offenders can be seen picking up highway litter.

In short, the notion of a "volunteer vacation" sounds like a disciplinary measure akin to assigning extra household chores to a balky teenager.

Happily, there are people like Bill McMillon (along with the hundreds of people who have taken volunteer vacations) to set us straight: volunteering for a worthy cause can be fun, fulfilling, and an adventure you'll anticipate year after year. Maybe working with livestock isn't your thing, but there's plenty of variety: go on archaeological expeditions; assist with health care in remote villages; maintain trails in beautiful mountain climes; or build homes for the homeless. Some programs encourage you to bring the kids; some pay part of your expenses.

Best of all, you'll be helping people who need you. These days our local, state, and federal government budgets (and many government budgets around the world) have cut "people programs" in favor of big business and the military. More and more, our nation and our world must look to volunteers to fill the gaps that governments are unwilling or unable to fill—in health care, education, and programs for the disabled and underprivileged.

Read this book . . . try a volunteer vacation. The world will be a better place and so will you.

Preface

YOUR COMMUNITY IS growing. Whether or not you want it to, whether or not you are aware of it, the bounds of where you can go, what you can do, and who you can meet grow almost every day. As technology improves, communities and countries that were once geographically and culturally isolated are coming into close contact with other cities and nations. We recall walking into a village in the middle of the rainforest of Suriname, commenting on how remote the village was and how little contact it had with the outside world, and then noticing a Nike swoosh shaved into the back of a villager's haircut. That this icon of American corporate culture had made its way to a village that lacked roads, running water, and electricity demonstrated what we already knew but had forgotten: there are very few communities left on Earth that you can't reach, and we are all quickly becoming interconnected.

This process of globalization has had both positive and negative aspects. More people have access to better health care. More children are being educated. More communities are getting basic services, such as clean drinking water and electricity. But these same communities are under attack from outside influences both cultural and economic. Is it a good thing when a child learns to read . . . but not in the language of her parents? What happens to a rural family who finally gets electricity . . . but the husband has to work—and live—in the nearest city in order to afford it? And why do so many people around the world seem to love American products, sports, and popular culture, but profess a disdain for our country?

There are no easy answers to these questions. But, as the definition of your community changes and more people become your "neighbors," you have a level of responsibility to try to figure these and other questions out.

We would argue that volunteering is one of the best ways to start to find these answers. As a volunteer, you can begin to halt the tide of the nastier effects of globalization and instead promote the benefits of international understanding and cooperation. Through personal, one-on-one exchanges and dialogues, individuals around the world—including people from different communities in the United States—will better understand and appreciate the people in their national and global neighborhoods.

Why turn a vacation into a volunteer vacation? After researching this book, we're hard-pressed to see why you wouldn't! First, the opportunities presented here are amazing. We challenge you to read this book and not find organizations that make you want to get on the next plane to Nepal, France, or California. Second, your help is desperately needed. The 150 organizations listed in this book exist for a reason—there is a lot of need in the world, and the skills that you have can be put to tremendously good use in helping to fulfill that need.

We hope that you'll take advantage of the chance that you have to turn a regular vacation into an experience that will truly benefit yourself, others, and your community. Almost everyone who undertakes these projects returns home proclaiming that their vacations benefited them at least as much as they did the people being served. And when this happens to you, we hope that you'll then take the next step: share the experience. Invite friends over to see pictures of your trip. (They'll be more interested in these pictures than those of your last trip to the beach, we promise!) Talk to a group at your place of worship about what you did. Write a column for the local newspaper. Call an elementary school and ask if you can come speak to a class. The medium isn't crucial; what's most important is that you share the lessons that you learned with a wider audience, because then your understanding of a new community is spread to more people.

And keep your mind open—you may even find that a volunteer vacation is so rewarding that you want to take on a longer-term commitment. If that happens to you, turn to the end of this book—for the first time in the nine editions of *Volunteer Vacations*, we've included a special section with information on some long-term volunteer programs.

Volunteer vacations can change your perspective on the world, teach you new skills, and greatly affect the lives of others. We hope that you are inspired to make an ordinary vacation extraordinary, and to use your talents to better yourself and your community.

—Doug Cutchins and Anne Geissinger

Acknowledgments

for Doug Cutchins and Anne Geissinger

OUR FIRST THANKS have to go to the organizations that form the heart of this book. For months, they put up with our requests, reminders, and questions, spending time and resources on e-mails and phone conversations. Each one was truly outstanding to work with. In addition to their cooperation, though, we are also thankful for the work they do, the opportunities they create, and the assistance they give to volunteers, all in order to help improve the planet and the human condition.

We are also thankful for the help and cooperation of the authors and photographers whose work appears in this book to help bring volunteer experiences to life. None of these artists received compensation; all agreed to have their work published as a way to help promote the volunteer organizations and to inspire others. We are indebted to them for their kindness.

It is one of the greatest oddities of our lives that we have never met Bill McMillon, or even talked to him on the phone. Yet we are deeply impressed and inspired by the years of work he put into the early editions of this book. There are many people about whom we can say, "This book would not be what it is without you." Without Bill, though, this book simply would not be at all.

We sometimes wonder what we did to deserve the faith that our friends at Chicago Review Press have shown in us. Cynthia Sherry recruited us out of the blue to take over authorship of this book, and she has always been there to answer our questions and give helpful, timely advice. Lisa Rosenthal showed tremendous patience as she guided two newbie authors in their work on the previous edition, and this book would be much the worse without her editorial skills. Brooke Kush has been wonderfully supportive and encouraging as we sought to make significant changes to this edition. And while many first-time authors dream of having their book mentioned in O, The Oprah Magazine, our publicist for the eighth edition actually made it happen . . . along with mentions in USA Today, the Boston Globe, the television show Today, and many, many other publications and radio and TV shows. Elisabeth Malzahn, our publicist for this edition, has already created several new and creative contacts for us. We are indebted to them all.

On more personal notes, the experiences of our pastor, Bob Molsberry of the Grinnell United Church of Christ, made us realize that we needed to include information for volunteers with disabilities. Russell Osgood, president of Grinnell College, has given us several life-changing opportunities. Our parents—a professor, a human-services administrator, a social worker, and a nurse—provided us examples of life-long service. And we have to thank our two immensely talented assistants, Leighton Aycock and Lara Janson, whose research and editing skills vastly improved the quality of this book.

Lastly, Emma and Bea have been our sources of inspiration and joy, and they have put up with endless Big Adult Conversations about volunteer vacations. (You know your kids pay attention to what you do when your three-year-old announces, "I'm going upstairs to work on my book now.") We couldn't be more thankful for their presence in our lives, and it is to our girls that this book is dedicated.

Introduction

SEE A NEW part of the United States or a completely different country.

Help other people.

Relax.

Make new friends.

Learn a few words in a new language or resurrect the Spanish that you haven't used since high school.

Change your perspective on what it means to be rich or poor, first world or third world, developed or underdeveloped.

How? Take a volunteer vacation.

"A volunteer vacation?" you might say. "Doesn't that imply work? But isn't that why I'm going on vacation, to get away from work?"

Yes and no. If you take advantage of one of the opportunities in this book, you'll certainly work. You'll build bridges and blaze trails (both real and metaphorical), teach people how to read, take care of injured wildlife, play with kids in an orphanage, or do any of a hundred other jobs that will make a real difference on our planet. That's work—hard work.

But it's completely different than what most of us do to bring home a paycheck every week.

You'll be in a new place, surrounded by people you don't know. You'll be using parts of your brain and body that haven't gotten good workouts in years. You're likely to experience some kind of paradigm shift and to look at yourself, your country, or the world in a new way. Not only will you come home refreshed and rejuvenated, as you would after any vacation, but you'll also have the knowledge that you've made a difference in someone's life or in the world.

Sounds good—what's next?

There are two ways to go about using this guide. The first is to open it up and begin to dream, to allow yourself to exclaim, "That's it, honey—pack your bags for Croatia! I hear it's beautiful this time of year." If you're open to new places to go and things to do, this is the approach for you; start reading and dreaming. Some people, though, need to be a little more intentional in their planning. If you know that you want to go to Europe, for example, or that you really want to work with kids, or that you can't spend more than five hundred dollars, then you need to be more selective in your reading. Make good use of the indexes in the back of this book and frequently check the Web sites of the organizations you're considering, since information can and does change over time.

What This Guide Does and Doesn't Do

This is a resource guide; it is not a review book. We provide basic information about select organizations that we have carefully vetted and that we feel good about recommending in order to allow you to begin to make decisions about what organizations are right for you and the experience that you want to have. Given that well over a hundred organizations run thousands of programs in scores of countries, we wouldn't want to try and make a judgment call for you as an individual; what is perfect for some people is horrible for others. Instead, we give you excellent information that you need to know about these organizations so that you can begin to make an informed decision. In fact, if you compare this edition of *Volunteer Vacations* with past editions, you'll notice that we've undergone an important transition: instead of focusing on giving you a little bit of information on as many organizations as possible, we've been very selective and pared down the list, but have given you much more in-depth information about each organization. Even with this additional information, though, we hope that nobody goes on a volunteer vacation without first talking with a staff member of the organization and, if at all possible, with people who have volunteered with the organization in the past. Every organization's listing in this book has extensive contact information, including e-mail addresses and Web site URLs. Research and evaluate organizations the same way you would go about making any other decision about how to use your time and money. (Speaking of money, it's important for you to know that none of the organizations listed in this book had to pay anything to be included. This book is free publicity for them, and they deserve it. We hope that their inclusion in *Volunteer Vacations* helps them to recruit volunteers like you.)

We've given you another valuable tool to start with, in addition to this expanded information. Sprinkled throughout this book you'll find volunteer vignettes, stories written by past volunteers about their experiences with some of these organizations, as well as photos of volunteers in action. These more personal glimpses into the daily lives of volunteers will give you a better sense of what your experience might be like, and they can help you to imagine yourself in the volunteers' places.

One last tool that we would recommend you use when researching your volunteer vacation is NetAid's "Volunteer Guru," available free at www.netaid.org/go/guru-vol-vacation.html. "Volunteer Guru" won't tell you which of these organizations to sign up with, but it will give you some excellent questions to think about, and it may help you define what you want to get out of your volunteer experience.

How Do I Evaluate an Organization to See If It Is Right for Me?

Here are 10 questions you should get answers to before signing on with a volunteer organization.

1. Does the work involved mesh with what I want to do on my vacation? Will it allow me to develop or use skills that are important to me?
2. Will the project take me to a place that I want to go?

3. Do I have the same goals and values as those of the organization? (This is especially important for organizations that have overt political or religious goals; you don't want to end up promoting a cause, directly or indirectly, that you don't believe in.)
4. What do past volunteers say about their experiences with this organization?
5. What are living conditions at the site like?
6. What will my exact job responsibilities be? How much scut work (cooking, cleaning, filing, and so on) will I be expected to do? Keep in mind that someone has to do this work, and it is often divided among all of the employees and volunteers, from top to bottom.
7. How much does it cost to participate? What exactly is included in a program fee?
8. When does the project take place, how long does it last, and does it fit with my schedule?
9. Will I be working in a group? What is the profile of the average volunteer? Age range? What are the motivations of the other people in the group?
10. What kind of training or orientation is offered? (This is crucial for international organizations, where you might be working in a culture very different from your own.)

Always check the U.S. State Department's lists of countries under travel warnings and public announcements to better understand the security situation in the places that you might be traveling. We would strongly discourage anyone from volunteering in a country that is under a travel warning, and we would caution you to do more research before volunteering in a country under a public announcement.

Getting the Most Out of This Book

Each listing in this book contains up to 12 sections:
1. General contact information, including (as available) postal address, phone and fax numbers, e-mail addresses, and Web site URLs.

2. *Project Type:* We asked each organization to place itself among approximately 20 categories, so that you can tell at a glance what an organization does, broadly speaking. You can use this section (in addition to the indexes) if you are glancing casually through the book looking for, say, opportunities to volunteer with orphans, or another specific type of opportunity.

3. *Mission Statement Excerpt:* This gives you an idea of how each organization defines itself.

4. *Year Founded* and 5. *Number of Volunteers Last Year:* Though numbers can certainly be misleading, you can get a sense of the scope of an organization's work by looking at how long it has been in existence and how many people they are used to serving. That said, don't reject small or recently founded organizations out of hand; some of our favorite organizations are young, but they have passionate, go-getter administrators behind them.

6. *Funding Sources:* To borrow the old dictum from the movie *All the President's Men*, "Follow the money." This is important, as knowing where an organization's funding comes from helps you know more about its reason for being and who supports its work. Luckily, most organizations are very up-front about this information; they don't want disaffected volunteers who don't share their mission.

7. *The Work They Do:* Here's where we get into the meat of the description. This part describes in broad terms what the work of the organization is, as well as how volunteers help with that work. Look for specifics on volunteer jobs and examples of how you'll be spending your time with this organization.

8. *Project Location:* This can range from incredibly specific for some of our smaller organizations, to "worldwide" for organizations that operate a large number of ever-changing global operations. This section also includes details, as we know them, about lodging accommodations so that you can be sure you'll be comfortable with the arrangements.

9. *Time Line:* Information here includes when applications are accepted, when volunteer positions begin, and how long positions last (minimum, maximum, and average time lengths).
10. *Cost:* Yes, virtually all of these opportunities cost money (the few that do not usually require very specialized skills or a long-term commitment). This section tries to detail as best it can what those costs will be, as well as what is included in the organizations' fees and what additional expenses you will need to bear. Pay close attention to insurance coverage; if the organization does not provide insurance, check with your insurance provider before departure to make sure that you will be covered overseas. If not, please consider purchasing a short-term supplemental policy.
11. *Getting Started:* This section gives information about how to best contact the organization or obtain an application, as well as details on training and orientation programs.
12. *Needed Skills and Specific Populations:* If an organization requires that you have mastered specific skills before volunteering with them, that information will be noted here. Also found here is information regarding age minimums and maximums, as well as information for volunteers with disabilities.

Another new aspect of this edition is our short section on long-term volunteer opportunities. We hope that you will seriously consider these as well as, or perhaps after undertaking, a shorter-term volunteer vacation. The opportunities listed here all have the added bonus of providing funding for your experience; you won't have to foot the bill for one of these long-term stints. Taking a volunteer vacation will change your perspective; a long-term volunteer commitment will change your life.

Expectations: What Is Reasonable and What Is Unreasonable

Be nice to the organizations that offer these services. Remember that many of them operate on extremely lean budgets with underpaid and overworked staff. Please don't request information from a group unless you are seriously considering volunteering with them. Make ample use of the vast resources of the Internet—all of the organizations in this book have Web sites that you can access for basic information. Be polite and understand that your request is one of many that the organization is dealing with at any given time. Act as a partner, not as a consumer. Consider sending a small check along with each request for information, and if the organization is based overseas, send them an international reply coupon (available at your local post office) to help defray the cost of postage. Remember: the more money these organizations spend on administration, the less they have to spend on what they're working to achieve.

That said, organizations have a responsibility to their volunteers as well. Organizations should live up to their promises and advertising. They should answer your questions fully, honestly, and in a timely manner. To some extent, there is also the aspect that "you get what you pay for." In other words, if you are paying thousands of dollars for an experience, you have a right (within limits) to expect more service than someone whose experience is wholly sponsored by the organization.

Last, don't expect to change the world overnight. Have reasonable expectations of the organization, yourself, and your ability to create long-term change. Recognize that the work you do is important, but that it is just one piece of the larger puzzle of improving global conditions. Let the process, not the product, be your measure of success.

ACDI/VOCA

50 F Street NW, Suite 1100
Washington, DC 20001
(800) 929-8622; Fax: (202) 626-8726
E-mail: volunteer@acdivoca.org
Web site: www.acdivoca.org

Project Type: Agriculture; Community Development; Economic Development; Natural Conservation (Land); Natural Conservation (Sea); Professional/Technical Assistance; Rural Development; Scientific Research; Women's Issues; Youth

Mission Statement Excerpt: "ACDI/VOCA's worldwide mission is to promote economic opportunities for cooperatives, businesses, and communities through the innovative application of sound business practices."

Year Founded: 1963

Number of Volunteers Last Year: More than 400

Funding Sources: ACDI/VOCA receives government funding from the U.S. Agency for International Development and the U.S. Department of Agriculture, as well as gifts, grants, and donations from private sources.

The Work They Do: ACDI/VOCA creates volunteer opportunities for experts in agriculture, business, finance, cooperative development, and natural resource management. ACDI/VOCA volunteers are typically mid-career professionals with significant experience who provide expertise to host organizations in economically developing countries. Many volunteers are members of teams, and many conduct repeat assignments.

Project Location: Projects are located around the world, including the Middle East, Africa, Latin America, Eastern Europe and the former Soviet Union, and Southeast Asia. Accommodations vary from country to country; in urban areas, volunteers are typically housed in moderate-quality hotels, guesthouses, or apartments that the project leases.

In rural areas, volunteers may be asked to stay with the host or in more rustic settings.

Time Line: Volunteers are placed year-round. Placements are typically two to six weeks in length.

Cost: ACDI/VOCA pays for all assignment-related expenses, including round-trip coach airfare, passport, visas, lodging, meals and incidentals, project materials, required immunizations, emergency medical evacuation, and supplemental health insurance.

Getting Started: Apply via the ACDI/VOCA Web site.

Needed Skills and Specific Populations: ACDI/VOCA volunteers are typically mid-career and senior professionals with a minimum of 15 years of experience in one of the following areas: accounting; agricultural extension and education; baking; banking and finance; business management; community development; cooperative and association development; domestic and international marketing; enterprise development; entrepreneurship; farm management; food and meat processing; food storage and handling; fruit, vegetable, and plant production and protection; grain and commodity inspection and storage, information technology and e-commerce; livestock production and disease control; manufacturing; natural resources management and ecotourism; policy reform; post-harvest handling; rural credit; sustainable agriculture; trade associations; and training of trainers. Many retired experts have volunteered with ACDI/VOCA. Because some work sites are in rural areas in economically developing countries, ACDI/VOCA may have problems accommodating volunteers with disabilities. Some programs require U.S. citizenship.

African Conservation Experience (ACE)

P.O. Box 28, Ottery St Mary
Devon, EX11 1ZN
United Kingdom
+ (0870) 241 5816; Fax: + (0870) 241 5816
E-mail: info@conservationafrica.net
Web site: www.conservationafrica.net

Project Type: Community Development; Natural Conservation
(Land); Natural Conservation (Sea); Scientific Research;
Trail Building/Maintenance

Year Founded: 1999

Number of Volunteers Last Year: 250

Funding Sources: No outside funding; ACE is self-funded

The Work They Do: ACE arranges opportunities for volunteers
to carry out conservation work on game and nature
reserves in southern Africa. ACE volunteers work in close
association with biologists, conservationists, wildlife veterinarians, and nature reserve managers on a variety of projects, including animal capture for tagging and relocation,
behavioral studies on lions and hyenas, counting and monitoring animals, veterinary work, animal rehabilitation, and
whale and dolphin research. Volunteers sleep in the African
bush and have the opportunity to learn firsthand how
game and nature reserves are run and maintained.

Project Location: Volunteers are placed in South Africa, Zimbabwe, and Botswana, where they live and work within
game and nature parks. Accommodation and food are provided, usually in shared dormitories, each with its own
bathing and kitchen facilities. Volunteers generally share
cooking and kitchen responsibilities.

Time Line: Projects are available throughout the year. Volunteers can work with ACE for four to twelve weeks at a
time.

Cost: Program fees run from £2,790 for four weeks up to
£4,000 for twelve weeks. The program fee covers international flights, accommodation, transfers, and all meals.

Travel insurance is compulsory but is not included in the placement cost.

Getting Started: Contact ACE to request further information and an application. No orientation is provided.

Needed Skills and Specific Populations: Volunteers should be enthusiastic about wildlife conservation and must be at least 17 years old (there is no maximum age limit). Prospective volunteers with disabilities will be assessed on a case-by-case basis to determine the feasibility of volunteering with ACE.

African Conservation Trust (ACT)

P.O. Box 310
Link Hills 3652
South Africa
+ 27 31-2016180
E-mail: info@projectafrica.com
Web site: www.projectafrica.com

Project Type: Archaeology; Community Development; Historic
Preservation; Natural Conservation (Land); Scientific Research

Mission Statement Excerpt: "The mission of the African Conservation Trust (ACT) is to provide a means for conservation projects to become self-funding through active
participation by the public. This gives ordinary people a
chance to make a positive and real contribution to environmental conservation by funding and participating in the
research effort as volunteers."

Year Founded: 2000

Number of Volunteers Last Year: 53

Funding Sources: None; self-funded through program fees and
contracts with other organizations

The Work They Do: Most of ACT's programs involve long-term
natural conservation or historic preservation efforts such as a
hippo project on Lake Malawi, a community game farm project in Botswana, and a rock art mapping project in South
Africa. Examples of specific work carried out by volunteers
include radio tracking of various species of African mammals,
sand trapping at holes dug under the perimeter fence to monitor entry and exit species and numbers, conducting monthly
game counts at water holes and perhaps walking transects,
clearing the fence line of vegetation and eradicating alien
invasive plants on the farm, exploring the Ukhalhamba-Drak-
ensberg Park in South Africa for new unrecorded rock art
painting and archaeological sites of the indigenous San people, or conducting a hippo census on Lake Malawi by boat.

Project Location: Projects are carried out in the sub-Saharan countries of South Africa, Botswana, and Malawi. Conditions vary by location. In South Africa, volunteers are based in the mountains at an extensive base camp. Volunteers in Botswana camp in the Kalahari Desert, which can be very hot in summer but can freeze at night in winter. The roughest conditions may be found in Malawi, where volunteers camp in expedition conditions. Volunteers usually provide their own camping gear.

Time Line: Volunteers are accepted in South Africa and Botswana year-round; they are only accepted at specific times, usually during June, for work in Malawi. Volunteers can commit to as little as a two-week period to as much as a one-year experience; the average stay is about four weeks.

Cost: ACT's program fee is $450 per month except for the hippo project in Malawi, which is more expensive and which will be priced closer to the project time. The program fee includes pick-up from and drop-off at the airport nearest the site, all in-country, project-related transport, accommodation, food, and training. Air transportation to and from the country involved (as well as to and from the airport nearest the project site) are not included in the program fee.

Getting Started: Prospective volunteers should contact ACT via e-mail or the organization's Web site. ACT will provide orientation and training if necessary. For example, in Botswana, a tracking course is given by a local Bushman tracker and is followed up by in-field experience and testing that results in a certificate.

Needed Skills and Specific Populations: In South Africa the work is very physical and includes working and walking on steep slopes, so volunteers must have hiking or backpacking experience. Volunteers must be at least 18 years old; there is no maximum age limit. ACT cannot accommodate volunteers with disabilities.

Alliance Abroad (AA)

1221 South Mopac Expressway, #250
Austin, TX 78746
(512) 457-8062; Fax: (413) 460-3502
E-mail: outbound@allianceabroad.com
Web site: www.allianceabroad.com

Project Type: Administrative; Archaeology; Community Development; Construction; Economic Development; Education; Medical/Health; Natural Conservation (Land); Orphans; Trail Building/Maintenance; Women's Issues

Mission Statement Excerpt: "We strive to provide diverse cultural exchange programs to participants around the world."

Year Founded: 1992

Number of Volunteers Last Year: 185

Funding Sources: None; AA is self-funded

The Work They Do: AA offers a variety of volunteer projects tailored to the wishes of the individual volunteer. Volunteers can work on a variety of projects such as teaching English, environmental conservation, helping to save sea turtles, working at orphanages, working in hospitals, working at an archaeological dig, working with communities, and others. AA claims that it can "provide a project for anyone's interests."

Project Location: Volunteers are placed in Argentina, Brazil, Costa Rica, Ecuador, Peru, and Spain. Accommodations and meals vary by work site, but in most cases volunteers are provided a home stay and food.

Time Line: Volunteers are accepted year-round for a minimum of two weeks and a maximum of twelve months.

Cost: Program fees range from $850 to $3,000. Fees include a pre-departure and post-arrival orientation, volunteer placement, airport transfer in the host country, accommodation, all meals, and insurance. Volunteers must pay for their own airfare.

Getting Started: Prospective volunteers should download an application from the AA Web site, complete it, and send it to AA by postal mail. Orientation is provided both before departure and after arrival, but no training is offered.

Needed Skills and Specific Populations: Volunteers must be at least 18 years old, and senior volunteers are welcomed. Most volunteer sites cannot accommodate volunteers with disabilities. Volunteers from outside the United States are welcomed as long as a visa for the host country can be obtained.

Amazon-Africa Aid (AAA)

P.O. Box 7776
Ann Arbor, MI 48107
(734) 769-5778; Fax: (734) 769-5779
E-mail: info@amazonafrica.org
Web site: www.amazonafrica.org

Project Type: Medical/Health
Mission Statement Excerpt: "Amazon-Africa Aid is dedicated
to helping people today and preventing suffering
tomorrow."
Year Founded: 1999
Number of Volunteers Last Year: 24
Funding Sources: USAID, foundations, corporations, and
individuals
The Work They Do: In conjunction with a partner organization, the Fundação Esperança, AAA operates a medical and
a dental clinic in the Brazilian Amazon. The medical clinic
provides quality service to patients, who pay only what
they are able to afford. It also serves as the referral center
for primary care programs, and it offers general medical,
pediatric, cardiology, and gastroenterology services. At the
dental clinic, volunteer dentists join with local dentists and
hygienists to provide quality care to the region's poor people. Services include restoration, root canal, and X-ray. In
addition, the dental clinic performs thousands of prophy-
lactic procedures, including cleaning and application of
fluoride and sealants. AAA only accepts board-certified
physicians and dentists as volunteers, who see patients and
work with local medical and dental students.
Project Location: AAA's clinic is located in Santarém, Brazil,
500 miles upriver from the mouth of the Amazon. Dental
volunteers provide general dental care to patients in the
six-chair, air-conditioned dental clinic. The clinic is
equipped with hydraulic chairs and Adec front delivery
units. The units have air, water, suction, one high-speed
drill, and one low-speed drill. Trained Brazilian hygienists

9

and assistants, many of whom speak English, help the volunteers. Physicians work in the air-conditioned medical clinic, but they may also have the opportunity to travel to rural villages to provide care. Volunteers stay in AAA's dormitory. There are ten rooms, with a bathroom shared between every two rooms.

Time Line: Volunteers are accepted year-round. Volunteers must stay at least two weeks and not more than two months, with the average volunteer staying one month.

Cost: There is no program fee to volunteer with AAA, but a $20-per-day donation is requested to help cover the cost of room and board. Volunteers must provide their own airfare to Brazil. Average total expenses range from $1,200 to $2,000 per volunteer stay.

Getting Started: Prospective volunteers should mail paper copies of their CV, diploma, licenses, and passport. Volunteers are provided a volunteer handbook and an on-site orientation.

Needed Skills and Specific Populations: AAA volunteers must have an M.D., D.D.S., or D.M.D. and a current license. Unfortunately, AAA does not offer volunteer opportunities for nurses, students, or other health care professionals. Senior volunteers and volunteers with disabilities are welcome to volunteer with AAA.

Ambassadors for Children (AFC)

3620 North Washington Boulevard
Indianapolis, IN 46205
(317) 536-0250; Fax: (317) 536-0258
E-mail: info@ambassadorsforchildren.org
Web site: www.ambassadorsforchildren.org

Project Type: Construction; Human Rights; Medical/Health; Orphans; Social Justice; Youth

Mission Statement Excerpt: "Ambassadors for Children (AFC) seeks to better the lives of children around the world who live, study, and play in impoverished communities, while offering volunteers a life-changing experience."

Year Founded: 1989

Number of Volunteers Last Year: Approximately 500

Funding Sources: Private donors and religious organizations

The Work They Do: AFC trips provide hands-on interaction with disadvantaged children around the world. Examples of volunteer work include partnering with Habitat for Humanity on home construction projects, setting up dental and medical missions or school lunch programs, building playgrounds, and painting classrooms. An important aspect of AFC's humanitarian trips is the delivery of specifically requested items to the children in each destination, in addition to donations of medicines, medical equipment, food, clothing, hygiene items, school supplies, and toys. Compared to many other organizations, AFC places a greater emphasis on the "vacation" part of this experience, and volunteers are able to have a relaxing vacation while experiencing the culture and customs of the area.

Project Location: AFC has operated volunteer programs in Mexico, Guatemala, Cuba, the Dominican Republic, Kenya, Ecuador, Peru, Brazil, Vietnam, Belize, and Serbia, and on Native American reservations in the United States. AFC volunteers often stay in a resort or destination hotel.

Time Line: AFC operates at least one trip almost every month of the year, and it usually offers more than twenty volunteer programs per year. Trips vary in length from three days to two weeks, with most falling on the shorter end of that spectrum.

Cost: Program fees can be as low as $400 for domestic programs that do not require transportation to as much as $2,500 for international programs. What is included in the program fee varies by project; these details are provided on AFC's Web site. AFC has fund-raisers throughout the year to cover its administrative costs, so virtually all program fees are used to offset the program costs.

Getting Started: Prospective volunteers should contact AFC via e-mail. AFC offers the opportunity to meet with its volunteer mission coordinators in Indianapolis before departure to help pack supplies and review the work that the volunteer group will be doing.

Needed Skills and Specific Populations: No specific skills are required, but AFC always needs more teachers, doctors, dentists, carpenters, and other skilled professionals. There is no minimum age limit, but volunteers under age 18 must be accompanied by an adult. Senior volunteers are welcomed. Volunteers with disabilities are also welcomed, provided that they are able to get into a truck or van.

The Other Cancún

❖ By Micki Wanzer ❖

Ambassadors for Children (AFC)

In October 2004 I had the opportunity to travel with Ambassadors for Children (AFC) to Cancún, Mexico, to visit several orphanages and schools in the areas outside of the Cancún Hotel Zone. Away from the lights, hotels, restaurants, and market shops, Cancún has a different face. This Cancún is not a vacationer's paradise of warm, sandy beaches and bright lights. This Cancún struggles with a depressed economy, poverty, and children who fend for themselves, don't know where their next meal is coming from, and are thankful for anyone who offers a warm smile and a hand to hold. The bright lights in this otherwise oppressive area are the orphanages and schools that we were privileged to visit.

The people who run the Casa Esperanza Orphanage are warm and caring. The children are happy, well fed, clothed, and educated on very little money and resources. They need so much and demand so little. Sewing machines donated by AFC are used to teach the children to make clothing, curtains, and tablecloths. Donated secondhand computers are used to teach basic computer skills. Our volunteer travelers brought piñatas to the children, which were a big hit. What was a big hit as well were the hugs and smiles from volunteers and the Polaroid pictures that each child could keep for themselves to remember the day. When Enrique Esquella School was started, children initially attended because they were given breakfast if they came to school for the day. AFC has helped to build a playground, donated soccer and sporting equipment, provided hygiene kits with possibly the first toothbrush a child has ever had, and donated school supplies and backpacks for the children and teaching aids for the teachers. Doctors and dentists have provided much-needed medical and dental care as well. I loved my visit to the "other" Cancún. The children were wonderful. They are beautiful and happy, and warmly welcome everyone who visits. They appreciate even the smallest expression of affection. They demand little and give so much.

I became involved with AFC because I wanted to give back some of what I have been blessed with in my life. My expectations as a volunteer were far surpassed by the actual experience. Children are the same everywhere. They smile, they love, they cry, they laugh, and they accept anyone who reaches out to take their hand. I wish everyone the joy of experiencing the "other" Cancún. It will change your ideas of how a vacation should look. You will like the change—I promise.

American Hiking Society (AHS)

1422 Fenwick Lane
Silver Spring, MD 20910
(301) 565-6704; Fax: (301) 565-6714
E-mail: volunteer@americanhiking.org
Web site: www.americanhiking.org

Project Type: Natural Conservation (Land); Trail
Building/Maintenance
Mission Statement Excerpt: "As the national voice for America's hikers, American Hiking Society promotes and protects foot trails and the hiking experience."
Year Founded: 1976
Number of Volunteers Last Year: 730
Funding Sources: Government, private, and corporate donors
The Work They Do: AHS protects and conserves trails through its National Trails Fund, supporting the volunteer-based organizations that construct and maintain trails. It recruits and deploys volunteer trail-maintenance crews all across America to repair trails and construct new ones.
Project Location: AHS has volunteer projects in 29 states, including Alaska and Hawaii. In some cases, food is provided by the host; in others, volunteers receive a daily stipend for food purchases and are reimbursed at the end of the project. Lodging is normally a tent site in either a campground or a backcountry location. Participants must provide their own tents, sleeping bags, pads, and all personal gear. AHS does have a few projects that feature cabin accommodations.
Time Line: AHS's volunteer projects are available from early January through the first week in November. Most of its projects are one week in length, but it occasionally has two-week projects.
Cost: Volunteers must first join AHS at a cost of $25 per year, then pay a $95 program fee per project. Food and lodging is provided, but volunteers must pay their own travel expenses.

Getting Started: Prospective volunteers can download a volunteer schedule from the AHS Web site, or they can call to request a printed version of the schedule. The host of each project provides on-site training.

Needed Skills and Specific Populations: Previous trail-building experience is not necessary, but volunteers do need to be in good physical condition. Volunteers must be at least 18 years old, but there is no maximum age limit, and a large percentage of AHS's trail volunteers are retirees. Prospective volunteers with disabilities will be considered on a case-by-case basis; acceptance depends on their specific disabilities and the specific projects they wish to work on.

It Is Beauty That Transforms the Soul

By Audrey Peterman

American Hiking Society (AHS)

Last spring we were invited to spend the Fourth of July kicking off a week-long American Hiking Society (AHS) Volunteer Vacation in beautiful Mount Rogers National Recreation Area, near Marion, Virginia. My husband and I drove the six hours up from Atlanta, anticipating a full week in the forest with volunteers who are making an effort to educate Americans about our public lands and the opportunities they provide. We finally turned off the busy highways onto a two-lane road that was forested on both sides, a canopy of green above us, and a picturesque stream running alongside. Ten miles later we arrived at the work site; our blood pressure already had dropped. What a great way to start the week!

The rest of the team had already arrived and included our AHS coordinator, a young French woman, a retired Federal Aviation administrator, a teacher, a retired nurse, and an engineer. We arrived from Atlanta, Philadelphia, Ohio, North Carolina, West Virginia, and Virginia. From the first moment to the last, we bonded like far-flung relatives who had eagerly anticipated coming together. Our delight grew over a week in which we:

- Became fast friends with each other.
- Cleared brush, dug postholes, fetched water from the river, mixed cement, and extended the rails on three bridges across an old railroad track, above a rushing river, along banks laden with ripe berries.

- Were thanked profusely by many people riding their bikes on the trail. Interestingly, we saw every age represented among the cyclists, but only two people of color in more than 1,000.
- Broke spontaneously into digging songs, singing "We've Been Working on the Railroad" followed by such classics as "Amazing Grace."
- Prepared meals together in the commercial-grade kitchen, including cultural specialties such as rice and beans with jerk chicken, a semi-vegetarian spread that included salmon, and fresh-baked brownies. We ate together in the communal dining room, with much joking, laughter, and shoulder-to-shoulder fellowship.
- Slept three to a cabin with single beds; shared a bathroom with four stalls, two showers, and laundry facilities.
- Built campfires and sat around at night talking, and watching fireflies and stars, with s'mores and popcorn as snacks.
- Watched a hummingbird go to and from its cleverly camouflaged nest right over the trail to our cabins.
- Hiked part of the Appalachian Trail across fields of wild ponies with foals, past rhododendron bushes and enjoying views for hundreds of miles, to the top of Mount Rogers, where we were enfolded in the heart of the forest.
- Left on Friday and Saturday with plans to visit new friends, knowing we could always have our memories of this week of work together.

I hope this brief account has sparked your desire to join a similar trip in the future. American Hiking Society is eager to get more Americans of color participating in Volunteer Vacations. The Forest Service, which partnered with American Hiking Society to serve as hosts and provide our food, instruction, and tools, is also eager to involve more people of color in its work.

As the old saying goes, "It is beauty that transforms the soul." You can experience beauty lavishly in the great outdoors!

American Jewish World Service (AJWS)

45 West 36th Street, 10th Floor
New York, NY 10018
(800) 889-7146; Fax: (212) 736-3463
E-mail: volunteer@ajws.org
Web site: www.ajws.org

Project Type: Agriculture; Community Development; Construction; Economic Development; Education; Human Rights; Legal; Medical/Health; Orphans; Professional/Technical Assistance; Rural Development; Social Justice; Women's Issues; Youth

Mission Statement Excerpt: "AJWS [was] founded . . . to help alleviate poverty, hunger, and disease among the people of the world regardless of race, religion, or nationality. It breathes life into Judaism's imperative to pursue justice and helps American Jews act upon a deeply felt obligation to improve the chances for survival, economic independence, and human dignity for all people."

Year Founded: 1985

Number of Volunteers Last Year: 80

Funding Sources: Private donors

The Work They Do: AJWS places Jewish professionals with grassroots organizations in Africa, the Americas, and Asia to provide training to nonprofit organizations. AJWS volunteers are placed as consultants to train specific staff members in their personal areas of expertise. By focusing on transferring skills, AJWS helps these nonprofit organizations to build their capacities, promote sustainable development, and achieve their overall missions. Volunteer placements are based on requests for volunteers from nonprofit organizations and each volunteer's professional background. Volunteers work in their areas of expertise; general areas of work include organizational development and strategic planning, fundraising, computer technology, small business, microfinance, health care, public health and

19

HIV/AIDS, mental health, social work and community organizing, education, and sustainable agriculture. Each work placement is developed individually.

Project Location: Volunteers are placed in Africa (Uganda, Ghana, South Africa, and Zambia), the Americas (Mexico, Guatemala, Honduras, Nicaragua, El Salvador, Peru, and the Dominican Republic), Asia (Thailand and India), and the former Soviet states of Russia and the Ukraine. Living and work conditions vary with each placement. In rural areas, conditions are very rustic, and often there is no running water or electricity. In urban areas, volunteers will have running water and electricity, but there are other concerns, such as overcrowding, heat, and pollution. The volunteer's host agency is responsible for arranging housing for the volunteer. Some volunteers live in guesthouses or inexpensive hotels or rent other appropriate housing for the length of their stay.

Time Line: Volunteers are accepted throughout the year, and they must commit to a minimum of two months. The average AJWS volunteer stays for three months.

Cost: There is no program fee, but the cost of the volunteer experience is split between AJWS and the volunteer. AJWS pays for airfare and emergency evacuation insurance, and it may provide a cost-of-living stipend. Volunteers pay for housing, food, visa fees, and vaccinations.

Getting Started: Prospective volunteers should download an application from AJWS's Web site or request one by e-mail. Orientation is done informally by AJWS staff.

Needed Skills and Specific Populations: There is no minimum age to participate, but AJWS volunteers should have at least several years of professional experience. Senior volunteers are welcomed. Volunteers with disabilities are welcomed, though all volunteers must be able to manage the challenges of living in an economically developing country for an extended period of time. Volunteers must be Jewish or part of an interfaith couple.

AmeriSpan

117 South 17th Street, Suite 1401
Philadelphia, PA 19103
(800) 879-6640 or (215) 751-1100
Fax: (215) 751-1986
E-mail: info@amerispan.com
Web site: www.amerispan.com

Project Type: Administrative; Community Development; Developmental Disabilities; Education; Medical/Health; Natural Conservation (Land); Orphans; Trail Building/Maintenance

Mission Statement Excerpt: "AmeriSpan . . . aims to facilitate second-language acquisition combined with temporary volunteer opportunities throughout Latin America."

Year Founded: 1993

Number of Volunteers Last Year: More than 300

Funding Sources: None; self-funded

The Work They Do: AmeriSpan represents more than 165 different host organizations in Latin America. Most of these organizations are small, local, nonprofit initiatives, but some, such as Common Hope and Habitat for Humanity, are worldwide organizations. Others, particularly those that host internship opportunities in Argentina, are for-profit organizations. Volunteer work varies depending on the host organizations, but it can range from highly professional projects to caring for orphans, and from teaching English to trail maintenance. Customized internship and volunteer placements are available.

Project Location: AmeriSpan offers volunteer sites throughout Latin America. The work site is most often a direct reflection of the type of volunteer work and the economic development of the host country. For example, volunteers at an under-funded orphanage in Bolivia should expect extremely basic living and work conditions and little supervision due to a lack of staffing. Conversely, a volunteer at a law firm in Buenos Aires will find work conditions similar to those in the United States. Volunteers stay with host families during the initial language part of the program, which lasts for two to six weeks, then stay in lodging just for volunteers, with shared rooms (two people per room), and shared kitchen facilities during the volunteer experience.

Time Line: Volunteers are accepted year-round, but only on the first Monday of every month. Volunteers must commit to a four-week volunteer experience plus a two- to six-week language training program. The average volunteer stays for an eight-week volunteer stint, plus two weeks of language training. There is no limit to how long one may volunteer with AmeriSpan.

Cost: Program fees range from $350 to $3,500, depending on location, project, and length of the volunteer experience. Fees include language instruction, lodging, full or partial board, and emergency medical service. Volunteers must provide for their own airfare, in-country transportation, and meals while at the volunteer placement. AmeriSpan makes direct donations to host organizations, including more than $250,000 worth of medical supplies reaching needy communities in Latin America in a single year.

Getting Started: AmeriSpan's application process includes an application, essay, resume, two reference letters, and a telephone interview. AmeriSpan's partner organizations conduct an in-country volunteer meeting before the work starts, covering details of the organization, the volunteers' duties, and cultural issues. If the placement is close to the language school, the volunteer coordinator will visit the placement with the volunteer before starting work. The training a volunteer receives at the placement varies by organization.

Needed Skills and Specific Populations: Some host organizations require proficiency in Spanish or Portuguese; some require education or experience related to the volunteer placement. Most host organizations will accept volunteers who are at least 18 years old, but some have a minimum age of 21 or 23. Senior volunteers are "absolutely" wel-

comed by AmeriSpan. Volunteers with disabilities are welcomed, but prospective volunteers should contact
AmeriSpan before applying, as not all countries and projects can make accommodations for them.

Amigos de las Américas

5618 Star Lane
Houston, TX 77057
(800) 231-7796; Fax: (713) 782-9267
E-mail: info@amigoslink.org
Web site: www.amigoslink.org

Project Type: Community Development; Education;
Medical/Health; Rural Development; Youth
Mission Statement Excerpt: "Amigos de las Americas builds
partnerships to empower young leaders, advance community development, and strengthen multicultural understanding in the Americas."
Year Founded: 1965
Number of Volunteers last year: 734
Funding Sources Include: Amigos receives donations from corporations, foundations, and individuals.
The Work They Do: Amigos de las Americas provides students
an opportunity to experience hands-on cross-cultural
understanding and leadership by volunteering in teams of
two or three as public health, education, and community
development workers in rural communities or semi-urban
neighborhoods. Collaborating with local sponsoring agencies and community members, volunteers usually help identify local resources, then implement community
improvement projects in their community's schools, health
clinics, or residences. Programs include, but are not limited
to community based initiatives, sanitation and development, environmental education, family nutrition, health
education, school renovations, home improvement, youth
group formation and collaboration, education, and leadership development. Examples of past volunteer projects
include teaching nutrition classes, forming local women's
groups, and facilitating creative expression workshops for
youth. Amigos de las Americas also offers several projects,
open to college or post-college students, that focus on

indigenous culture, community nutrition, child health pro-
motion, and other themes. Since its inception, more than
20,000 Amigos de las Americas volunteers have lived and
worked in 15 Latin American and Caribbean countries.

Project Location: Amigos de las Americas currently offers 12
summer projects located in nine countries: Brazil, Costa
Rica, the Dominican Republic, Honduras, Mexico,
Nicaragua, Panama, Paraguay, and Uruguay. Volunteers
live with host families along with one or two project partners who are also Amigos de las Americas volunteers. In
many of the rural communities, electricity (and, sometimes,
running water) is not available. Many of the communities
are located in mountainous regions that require hiking and
walking.

Time Line: Exact dates vary by year, but almost all projects
take place during the summer. Projects are four, six, or
eight weeks in length, and all have set start and end dates;
most end in early to mid-August.

Cost: The program fee is $3,650, which includes international
airfare from Houston or Miami, insurance, training, all
room and board, and in-country transportation.

Getting Started: Prospective volunteers can download an application from the Web site or contact Amigos de las Americas by phone or e-mail to request one. The application
deadline is April 1. Volunteer training includes Spanish or
Portuguese language instruction, Latin American history
and cultural awareness, health and safety, first aid, positive
development approaches, human relations, leadership, management, and presentation skills. Volunteers who live in
one of 26 cities in the United States undergo in-person
training over an eight-month period, meeting once or twice
per month. Volunteers outside of these cities receive their
training by correspondence.

Needed Skills and Specific Populations: Volunteers must have
taken at least two years of high school Spanish or have an
equivalent skill level. Volunteers must be at least 16 years
old and have completed their sophomore year of high

school. Senior volunteers are welcomed, but they are not the focus of the volunteer program. Every effort will be made to successfully place volunteers with disabilities, but those volunteers may be hindered by the conditions present in Latin America.

Volunteers live with families in host communities and participate in the activities of daily village life, such as learning to successfully milk the family's cow. *Photo courtesy of Amigos de las Americas*

Amizade

P.O. Box 110107
Pittsburgh, PA 15232
(888) 973-4443 or (412) 441-6655; Fax: (412) 441-6655
E-mail: volunteer@amizade.org
Web site: www.amizade.org

Project Type: Administrative; Agriculture; Community Development; Construction; Developmental Disabilities; Economic Development; Education; Historic Preservation; Human Rights; Medical/Health; Natural Conservation (Land); Orphans; Rural Development; Trail Building/Maintenance; Women's Issues; Youth

Mission Statement Excerpt: "Amizade encourages intercultural exploration and understanding through community-driven service-learning courses and volunteer programs."

Year Founded: 1994

Number of Volunteers Last Year: 459

Funding Sources: Some funding from private individuals

The Work They Do: Amizade carries out a number of projects in the areas of community empowerment, education, the environment, health care, housing, infrastructure, building of peaceful relationships, and creation of responsible individuals. Current projects open to volunteers include constructing an orphanage and working with physically challenged youth in Bolivia; working with street children in Brazil; constructing a school in Jamaica; establishing a vital health care clinic in Tanzania; performing agricultural and construction work in Australia; participating in historic preservation activities at concentration camps in Poland; constructing primary and secondary schools, roads, and hospitals in Ghana; helping in the healing of social, religious, and political divisions in Northern Ireland; renovating a school in Nepal; participating in historic preservation and environmental cleanup at the OTO Ranch near Yellowstone National Park; tutoring elementary children at the

Navajo Nation in Arizona; and feeding the hungry and homeless in Washington, DC.

Project Location: Amizade carries out projects in Santarém, Brazil; Cochabamba, Bolivia; Petersfield, Jamaica; Hervey Bay, Australia; India; Belfast and Bellycastle, Northern Ireland; Berlin, Germany; Auschwitz-Birkenau, Poland; Tanzania; Puerto Morelos, Mexico; Ghana, Africa; Gardiner, Montana; the Navajo Nation, Arizona; and Washington, DC. Given the huge differences between these places, the work sites and accommodations vary, from an aboriginal farm in Australia to an Andean valley; from the heart of Belfast to a coastal village in Mexico; from a Navajo reservation to a Kenyan village; and more. However, at all sites, Amizade provides lodging and meals. Lodging varies by site and ranges from home stays to dorms to hotels. Meals incorporate locally available food and are cooked and served by Amizade staff.

Time Line: Various programs are offered throughout the year, but each has a specific start and end date, and not all are available at all times. Almost all of the volunteer programs run from one to three weeks, with the average volunteer serving for two weeks. At projects in Bolivia and Jamaica, volunteers have the opportunity to stay for up to a year, and there are no start and end dates.

Cost: Program fees start at $425 and go up to $2,640, depending on the program. This fee covers lodging, meals, educational activities, recreational activities, and, in most cases, local transportation. Volunteers are responsible for transportation to the work site, immunizations, travel insurance, and departure taxes.

Getting Started: Prospective volunteers can download an application and other documents from Amizade's Web site or call the office. Every volunteer site offers cultural orientation, and the Australian program offers orientation on indigenous wildlife.

Needed Skills and Specific Populations: No specific skills are required, though the Brazil program needs doctors, dentists, surgeons, and teachers in addition to volunteers with more generalized skills. Volunteers must be at least 18 years old to work on their own; a parent or guardian must accompany volunteers aged 12–17. Only the Montana program accepts volunteers under age 12. Senior volunteers are welcomed at all programs. Volunteers with disabilities are encouraged and welcomed to participate in Amizade's programs, though some program community conditions are better suited to volunteers with disabilities than others.

Appalachian Mountain Club (AMC)

P.O. Box 298
Gorham, NH 03581
Phone: (603) 466-2721 x192; Fax: (603) 466-2720
Web site: www.outdoors.org

Project Type: Trail Building/Maintenance

Year Founded: 1876

The Work They Do: AMC is the nation's oldest nonprofit conservation and recreation organization. Its 12 Northeast chapters maintain more than 1,400 miles of trail, including 350 miles of the Appalachian Trail. Previous projects include the construction of new trails in Acadia National Park, Maine; a canoe portage trail in Baxter State Park, Maine; a loop trail to the Appalachian Trail in Grafton Notch, Maine; the construction of bog bridges in the New Hampshire White Mountains; reconstruction of the Appalachian Trail in the Berkshire region of western Massachusetts; and rock work on alpine trails near the peak of Mount Washington in New Hampshire. Volunteers build, maintain, and repair trails, all of which involve moderate to strenuous physical labor.

Project Location: AMC offers trail crews and skills workshops in the White Mountain National Forest of New Hampshire and Maine, in Acadia National Park and Baxter State Park in Maine, in the Berkshire Mountains of Massachusetts, and in other locations in the Appalachian region. Many of the project sites are in remote locations. Volunteers should be prepared to work outside in all weather conditions and sometimes in steep terrain. Accommodations are provided in the form of tents or bunkhouses, and they are, necessarily, quite basic.

Time Line: Openings for work crews are usually offered from March through November. Most programs last from one to ten days. A 15-day Teen Stewardship training program is also available.

Cost: Most program fees range from free to $350, with the average being about $120; the Teen Stewardship training program is $650. Included in the program fee are training, tools, logding in a tent or bunkhouse, food, cooking and eating equipment, and first aid supplies. Volunteers must supply their own personal gear and transportation to and from the site.

Getting Started: Information about the coming year is posted each January on AMC's Web site. Prospective volunteers can apply through the Web site or by calling the Chapter Trails Chair. AMC members receive *AMC Outdoors* magazine, which also lists all volunteer opportunities. (Membership is not required in order to participate in volunteer programs, however.) All training and orientation is done on the trail.

Needed Skills and Specific Populations: Volunteers should be in good physical condition and have an enthusiastic willingness to work. Some backpacking experience is helpful, as is previous experience in trail building. Training in the use and maintenance of tools is given at each project site. The minimum age of volunteers is generally 15, but this varies by program. Senior volunteers are welcomed, as are volunteers with disabilities. Specialty crews are often scheduled for groups of teens, adults, and women.

Appalachian Trail Conservancy (ATC)

1280 North Main Street
Blacksburg, VA 24060
(540) 961-5551; Fax: (540) 961-5554
E-mail: crews@appalachiantrail.org
Web site: www.appalachiantrail.org

Project Type: Historic Preservation; Natural Conservation
(Land); Trail Building/Maintenance

Mission Statement Excerpt: "The Appalachian Trail Conservancy (ATC) is a volunteer-based organization dedicated to
the preservation and management of the natural, scenic,
historic, and cultural resources associated with the
Appalachian Trail, in order to provide primitive outdoor-
recreation and educational opportunities for Trail visitors."

Year Founded: 1925

Number of Volunteers Last Year: More than 4,500

Funding Sources: Government and private donors; the USDA
Forest Service and the National Park Service cosponsor the
ATC volunteer trail crews

The Work They Do: The Appalachian National Scenic Trail is
the longest continuously marked footpath in the world and
America's first national scenic trail. It follows the crest of
the Appalachian Mountains for more than 2,100 miles
along ridges and through rural farm valleys and rugged
high country. ATC member clubs are assigned a section of
the Appalachian Trail to maintain, and clubs are assisted in
their efforts by the volunteer trail crews. ATC organizes
and supports the volunteer efforts to maintain and build
the Appalachian Trail. Trail work is hard, physical labor.
Volunteer work assignments include new trail construction,
rock work, log work, shelter construction, and other physically demanding tasks. Trail crews of six to eight volunteers
work under the supervision of a skilled leader. Trail construction involves working with hand tools, and getting
dirty is guaranteed. The crews work eight-hour days, rain

A trail crew works hard, crushing rock (foreground) and filling treadway (background) to widen the beautiful Appalachian Trail north of Wayah Bald, North Carolina, in June 2004. *Photo courtesy of Appalachian Trail Conservancy*

or shine, hot or cold, regardless of black flies, mosquitoes, and other insects.

Project Location: Volunteers can work anywhere along the length of the Appalachian Trail. Crew base camps are located in northern Maine, central Vermont, Pennsylvania, southwestern Virginia, and the Great Smoky Mountains in Tennessee. Volunteer crew members backpack into a backcountry campsite and set up a primitive tent camp near the project site. The hike, which may be up to four miles up a mountain, can be very strenuous. In addition to personal gear, crew members carry all the food, tools, and group gear needed for the week in the woods. Crews may also work from car camps or developed campgrounds. During the course of the crew season, the weather can vary from sweaty, summertime heat to freezing, winter-like cold.

Time Line: The Maine Trail Crew operates from June through mid-August. The Vermont Volunteer Long Trail Patrol operates mid-July through mid-September. The Mid-Atlantic

Trail Crew works during September and October. The Virginia-based Konnarock Trail Crew operates from mid-May through August. Based in the Great Smoky Mountains, the Rocky Top Volunteer Trail Crew works in September and October. Prospective participants in any of these crews' programs may volunteer for one to six weeks; the average volunteer stint is ten days.

Cost: There is no program fee, though volunteers are responsible for their own transportation to and from their base camp. Once volunteers reach the base camp, most expenses are covered, including shelter, food, transportation to and from work projects, tools, safety equipment, and group camping gear (as available). Crew members need to bring work clothing, sturdy boots, and their own basic camping gear.

Getting Started: Prospective volunteers can download an application from the Web site or contact ATC's office and request one. Volunteers receive training in "leave no trace" camping techniques and trail crew safety the evening before their project starts. All skills training is provided in the field during the course of the project.

Needed Skills and Specific Populations: Good health, willingness to cooperate, community spirit, and enthusiasm are more important than previous trail experience. Participants should be comfortable living and working in a primitive outdoor setting. Volunteers must be at least 18 years old; senior volunteers are "welcome and encouraged!" ATC will work with volunteers with disabilities to accommodate individual needs. ATC also welcomes international volunteers, but it cannot assist them in obtaining entry to the United States.

ARCHELON, The Sea Turtle
Protection Society of Greece

Solomou 57, 10432
Athens, Greece
(30) 210 5231342
E-mail: stps@archelon.gr
Web site: www.archelon.gr

Project Type: Natural Conservation (Sea)
Year Founded: 1983
Number of Volunteers Last Year: 450
Funding Sources: Government, faith-based, and private sources
The Work They Do: ARCHELON helps to protect Greece's
  three major turtle nesting areas, which cover about 60
  miles of shoreline. They accomplish this mission by protecting more than 2,500 nests from human and animal
  threats, tagging turtles for monitoring purposes, treating
  injured and sick turtles (more than 50 per year, on average), teaching more than 18,000 students in environmental
  education programs, and maintaining a public education
  campaign that reaches tens of thousands of visitors. Volunteers assist with nest management and habitat protection
  by conducting morning and night surveys via beach patrols
  and excavations, and they also provide protection to turtles
  and their nests. Volunteers can also help with the public
  awareness campaign by staffing information stations and
  presenting slide shows. There are also opportunities to
  assist with the daily treatment of injured sea turtles.
Project Location: Volunteers work at one of the three turtle
  nesting areas, located in Zakynthos, Peloponnesus, and
  Crete, or at the Sea Turtle Rescue Center in Athens. In
  Zakynthos, where the first national marine park for sea
  turtles in the Mediterranean was established in 1999,
  volunteers assist in protecting the nesting beaches. In
  Peloponnesus, volunteers protect nests from foxes and
  other mammals, help with sand dune restoration and the

maintenance of nature trails, and assist in the newly established Nature Information Centres. On the island of Crete, volunteers help manage nesting areas. Volunteers stay free, in campsites that are restricted to ARCHELON volunteers, with very basic outdoor sanitary and cooking facilities that feature cold-water showers, gas stoves, and refrigerators. Volunteers must provide their own camping gear, including a tent and a sleeping bag, as well as their own food to cook.

Time Line: Volunteers are welcomed year-round at the Sea Turtle Rescue Center. At the other three sites, volunteers are accepted between May and October. Volunteers must commit to a minimum of 28 days.

Cost: Volunteers pay a nonrefundable participation fee of €100 or €70 (field-work volunteers who arrive before May 15 or after September 20 receive a 50 percent discount). The fee helps to cover administrative costs as well as the cost of the annual subscription to the ARCHELON newsletter, an exclusive "volunteer" T-shirt, and a booklet on turtle biology. Free campsites are provided, but volunteers are responsible for all travel and food expenses. Volunteers should budget a minimum of €15 per day for food.

Getting Started: Contact the organization via e-mail, phone, or its Web site. ARCHELON provides training upon arrival, as well as direct supervision during the first week.

Needed Skills and Specific Populations: The only needed skill is the ability to communicate in both spoken and written English. Volunteers must be at least 18 years old; there is no maximum age limit. Volunteers with disabilities will find it difficult at best to work with ARCHELON, given the nature of the work and the basic sanitary facilities at the camp.

Asociación ANAI

Apartado 170 (2070)
Sabanilla, San Jose
Costa Rica
+ (506) 224-3570, 224-6090, or 224-8815
Fax: + (506) 253-7524
E-mail: volunteers@racsa.co.cr
Web site: www.anaicr.org

Project Type: Agriculture; Community Development; Natural
Conservation (Land); Natural Conservation (Sea); Rural
Development; Scientific Research

Mission Statement Excerpt: "Asociación ANAI has put into
practice a strategy that links conservation and sustainable
development through activities that directly benefit both
the people and the environment. The focus has been on
establishing the conditions for a self-sustaining process
involving work in the broad areas of conservation, economic development, training and education, organization,
and advocacy."

Year Founded: 1978

Number of Volunteers Last Year: 578

Funding Sources: Some funding from private donors

The Work They Do: Asociación ANAI focuses on projects that
include the intersection of conservation and human development. Its current programs include supporting organic
agriculture, biomonitoring, maintaining a conservation
program for sea turtles, and supporting local, national, and
regional initiatives for sustainable development and conservation. Volunteer work varies widely by project, but one
good example of a volunteer experience is the sea turtle
project. In this project, volunteers work mainly on night
patrols and in the hatchery. Night-patrol volunteers walk a
seven-mile beach, searching for nesting turtles. Once a turtle is found, volunteers take its measurements, help embed
a microchip into it, and collect and relocate eggs (perhaps

to the hatchery). Volunteers can also help with data analysis of, among other things, hatchling survival rates, as well as with beach cleanup and other small projects.

Project Location: Asociación ANAI works on the Caribbean coastline of Costa Rica, mainly in the biologically rich and diverse region of Talamanca. Some of the villages and work sites are quite remote or are in wildlife refuges. Accommodations and food tend to be fairly basic, and most volunteers live with host families in shared rooms. Volunteers may also have the option to camp. Most sites have electricity, though running water may not be available. Volunteers should be aware of the strong likelihood of large numbers of biting insects, such as mosquitoes, in the area.

Time Line: Volunteers are accepted as early as March, and they can volunteer at some sites through the end of November. Volunteers stay for one week to several months, with the average stay being two to three weeks.

Cost: Asociación ANAI charges a $30 administrative fee and $12 to $15 per day for lodging and food (volunteers who choose to camp pay only $7 per day). Volunteers are responsible for all travel costs. Because of the remoteness of the sites, volunteers usually incur very few other costs.

Getting Started: Prospective volunteers should contact Asociación ANAI's volunteer coordinator by postal mail, e-mail, phone, or fax and request a registration form. Volunteers must visit the organization's headquarters in San Jose, Costa Rica, before heading to site. At the office, volunteers watch a short video and receive a training manual and directions to the work site. Further training is given at the site.

Needed Skills and Specific Populations: Volunteers should be in good physical condition and able to work at night without artificial light in difficult and uncomfortable conditions. Volunteers must be at least 18 years old unless accompanied by a family member. There is no maximum age limit. Prospective volunteers with disabilities are welcome to apply, but Asociación ANAI cannot make special accommodations for them.

Asociación de Rescate de Fauna (ARFA)

Edif. La Vista, Ap. 11-B, Calle Bella Vista
Colina de los Caobos, Caracas 1050
Venezuela
0058-212-782.4182; Fax: 0058-212-793.4421
E-mail: lucyalio@cantv.net
Web site: www.geocities.com/arfavenezuela

Project Type: Natural Conservation (Land)

Mission Statement Excerpt: "To create awareness through rescue, rehabilitation, and release of wildlife."

Year Founded: 1999

Number of Volunteers Last Year: 5

Funding Sources: Some private donors

The Work They Do: ARFA runs the only wildlife rescue and environmental education center in Venezuela. Examples of its work include an awareness campaign in schools of neighboring communities, and teacher training in the area of animal conservation in the states of Cojedes and Caracas for veterinarians and environmental police. Volunteers who are veterinarians or who are in their last year of veterinary school help supervise the care of wildlife at the center, while non-veterinarians help to feed the animals and maintain the facility.

Project Location: ARFA's center is located in the central plains of Venezuela, on an isolated cattle farm one hour away from San Carlos. Lodging is provided at the center, which has power, a rural phone system, and running water. Occasional transportation into town is provided so that volunteers can take care of personal matters and access the Internet.

Time Line: Volunteers are accepted year-round, and there is no minimum required stay. Volunteers are usually limited to a maximum stay of 90 days due to visa regulations, though veterinarians can usually extend their visas to six months. ARFA asks that volunteers work with them to coordinate their stays so that a subsequent volunteer arrives before the previous one leaves.

Cost: The program fee for 90 days is $300, which includes room and board. Airfare to Venezuela is not included. ARFA estimates that most volunteers spend only about $200 for personal expenses for three months.

Getting Started: Prospective volunteers should e-mail a letter outlining their qualifications, goals, and desired arrival and departure dates to the address listed above, along with two letters of reference. ARFA provides on-site training.

Needed Skills and Specific Populations: It is preferred that volunteers be qualified veterinarians or veterinary students in their final year of veterinary school; others should have a degree in biology or work in a related field. Volunteers must be at least 22 years old. Senior volunteers and volunteers with disabilities are not accepted.

Australian Tropical Research Foundation (ATRF)

PMB 5 Cape Tribulation
Queensland, Australia 4873
+ 61 7 4098 0063
E-mail: austrop@austrop.org.au
Web site: www.austrop.org.au

Project Type: Natural Conservation (Land); Scientific
Research; Social Justice

Mission Statement Excerpt: "To conduct and facilitate research
into terrestrial and aquatic ecosystems in Australia and
elsewhere; to research human impact on the Australian
tropics and develop and promote sound management practices for the tropics."

Year Founded: 1988

Number of Volunteers Last Year: 54

Funding Sources: Specific project-based funding for research,
plus some private donations for station operation

The Work They Do: Previous and current ATRF research projects include the development of techniques for assisted
regeneration of rainforests; the development of appropriate
technology (particularly energy conservation) for living in
the wet tropics; research on the productivity, phenology,
and pollination of cluster figs, on the ecology of flying
foxes (fruit bats) and their relatives, and on rainforest and
reef conservation; and the chemical analysis of plant and
insect materials. Volunteers assist in many research and station activities, including radio-tracking bats, counting figs,
stomping grass for forest regeneration, constructing buildings, digging holes, collecting coconuts, and running the
Bat House (ATRF's visitors center).

Project Location: The station is located in the Daintree tropical lowlands. Considered the "jewel" of the Australian Wet
Tropics World Heritage Area, the lowlands are sandwiched
between the coastal fringe and the coastal mountain range.
The area features a wide variety of habitats, from coastal

reefs to tropical rainforest, though it claims to be "one of the most benign tropical rain forest environments anywhere in the world . . . there are no seriously nasty things here." The station is based on 25 acres of regenerated pasture less than half a mile from the coast. Accommodation is in light and airy bunkhouse-style buildings. Breakfast and lunch are self-catered, whereas dinner is taken as a group. Food tends to be plentiful, which has led to the site's tongue-in-cheek nickname, "the Cape Tribulation Cooking Camp."

Time Line: Volunteers are accepted year-round. Volunteers must stay at least two weeks; the maximum length of stay is open for negotiation. The record length of stay is about one year.

Cost: The program fee for volunteers is $20 per day, which covers all food and accommodations. Volunteers who stay for more than two months may be able to negotiate a lower fee. The program fee does not include transportation to Australia or to the work site. Volunteers have very few on-site expenses, since there is nowhere to spend money.

Getting Started: Prospective volunteers should contact the station by e-mail and inquire about potential dates. No formal orientation or training is offered, but the station will provide these as needed.

Needed Skills and Specific Populations: ATRF prefers volunteers who are at least 20 years old; there is no maximum age limit. Those who use wheelchairs will find that the station is not accessible; prospective volunteers with other physical disabilities will probably be able to be accommodated, though they should discuss this with the organization well in advance of their planned trip.

AVIVA

P.O. Box 60573
Flamingo Vlei 7439
South Africa
+27 21 557 5996; Fax: +27 21 557 9609
E-mail: info@aviva-sa.com
Web site: www.aviva-sa.com

Project Type: Administrative; Agriculture; Community Development; Construction; Education; Medical/Health; Natural Conservation (Land); Natural Conservation (Sea); Orphans; Rural Development; Trail Building/Maintenance; Youth

Mission Statement Excerpt: "AVIVA is dedicated to providing value for money volunteering experiences in South Africa with carefully researched projects throughout the country."

Year Founded: 2001

Number of Volunteers Last Year: 93

Funding Sources: None

The Work They Do: Volunteers work in one of seven disparate projects. At the Wildlife Rehabilitation Centre, volunteers work closely with baboons and a variety of other small mammals and birds. At Monkey Town, volunteers educate visitors about the 25 different primate species at the center. Volunteers with African Penguin Conservation help feed and care for penguins at the world's leading marine bird rehabilitation center. In Zeekoevlei, environmental education is the focus of volunteers, who work outdoors with local school and community groups. Volunteers who want to work with orphans can do so at the Baphumelele Children's Home by assisting with child development, baby feeding, homework, nursing, food collection, and a variety of other tasks. "Learn, then teach" is the mantra at Gary's Surf School, where volunteers do exactly that in regard to surfing. Last, Rustler's Valley Mountain Retreat is creating a model for sustainable African existence by promoting the conservation and use of renewable natural resources, the practice of permaculture, and the development of alternative energy production. Volunteers there help in a variety of roles, including working in the permaculture garden, bar, and Saucery Restaurant (which uses Rustlers-produced fruit and vegetables in its dishes) and teaching environmental education classes to local school children.

Project Location: Most projects are situated in and around Cape Town. Accommodation and self-service breakfasts are provided for all volunteers staying at the AVIVA House in Cape Town. All meals are provided for volunteers who participate at the Penguin Conservation Centre, the Wildlife Rehabilitation Centre, and Rustler's Valley Mountain Retreat.

Time Line: Projects are available year-round, though not all projects are available at all times of year. Start dates are flexible. The minimum period for volunteer projects varies from four to thirteen weeks, and volunteers can stay as long as they choose. Visas are required for those who wish to stay more than 90 days; AVIVA can assist with the application process. Volunteers normally stay an average of eight weeks, though volunteers have stayed for periods ranging from four weeks to ten months.

Cost: Program fees range from $1,069 to more than $1,600, with most in the $1,500 range. Some programs' fees include all meals, as well as required flights between Cape Town and Johannesburg. Volunteers who stay on for a second project or more receive reduced program fees for these subsequent projects. All program fees include airport transfers, orientation, a comprehensive welcome pack, accommodations, some or all meals, transportation to the volunteer site, an AVIVA fleece, and tours of Table Mountain, the city of Cape Town, Cape Point peninsula, a township, the Cape wine lands, and Robben Island. Volunteers must provide their own airfare to Cape Town.

Getting Started: Prospective volunteers can apply via the online application form found on the AVIVA Web site. Each volunteer receives a thorough welcome brief from a member of the AVIVA team, and orientation activities are included with most projects to introduce volunteers to Cape Town's cultural and natural attractions. When volunteers join a project, they are given relevant training and supervision.

Needed Skills and Specific Populations: No special skills are needed, though volunteers should be able to speak English reasonably well. Volunteers should indicate any previous experience or qualifications on their application form. Volunteers must be at least 16 years old, and all projects are open to senior volunteers. People with disabilities are welcome to apply, though the nature of the disability may dictate whether or not a project is suitable for them. Due to the nature of the work and location of many projects, facilities for disabled people may be limited or nonexistent.

Azafady

Studio 7, 1a Beethoven Street
London W10 4LG
United Kingdom
+ 44 (0) 20 8960 6629; Fax: + 44 (0) 20 8962 0126
E-mail: info@azafady.org
Web site: www.madagascar.co.uk

Project Type: Agriculture; Community Development; Construction; Economic Development; Medical/Health; Natural Conservation (land); Rural Development; Scientific Research; Social Justice

Mission Statement Excerpt: "Azafady is a registered U.K. charity and Malagasy NGO working to alleviate poverty, improve well-being, and preserve beautiful, unique environments in southeast Madagascar."

Year Founded: 1994

Number of Volunteers Last Year: 41

Funding Sources: Private donors

The Work They Do: Azafady works in Madagascar on a combination of environmental and humanitarian projects that bring measurable benefits to the poorest members of the village communities, where help is needed most. Although the organization was founded to protect the environment, its work is all about people: their health, their education, their workload, and their ability to raise their families and survive alongside the forest that they—and the wider global community—so depend upon. Azafady's goals in Madagascar are to raise global awareness in the country, to promote sustainable livelihoods, to improve health, and to protect the environment. Volunteer work varies greatly and might include conservation and research, building and equipping schools, setting up tree nurseries, conservation education, building improved stoves, food security, building beehives and fruit driers, promoting ecotourism, and promoting health.

Project Location: All of Azafady's volunteers work in southeast Madagascar. Volunteers move around the region but should plan on camping the entire time. Azafady's more established sites have basic amenities, but others may be simply an area to pitch a tent with a nearby well. Electricity is available in the town of Fort Dauphin, but not in rural villages, where field work is done. Volunteers should be prepared for physical work, adventurous road journeys, and long walks to reach remote project sites. Simple, nutritionally balanced food is provided by Azafady.

Time Line: Volunteer projects start in January, April, July, and October each year for a minimum of four weeks and a maximum of ten weeks.

Cost: The program fee is £2,000, which covers all in-country travel costs, training and orientation, all meals, and use of the campsites. Not included in the program fee are airfare to Fort Dauphin, Madagascar, or visa and travel insurance costs.

Getting Started: Prospective volunteers should download an application form from the Azafady Web site or phone or write to request the form. A comprehensive one-week orientation is provided to give volunteers lessons in the Malagasy language as well as a background on local culture, the region, practicalities of living in Madagascar, medical information, and the history of Azafady.

Needed Skills and Specific Populations: No special skills are needed, as all required skills are learned while working; Azafady requires only enthusiasm and sensitivity. Volunteers must be at least 18 years old; there is no maximum age limit as long as volunteers are able-bodied and capable of dealing with the sometimes basic conditions. Azafady is limited in the types of disabilities it can accommodate; prospective volunteers with disabilities are asked to contact Azafady for further information.

Bangladesh Work Camps Association (BWCA)

289/2 Workcamp Road
North Shajahanpur, Dhaka—1217
Bangladesh
+ 88 2 935-8206; Fax: + 88 2 956-5483
(mark faxes to the attention of BWCA)
E-mail: bwca@bangla.net
Web site: www.mybwca.org

Project Type: Agriculture; Community Development; Construction; Developmental Disabilities; Economic Development;
Education; Human Rights; Medical/Health; Natural Conservation (Land); Orphans; Rural Development; Social Justice; Youth

Mission Statement Excerpt: "Let's work together to have a better world through promoting peace and solidarity in the
spirit of 'learning while working and living together,'
which is aimed at the young generation around the world."

Year Founded: 1958

Number of Volunteers Last Year: 23

Funding Sources: None

The Work They Do: Bangladesh Work Camps Association
(BWCA) short-term volunteers can become involved in a
number of types of work, such as building renovations,
community development work, health care, helping to prepare for festivals, social and environmental work, and relief
and rehabilitation work after natural disasters. Volunteers
who work with BWCA for two months or more can assist
on more involved projects such as working with people
with disabilities, teaching, or assisting with agricultural
projects. Specific examples of volunteer work with BWCA
include installing low-cost latrines, planting trees, and giving "Greening Asia" presentations in local schools and
communities. BWCA also organizes temporary eye clinics
for cataract patients at the work site, and volunteers can

assist volunteer surgeons and doctors both inside and outside the operating theater.

Project Location: Work camps and projects are situated in rural villages that do not have access to modern conveniences. The work conditions and accommodations are therefore quite basic in nature. Volunteers usually stay in dormitory-like settings, and cooking is done communally. Since BWCA tends to attract volunteers from all over the world, it asks that volunteers come prepared to cook food that is native to their homeland to share with others.

Time Line: Short-term work camps operate between October and March for a maximum of two weeks. Medium-term volunteers can stay for two months up to one year and can start anytime.

Cost: Short-term volunteers pay a program fee of $150. Medium-term volunteers also pay $150 plus a per-day fee of $2 for the first three months. After these first three months, volunteers pay $50 per month plus $2 per day. The program fee includes lodging, food, and in-country transportation, but not travel to Bangladesh.

Getting Started: Prospective volunteers must apply at least one month before they wish to start. Applications may be obtained by e-mailing BWCA. BWCA holds an orientation session one day before each program begins, which includes an overview of program activities, basic language training, and information on the social, cultural, and economic conditions of Bangladesh.

Needed Skills and Specific Populations: Short-term volunteers do not need any special qualifications or experience. Medium-term volunteers should have some proven skills in the area in which they wish to volunteer. Volunteers must be 18–35 years old. BWCA is unable to accommodate volunteers with disabilities.

Bike-Aid

2017 Mission Street, Suite 303
San Francisco, CA 94110
(800) RIDE-808; Fax: (415) 255-7498
E-mail: bikeaid@globalexchange.org
Web site: www.globalexchange.org/getInvolved/bikeaid

Project Type: Agriculture; Community Development; Economic Development; Human Rights; Legal; Medical/Health; Natural Conservation (Land); Political Action; Rural Development; Social Justice; Women's Issues; Youth

Mission Statement Excerpt: "Global Exchange is an international human rights organization dedicated to promoting political, social, and environmental justice globally. . . . We [work] to increase global awareness among the U.S. public while building partnerships around the world through programs like Bike-Aid."

Year Founded: 1988

Number of Volunteers Last Year: Approximately 35

Funding Sources: Private donors

The Work They Do: Bike-Aid is a cross-country bike trip that combines service learning, physical challenge, group living, and political education. While biking across the country, Bike-Aid volunteers stop once per week in a community along the route. There they learn more about the challenges faced by people in these communities and undertake volunteer projects to help with these challenges. Throughout the summer riders engage in antiracism trainings and critical consciousness workshops about the global economy and current international events. Meeting with community-based organizations along the route and interacting with International Partner riders, who are affiliated with Global Exchange's international human rights campaigns, enable global solidarity and community alliances to be built. Examples of past projects include sending books to women in prison, painting a house, and cleaning up a park. The

average day starts between 6:00 and 10:00 A.M., depending
on the mood of the group, temperature readings, and distance to travel for the day. About once a week, volunteers
do not pedal at all.

Project Location: The cross-country ride itineraries start from
either Seattle or San Francisco. Shorter rides, from San
Francisco to Tijuana and around the Hawaiian islands, are
also available. Bike-Aid organizes community host stays in
towns along the route. Volunteers unroll their sleeping bag
in YMCAs, churches, gymnasiums, campgrounds, and people's homes. Frequently, local community members invite
riders to potluck suppers, pancake breakfasts, or community activities. Occasionally, riders will have to provide
their own food and lodging.

Time Line: Cross-country and West Coast rides take place in
the summer, and Hawaiian rides are in December. The
shortest rides are two weeks long; the longest rides are ten
weeks long.

Cost: Bike-Aid's program fee is $3,800, which includes most
lodging expenses and some food. Volunteers must pay for
their transportation costs to the start and from the finish
of the ride, as well as bicycling equipment needs.

Getting Started: Prospective volunteers can download an application from the Web site or call to request that one be
mailed to them. An orientation is provided before departure, and a bicycling training schedule is sent to volunteers
along with a "welcome packet" of information.

Needed Skills and Specific Populations: Given the nature of
Bike-Aid, volunteers must obviously be in good physical
condition, but beginning athletes are welcomed. Riders
aged 16 to 60 have completed Bike-Aid rides. All riders
must provide a signed medical release form from a physician before the ride. Volunteers with disabilities are not
only welcomed, but are "strongly encouraged" to participate in Bike-Aid rides.

Bimini Biological Field Station

9300 SW 99th Street
Miami, FL 33176
(305) 421-4146; Fax: (305) 421-4600
E-mail: sgruber@rsmas.miami.edu
Web site: www.miami.edu/sharklab

Project Type: Natural Conservation (Sea); Scientific Research; Youth

Mission Statement Excerpt: "Reveal the life history of elasmo-branch fishes (sharks) and foster their conservation."

Year Founded: 1990

Number of Volunteers Last Year: Approximately 100

Funding Sources: Government and private donors

The Work They Do: The Bimini Biological Field Station carries out genetic, ecological, and behavioral research on lemon sharks (*Negaprion brevirostris*). Volunteers at Bimini help with all of the duties involved in field research, as well as the maintenance of this remote island-based research facility.

Project Location: The field station is located on the island of Bimini in the Bahamas. Research is conducted in a shallow lagoon. The station's facilities are small but modern and air conditioned. Accommodations are provided at the field station.

Time Line: Volunteers are accepted year-round for a minimum of one month; there is no maximum time limit. On average, volunteers stay for about two and a half months.

Cost: Volunteers pay $575 per month for room and board and must also pay for all other personal expenses, including flights to Bimini, which can be reached directly from Ft. Lauderdale.

Getting Started: Prospective volunteers should contact Bimini Biological Field Station via the e-mail address or Web site listed above. All volunteers go through an extensive orientation that includes classes on research and field techniques.

Needed Skills and Specific Populations: Volunteers must have university experience and a background in the basics of biology; they must also know how to swim. Volunteers must be 20–35 years old. The organization cannot accommodate volunteers with disabilities.

Biosphere Expeditions

Sprat's Water, near Carlton Colville
Suffolk NR33 8BP
United Kingdom
(44) 870 4460801; Fax: (44) 870 4460809
E-mail: info@biosphere-expeditions.org
Web site: www.biosphere-expeditions.org

Project Type: Natural Conservation (Land); Natural Conservation (Sea); Scientific Research

Mission Statement Excerpt: "Biosphere Expeditions promotes sustainable conservation and preservation of the planet's wildlife by forging alliances between scientists and the public. Our goal is to make, through our expedition work, an active contribution toward a sustainable biosphere where each part can thrive and exist. At Biosphere Expeditions we believe in empowering ordinary people by placing them at the centre of scientific study and by actively involving them out in the field where there is conservation work to be done."

Year Founded: 1999

Number of Volunteers Last Year: 200

Funding Sources: Corporate partnerships and in-kind donations; donors include Land Rover, Motorola, Silva, Globetrotter, and Cotswold Outdoor

The Work They Do: Biosphere Expeditions allows the general public to have meaningful, hands-on engagement with conservation tasks by partnering them with scientists in the field. Volunteers are involved with all aspects of the scientific field research. Examples of past projects include snow leopard research in the Altai; cheetah conservation in Namibia; a biodiversity study in the Peruvian Amazon; whale, dolphin, and turtle research in the Azores; elephant-human conflict resolution in Sri Lanka; and wolf and bear research in Slovakia. All data collected during each volunteer vacation is published in a report that

A volunteer carries a sedated cheetah to a temporary field lab, where it will be radio collared. The purpose of this project is to find out how many cheetahs live in Namibia. Part of this work is to trap, radio-collar, and study the cheetahs. *Photo courtesy of Biosphere Expeditions*

includes a review of the expedition and its conservation research. The report is sent to all volunteers within a few months of the end of the expedition, and any suitable material will be published in scientific journals or other publications to make sure as many people as possible know about and benefit from the research performed. Volunteers' names will appear in the acknowledgements of all scientific papers. Volunteers will be sent copies of any publications arising out of their expeditions.

Project Location: Projects can take place anywhere in the world and locations are constantly changing with the scientific research being conducted. Biosphere Expeditions does not believe adverse conditions need to be a part of this scientific research; instead, it strongly believes that volunteers need to be well fed and comfortable in order to become proficient research assistants. Accommodations are always locally owned and vary from simple bed-and-breakfasts to lodge research centers to tent base camps in a mountain valley. Lodging and food is provided by Biosphere Expeditions.

Time Line: Project dates vary from year to year. The shortest project is two weeks long; the longest is two months long. Most volunteers work for two or four weeks.

Cost: Program fees range from $1,500 to $2,300 per two-week slot, which does not include airfare. Once the expedition starts, all reasonable expenses (excluding personal items and souvenirs) are included in the program fee. On average, two-thirds of the program fee benefits the project directly and locally, while the rest goes toward administrative overhead, research, and the establishment of new expeditions. Each project's expedition report (mentioned above) includes details on how the project's program fees were spent in supporting the research project.

Getting Started: Prospective volunteers should start by thoroughly reading the information found on the Web site and by selecting an expedition. Spots on expeditions are reserved with a £300 deposit, which can be sent electronically. Training is part of the expedition. Biosphere Expeditions plans to open a North American office in 2006.

Needed Skills and Specific Populations: Biosphere Expeditions works hard to allow many people to take a meaningful part in scientific research. There is no minimum or maximum age limit, and the organization proudly notes that its oldest volunteer to date was 82 years old. Some degree of fitness is required, but if one is healthy and enjoys the outdoors, his or her fitness level is probably sufficient. Individuals with disabilities are welcomed, but they should contact Biosphere Expeditions to find out about the suitability of specific expeditions.

Blue Ventures

52 Avenue Road
London N6 5DR
United Kingdom
44 (0) 208 341 9819; Fax: 44 (0) 208 341 4821
E-mail: volunteer@blueventures.org
Web site: www.blueventures.org

Project Type: Community Development; Education; Natural
Conservation (Land); Natural Conservation (Sea); Scientific
Research; Rural Development; Youth

Mission Statement Excerpt: "Blue Ventures is dedicated to
facilitating projects that enhance global marine conservation and research."

Year Founded: 2001

Number of Volunteers Last Year: 90

Funding Sources: Blue Ventures receives a small amount from
government and private sources.

The Work They Do: Blue Ventures coordinates teams of scientists and volunteers to carry out research and environmental awareness and conservation programs in threatened
coral habitats around the world. Its research aims to identify strategies that Blue Ventures, local communities, and
local nonprofit organizations can use to develop sustainable
local environmental management plans for these unique
reef systems. Volunteers carry out field research and manage field camps. Volunteers are given scuba, scientific, and
management training. Volunteers may explore previously
uncharted coral ecosystems, teach in local schools, undertake socioeconomic work, and interact with local people.
Throughout the duration of each expedition, volunteers are
required to take part in a range of non–diving related
research activities, such as socioeconomic studies that
focus on monitoring local fishing catches.

Project Location: Blue Ventures currently works in
Andavadoaka, in southwest Madagascar. Because the coral

reefs in this area are so remote, they are thought to possess a significantly different and higher abundance and diversity of species than other reefs in Madagascar. Volunteers stay in cabins that are equipped with bunk beds, shower facilities, storage space, and a desk. The cabins are located on Blue Ventures's private beach. Food is provided by Blue Ventures and highlights the local cuisine. Blue Ventures believes that "a volunteer needs comfortable accommodation and good food to be able to enjoy the project fully. Just because you are on an expedition doesn't mean that you have to suffer!"

Time Line: Volunteers are accepted every six weeks for a minimum of four weeks; there is no maximum time limit for a volunteer stay.

Cost: The program fee is £1,780 for volunteers without diving experience. This fee includes room and board as well as diving and scientific training. Volunteers must provide their own flights, visas, and insurance.

Getting Started: An application can be downloaded from the organization's Web site or requested via e-mail. Diving training is given up to PADI Advanced Standard, and the opportunity for further certification is offered. Scientific training is provided both onshore and in the water. Blue Ventures accepts only 16 volunteers per expedition.

Needed Skills and Specific Populations: Volunteers must be at least 17 years old; senior volunteers who are medically and physically fit are welcomed. Blue Ventures tries to accommodate as many volunteers with disabilities as possible.

Bridges for Education (BFE)

8912 Garlinghouse Road
Naples, NY 14512
(585) 534-9344
E-mail: mdodge@frontiernet.net
Web site: www.bridges4edu.org

Project Type: Education

Mission Statement Excerpt: "The purpose of Bridges for Education (BFE) is to promote tolerance and understanding using English as a bridge."

Year Founded: 1994

The Work They Do: BFE offers the opportunity to teach conversational English at an international language camp. Since its founding, students from a total of 33 countries have attended this camp. BFE volunteers teach three hours of classes in the morning, supervise two hours of activities in the afternoon, and spend two to three hours on evening activities with the students. All of the BFE students have had at least one year of English language classes before attending this camp. In the BFE classroom, students are divided into beginning, intermediate, and advanced groups, each of which rotates through each team of teachers. The three-week camp is then followed by a paid one-week vacation in the host country.

Project Location: BFE primarily operates in Central and Eastern Europe and in the Newly Independent States, though it has also held camps in China. Belarus, Bulgaria, Estonia, Romania, and Poland have all hosted BFE camps in the past. Accommodations for teachers may be basic, depending on the country and school. Teachers stay in dormitories, two to a room, with shared bathrooms down the hall. Dormitories are not air conditioned. Teachers take their meals in a cafeteria that usually serves local fare; special or restricted diets generally cannot be accommodated.

Time Line: BFE's language camps are usually held during the first three weeks of July, with the group vacation and travel during the last week of that month.

Cost: The program fee to teach with BFE is between $900 and $950. This program fee includes all accommodations and food during both the language camp and the week of travel, as well as weekend activities throughout the month. Airfare to the country of service is not included in the program fee, and it must be arranged through BFE's official travel agent. Volunteer teachers are paid by the host country for their three weeks of teaching, though the amount is usually only enough to cover the cost of some wonderful souvenirs.

Getting Started: Prospective teachers can download an application from BFE's Web site. A deposit on the program fee is due by the end of March. All inexperienced ESL (English as a Second Language) teachers must complete a five-session training that includes lesson planning and basic ESL methodology.

Needed Skills and Specific Populations: Volunteer teachers must already have state certification or teaching experience in a private school or college; all subject areas are accepted. BFE also accepts educated adults, student teachers, and college students as teaching assistants. Families with teenagers are welcomed. Native speakers of English are requested, but no other language proficiency is required.

BTCV

Conservation Centre, Balby Road
Doncaster DN4 0RH
United Kingdom
(44) 0 1302 572244 Fax: (44) 0 1302 310167
E-mail: information@btcv.org.uk
Web site: www.btcv.org

Project Type: Community Development; Natural Conservation (Land), Rural Development, Trail Building/Maintenance

Mission Statement: "To create a more sustainable future by inspiring people and improving places."

Year Founded: 1959

Number of Volunteers Last Year: 4,000

Funding Sources: Government and private sources, including lottery revenue

The Work They Do: BTCV is a huge organization that offers many, many kinds of volunteer opportunities. BTCV partners with local organizations to offer volunteer opportunities around the world, including Australia, the Gambia, Namibia, New Zealand, Thailand, and the United States. Many of the projects are conducted outdoors and are conservation-oriented, but many others deal with aspects of community or rural development. Examples of past projects include joining workers at an organic farm in Kyushu, Japan, to restore drystone retaining walls around rice paddies; enhancing the biodiversity potential of woodlands in England's Peak District; and planting living willow riverbank revetments in West Yorkshire to provide habitat for water voles. There are 2,000 U.K.-based volunteer options, some of which are just a day long. Given its range of locations and types of work, BTCV is a great organization to look into, especially if you want a short-term, conservation volunteer opportunity in the United Kingdom. Please note that BTCV used to be known as the British Trust for Conservation Volunteers. The acronym BTCV is currently exclusively used in place of this longer name.

Project Location: Seventy-five percent of BTCV's volunteers work within the United Kingdom; the remaining 25 percent are spread around the world at partner organizations. Work sites and conditions vary widely depending on the placement. Food and lodging are provided and are covered by the program fee, but the exact arrangements depend on the work site.

Time Line: Placements are available year-round. Day projects run from 10:00 A.M. to 4:30 P.M. with a break for lunch. Other "BTCV Holiday" programs run for a minimum of two days and a maximum of three weeks, with an average of one week for U.K. programs and two weeks for non-U.K. programs.

Cost: In the past, program fees have run the gamut from free (for nonresidential programs in the United Kingdom) all the way up to £250 per week in the United Kingdom and £1,450 for six weeks in Grenada. Program fees for projects in the United Kingdom include food and lodging; fees for projects outside of the United Kingdom may also cover some local transportation costs or leisure activities. In most cases, transportation costs to the volunteer site are the responsibility of the volunteer. Most of the fees go toward administrative expenses, although some community-based non-U.K. host organizations do benefit financially from the program fees.

Getting Started: The entire process is Web site based, from selection of a program to registration to payment of the program fee. Go to the Web site listed above and click on "Holidays." You may also contact a BTCV office in the United Kingdom to ask about opportunities. Training is provided on-site.

Needed Skills and Specific Populations: No special skills are required of volunteers. The minimum age to participate is 18. There is no maximum age limit, but BTCV cannot offer insurance to those over 81 years old. Volunteers with disabilities are welcomed, but they should work with the BTCV office to find an opportunity that can meet their needs.

Camp AmeriKids

88 Hamilton Avenue
Stamford, CT 06902
(800) 486-4357; Fax: (203) 658-9615
E-mail: camp@americares.org
Web site: www.campamerikids.org

Project Type: Medical/Health; Youth

Mission Statement Excerpt: "Enhance the lives of children ages 7 to 15 [who are] affected by or infected with HIV/AIDS by providing a traditional camp experience complemented by off-season programs, while providing a respite for their families."

Year Founded: 1995

Number of Volunteers Last Year: 130

Funding Sources: Faith-based and private sources

The Work They Do: Camp AmeriKids's program is dedicated to providing a summer experience to inner-city children living with HIV/AIDS, for whom camp is a chance to leave the city and just be kids. Children participate, under the guidance of volunteers, in swimming, boating, dance, drama, arts and crafts, sports, and nature activities. Volunteers serve as camp counselors and work with children on a 24-hour-a-day basis during one eight-day camp session. Volunteers are expected to participate fully in all of the camp activities listed above.

Project Location: Camp AmeriKids is located in Carmel, New York, on 250 acres of countryside that features a freshwater lake. Campers and staff reside in designated cabins, which are carpeted and which contain five bathrooms each. All meals are served family style in the dining hall.

Time Line: Camp AmeriKids operates in late July and early August. Volunteers commit to nine full days, which includes one and a half days of training.

Cost: There is no program fee to participate in Camp AmeriKids, and accommodations and food are provided to volunteers. Volunteers must pay for their own travel costs to and from the work site.

Getting Started: Prospective volunteers should visit the Camp AmeriKids Web site or call its office at the toll-free number listed above. The opening orientation and training takes place at the camp facility, lasts one and a half days, and covers camp policies, HIV education, and information on child development.

Needed Skills and Specific Populations: Volunteers do not need to have any particular previous experience—just an open mind and a willingness to share their summer with children. Volunteers must be at least 18 years old. Senior volunteers and volunteers with disabilities are not encouraged to volunteer with Camp AmeriKids.

Camphill Special School

1784 Fairview Road
Glenmoore, PA 19343
(610) 469-9236; Fax: (610) 469-9758
E-mail: brvolunteer@aol.com
Web site: www.beaverrrun.org

Project Type: Developmental Disabilities; Education; Youth

Mission Statement Excerpt: "Our mission is to provide healing and wholeness for children with developmental disabilities. Through extended-family living, an individualized education program, and a full range of therapies, disabilities are moderated and potential unfolds, enabling a more complete and meaningful participation in life—within our community and beyond."

Year Founded: 1963

Number of Volunteers Last Year: 40

Funding Sources: Government and private donors

The Work They Do: Camphill Special School provides training, education, and therapy for children and youth with developmental disabilities. Volunteers care for, supervise, and guide students with developmental disabilities in a school setting, in a prevocational program, and in a home.

Project Location: Volunteers live and work at a residential school in a beautiful rural setting. All volunteers and students live in family-style homes. Mealtimes form an integral part of the day. Volunteers join the students at all mealtimes. These occasions provide time for social interaction and offer students the opportunity to practice social and living skills.

Time Line: Volunteers all begin on the same day, usually in late August. The minimum commitment is six months and the maximum is four years; the average volunteer stays one year.

Cost: There is no program fee. Volunteers are provided full room and board, a monthly stipend, health insurance, and use of a shared car.

Getting Started: An online application is available on the organization's Web site. Applications are accepted throughout the year for the August start date. A one-week orientation is provided to new volunteers, with ongoing courses and trainings offered throughout the year. Camphill also offers a four-year training course in curative education.

Needed Skills and Specific Populations: Volunteers must have a sincere interest in working with children with disabilities, be mature and flexible, and have a sense of humor. The hours are long and the work is demanding and challenging. Volunteers must be at least 20 years old. Applications from volunteers with disabilities and senior volunteers will be considered on an individual basis. Volunteers are accepted from many different countries.

Caretta Research Project (CRP)

P.O. Box 9841
Savannah, GA 31412
(912) 447-8655; Fax: (912) 447-8656
E-mail: WassawCRP@aol.com
Web site: www.carettaresearchproject.org

Project Type: Natural Conservation (Sea); Natural Conservation (Land); Scientific Research

Mission Statement Excerpt: "The Caretta Research Project is a highly interactive educational research project that trains participants in the disciplines of fieldwork as they gather data on threatened nesting loggerhead sea turtles on Wassaw National Wildlife Refuge, Georgia."

Year Founded: 1956

Number of Volunteers Last Year: More than 90

Funding Sources: Private donors and grants

The Work They Do: CRP is a research, education, and conservation project that protects the threatened loggerhead turtles that nest on Wassaw Island. Volunteers help patrol the beaches each night, looking for nesting turtles. When nests are located, the turtles are tagged and nests are protected. Scientific data is also collected for collaborative projects with other organizations.

Project Location: The project is located in the Wassaw National Wildlife Refuge, an island off the coast of Georgia. The work site and available accommodations are basic and rustic, and there is no electricity or hot water.

Time Line: The research project runs from mid-May through early September. Volunteers must commit to at least one week of work, Saturday to Saturday. Volunteers may stay for as many weeks as they wish.

Cost: The program fee is $650. The fee includes food, lodging, and transportation to and from the island on Saturdays. Volunteers should not incur any costs once on the island. Volunteers are responsible for their own transportation to and from Landings Harbor Marina, near Savannah. One hundred percent of the program fee is used to offset the cost of this program.

Getting Started: To ensure that volunteers can work on the dates they desire, they should check the Web site for available dates and call to make a reservation. After a reservation has been confirmed by phone, volunteers should print the application from the Web site, complete it, and send it in with a check. Training is provided once volunteers arrive on Wassaw Island.

Needed Skills and Specific Populations: Volunteers should be physically fit, as this volunteer position requires a lot of walking. Flexibility and a sense of humor are also important, as volunteers share close living quarters (both with other humans and a lot of bugs!) in the summer heat of the American south. Volunteers must be at least 15 years old; and senior volunteers are welcomed as long as they are in good physical condition. Prospective volunteers with disabilities should call first to discuss their specific needs, as Wassaw is a remote island with no medical facilities.

Caribbean Conservation Corporation (CCC)

4424 NW 13th Street, Suite A-1
Gainesville, FL 32601
(800) 678-7853; Fax: (352) 375-2449
E-mail: resprog@cccturtle.org
Web site: www.cccturtle.org

Project Type: Natural Conservation (Land); Natural Conservation (Sea); Scientific Research

Mission Statement: "To ensure the survival of sea turtles within the wider Caribbean basin and Atlantic through research, education, training, advocacy, and the protection of the natural habitats upon which they depend."

Year Founded: 1959

Number of Volunteers Last Year: 25

Funding Sources: CCC receives funds from individual members and private foundations as well as grants from government agencies.

The Work They Do: CCC takes on research, habitat protection, public education, community outreach, networking, and advocacy projects. Because the colonies of green, loggerhead, hawksbill, and leatherback turtles that nest in Costa Rica, Panama, and Florida are among the largest remaining in the western hemisphere, CCC weights its efforts toward these critical nesting beaches. Volunteers assist sea turtle biologists by helping tag and measure turtles, counting eggs, marking nests, recording data, conducting morning nest surveys, conducting track surveys, and helping with nest inventories. The work is strenuous and requires a great deal of walking (generally five to seven miles per night and during morning nest surveys) in a humid, tropical climate without flashlights, in soft sand, and in all weather conditions, all while wearing a five-pound backpack.

Project Location: CCC volunteers work in Tortuguero, Costa Rica, at the John H. Phipps Tortuguero Biological Field

Station. Snakes are present, although encounters are unlikely. Volunteers stay at CCC's station. Sleeping accommodations are dormitory style with up to six people per room. Modern plumbing, indoor showers, and potable water allow for a rustic yet comfortable stay. Caribbean-style meals, prepared by a local cook, are served with plenty of fresh fruits and vegetables. Private rooms at the field station or accommodations at a local ecolodge are also options.

Time Line: The Leatherback Sea Turtle Project runs from mid-March to early June, and the Green Turtle Project runs from late June to the end of October. Programs begin each Saturday during the season. The minimum stay with CCC is one week, and the maximum stay is four weeks.

Cost: CCC's program fee for one week is $1,554. This covers first- and last-night hotel accommodations in San José, land and boat transport to Tortuguero, all meals and shared accommodations at the field station, a guided tour by a local naturalist (either along a rainforest trail or by boat through the canal system), and all scheduled in-country transfers. Volunteers have to pay for their transportation to and from San José, Costa Rica, and for all meals while they are in San José.

Getting Started: Prospective volunteers should apply by either submitting an online registration form or by calling or mailing CCC to register, confirm dates, and obtain a contact number for travel information. Research protocol and sea turtle biology training is provided on-site the afternoon the volunteers arrive in Tortuguero.

Needed Skills and Specific Populations: This work is very strenuous, and good health and good physical condition are musts for all participants. Since most turtle tracking is done at night, phobias about being in the dark may pose a problem. The minimum age for volunteers traveling without a parent or legal guardian is 18; for volunteers traveling with a parent or legal guardian, it is 15. While CCC does not discourage any volunteers, seniors must judge for themselves (as all volunteers must do) if they can physically handle the work involved. Unfortunately, due to the remoteness of the location and the requirements of the work, CCC cannot accommodate people with disabilities at this time. Volunteers must speak English or Spanish.

Caribbean Volunteer Expeditions (CVE)

P.O. Box 388
Corning, NY 14830
(607) 962-7846; Fax: (607) 936-1153
E-mail: ahershcve@aol.com
Web site: www.cvexp.org

Project Type: Archaeology; Construction; Historic
    Preservation
Year Founded: 1990
Number of Volunteers Last Year: Approximately 40
Funding Sources: None; entirely self-funded
The Work They Do: CVE carries out historic preservation
    projects such as building surveys, reports, cemetery inven-
    tories, and actual construction on historic projects. Volun-
    teers help by recording buildings through photography and
    drawings, filling out forms, painting, and performing car-
    pentry work.
Project Location: Projects are located throughout the
    Caribbean. Most are in towns, but some are in more rural
    locations. Volunteers usually stay in cabins, hotels, or
    guesthouses.
Time Line: Projects go on throughout the year, usually for a
    week at a time.
Cost: $500 to $1,000 for one week. This program fee does not
    include airfare, but it does include lodging and food, which
    are arranged by CVE, as well as local transportation.
Getting Started: Prospective volunteers should call or e-mail
    CVE and request an application form. Training is provided
    to volunteers.
Needed Skills and Specific Populations: Volunteers under 18
    must be accompanied by a parent or guardian. Senior citi-
    zens are welcome to apply. CVE cannot accommodate vol-
    unteers with disabilities.

Anguilla Is a Family Affair

❖ By Karen Alpha ❖

Caribbean Volunteer Expeditions (CVE)

For vacation this year, we decided to go with two other families (friends!) on yet another Caribbean Volunteer Expedition. This multigenerational group of veteran CVEers arrived on the island of Anguilla, just a short ferry ride from St. Martin, to begin a new project and initiate a new CVE venue. As our family's luggage was lost en route, we immediately set to work visiting the site for a preliminary survey. Note for next trip: the bathing suit for that first welcome-to-the-islands swim goes in the carry-on!

Our project on Anguilla was to generate a property site plan and measure drawings of the buildings at Wallblake House, a remarkably well-preserved plantation house dating from 1787—much of it original—which has been nearly continuously inhabited for 200 years, most recently as a rectory. Severe hurricanes in recent years have damaged Wallblake to the extent that a complete restoration is being undertaken by CVE and the Wallblake Trust.

There were few plantations on Anguilla in colonial times, as the island is semiarid and relatively flat and so did not lend itself well to agriculture. Anguillans relied on fishing and boat building, as a rule—an altogether healthier and more democratic lifestyle, all agree—and participated in sea trade and the profitable salt industry. Wallblake was a cotton plantation, and its grounds are still extensive. We discovered overgrown ruins in the outlying areas and noted an obvious raised animal round that became a good vantage point for shooting

Two children figure out how to use a transit to survey the grounds of an ancient sugar plantation on the beautiful island of Anguilla. Helpful adults were part of the team as well! *Photo courtesy of Caribbean Volunteer Expeditions*

angles and distances with the transit. Closer to the house, we documented a large cemetery ground, an enormous stone cistern, and three lovely stone outbuildings, one of which, the bakery, held an amazing plastered stone recurve arch beehive oven in the end wall.

But the best thing about Wallblake is the interior of the house itself. Relatively small for a plantation house, the rooms are comfortably human-scaled but still elegant, reminiscent of a more gracious time. Most notable is the remarkable hand-carved woodwork that extends overhead into extraordinary tray ceilings highlighted with roped molding. Later we learned from the distinguished Sir Emile Gumbs, former prime minister of Anguilla, how this roping was carved, as his house also contains examples of it. "My grandfather had a shipwright who cut teeth into an old worn-out machete with a curved blade he had from Santo Domingo," confided Sir Emile, "and he set about hand cutting all the woodwork in this house." We can assume a similar endeavor at Wallblake; at every turn the island exhibits such colorful and engaging glimpses into its history.

We spent our mornings at the site, and during our afternoons we set out to explore the island, the villages, and especially the fabulous white beaches for which Anguilla is renown. The snorkeling was incredible, full of darting silver, yellow, and purple multicolored fish, cowries, limpets and giant conches.

And in the evenings we visited the Dune Preserve, home (literally! Pull up a hammock!) of reggae star and international recording artist Banky Banx, who provides a rum punch, an open-air dinner, and a show not soon forgotten.

Altogether we had a terrific trip, mixing island history, island vistas and island food (locri, salt fish, and johnnycake for lunch, Uncle Ernie's barbecue on the beach, a midmorning snack of coconut pie and Tang for the kids). This family of CVEers hopes to return to Anguilla and get a crew busy restoring the charming interiors of Wallblake.

Catalina Island Conservancy

P.O. Box 2739
Avalon, CA 90704
(310) 510-2595; Fax: (310) 510-2594
E-mail: volunteers@catalinaconservancy.org
Web site: www.catalinaconservancy.org

Project Type: Administrative; Construction; Historic Preservation; Natural Conservation (Land); Scientific Research; Trail Building/Maintenance

Mission Statement: "The mission of the Catalina Island Conservancy is to be a responsible steward of its lands through a balance of conservation, education, and recreation."

Year Founded: 1972

Number of Volunteers Last Year: 667

Funding Sources: Private donors

The Work They Do: The Catalina Island Conservancy protects and restores the environment on Catalina, promoting and modeling ecologically sustainable communities to create a healthier future for the island. Sample programs include research projects on flora and fauna; a native plant nursery; educational projects for schools, the community, and visitors; maintenance; and construction projects to support programs and provide recreational access. Examples of volunteer projects include building enclosures around rare and sensitive plant species unique to Catalina Island; processing and cleaning native seeds; transplanting native plants; assisting in monitoring of research projects; removing fences; assisting with maintenance and construction projects; removing weeds; and constructing trails. Volunteers work alongside staff members who manage each of the projects. This enables volunteers to gain in-depth knowledge of each project and how their work plays a vital part in the conservation and protection of open space on Catalina Island for future generations to enjoy.

Project Location: All work is done on Catalina Island, California. Most projects are conducted outside in beautiful, remote areas of the island with vistas, and they may require short hikes. Shade is not always available, but temperatures tend to be mild. Work usually entails a mixture of moderate to strenuous activities. Housing is provided at a private camp overlooking the ocean, with two large permanent tents with bunks, an outdoor kitchen, bathrooms with plumbing, indoor/outdoor showers, a fire pit, and a deck. Volunteers bring their own food for breakfast and lunch. A local volunteer chef cooks evening meals.

Time Line: Volunteers are accepted during specific weeks in the months of May, June, August, and September. Volunteer vacations begin on Monday at 1:00 P.M. and end on Friday around 2:00 P.M. Trips typically include three days of project service, working from 8:30 A.M. to 2:30 P.M., a half-day of beach cleanup at a remote beach, and a naturalist activity.

Cost: Volunteers pay a program fee of $130 per person, which includes accommodations for four nights, four evening meals, on-island transportation to and from projects, training, work supplies, and a naturalist activity. Volunteers must pay for transportation to the island and food for breakfast and lunch for four days.

Getting Started: Prospective volunteers should call or e-mail the Catalina Island Conservancy office. Orientation is held on Mondays in Avalon, California; the orientation includes an overview of the week's projects and activities, as well as a brief video. Volunteers are then transported to the volunteer camp, where they receive a camp orientation. Training is provided each day that the volunteers complete a new task. This training includes an overview of the larger project, tasks that will be accomplished that day, the importance of the tasks being accomplished, and how the project benefits the community. Instructions for handling tools safely are provided.

Needed Skills and Specific Populations: Volunteers should be in good physical condition and possess a willingness to work, get dirty, and try new things. The minimum age for volunteers is 18, though youth aged 12–17 may attend if accompanied by a parent or guardian. Senior citizens are encouraged to volunteer. The camp is supplied with a ramp to the tents for wheelchair access, but some projects may not be accessible to persons with disabilities.

Catholic Medical Mission Board (CMMB)
10 West 17th Street
New York, NY 10011
(800) 678-5659 or (212) 242-7757; Fax: (212) 242-0930
E-mail: info@cmmb.org or rdecostanzo@cmmb.org
Web site: www.cmmb.org

Project Type: Medical/Health

Mission Statement Excerpt: "[R]ooted in the healing ministry of Jesus, Catholic Medical Mission Board (CMMB) works collaboratively to provide quality health care programs and services, without discrimination, to people in need around the world."

Year Founded: 1928

Number of Volunteers Last Year: 110 short-term volunteers and 84 long-term volunteers

Funding Sources: Individual donors provide most of CMMB's funding, but it also receives USAID money for specific projects in Haiti and Kenya.

The Work They Do: CMMB primarily places medical volunteers in developing countries and distributes donated pharmaceuticals in those same countries.

Project Location: CMMB places volunteers in 24 countries in Africa, Asia, Latin America, and the Caribbean. Most volunteers work in mission hospitals. Many of these hospitals are in rural areas with limited resources, though some are in urban areas. Accommodations and food are provided by the host hospitals.

Time Line: CMMB places volunteers throughout the year. While a few sites accept volunteers for a few weeks or months, most CMMB volunteers make a six-month to one-year commitment.

Cost: There is no program fee to volunteer with CMMB, but the extent of support given by the host hospital depends on the length of the volunteer's stay. All volunteers receive free housing and food. Volunteers who commit to one year or more also receive full health insurance, all travel expenses, and a modest monthly stipend. Those volunteering for less than one year receive only insurance coverage.

Getting Started: Prospective volunteers should either download, complete, and send in an application or call the volunteer office. Applications are accepted on a rolling basis, and applicants are expected to interview in person at CMMB's office in New York City. Orientation is done on an individual basis.

Needed Skills and Specific Populations: CMMB only places medical professionals who are licensed in the United States or Canada, including, but not limited to, doctors, surgeons, nurses, physical therapists, occupational therapists, lab technicians, and pharmacists. Some placement sites accept families. Volunteers must be between the ages of 21 and 72. Volunteers with disabilities will find that not all sites can accommodate all disabilities. CMMB does not require that volunteers be Catholic, but volunteers must be willing to abide by the morals and ethics established by the host facility. Almost all of the host facilities are Catholic mission hospitals and clinics.

Cetacean Research and Rescue Unit (CRRU)

P.O. Box 11307
Banff AB45 3WB
Scotland
+44 (1261) 851 696; Fax: +44 (1261) 851 198
E-mail: volunteer@crru.org.uk
Web site: www.crru.org.uk

Project Type: Natural Conservation (Sea); Scientific Research

Mission Statement Excerpt: "The Cetacean Research and Rescue Unit (CRRU) is dedicated to the understanding, welfare, conservation, and protection of cetaceans (whales, dolphins, and porpoises) in Scottish waters through scientific investigation, environmental education, and the provision of professional veterinary assistance to sick, stranded, and injured individuals."

Year Founded: 1997

Number of Volunteers Last Year: 48

Funding Sources: Some corporate and commercial sponsorship, along with public donations and small grants.

The Work They Do: CRRU primarily focuses on an individually identified population of bottlenose dolphins that spend a large portion of the year in the rich coastal waters of the southern Moray Firth, as well as on a subpopulation of minke whales that frequent particular sites along the northeast coastline during the fall. The CRRU also operates the only 24-hour emergency rescue team for whales and dolphins in Scotland. Volunteers participate fully in all aspects of the project, including counting animals, recording behavior, determining geographical positions, and taking photographs. Back at the base, volunteers help identify the animals encountered, catalog slides and photographs, and analyze data. Volunteers have numerous opportunities to discuss methodologies, findings, and experiences; furthermore, volunteers are encouraged to formulate their own interpretations with the researchers and other volunteers.

The project staff may present informal lectures. Volunteers may be required to assist the team with rescue work, education, and public awareness activities.

Project Location: Volunteers are based and live in one of two cottages in the village of Gardenstown, in Gamrie Bay near Banff, on the southern coastline of the outer Moray Firth. Bedrooms are usually shared with up to three other people. All volunteers are expected to do their share of cooking, cleaning, and other similar tasks.

Time Line: Volunteers are accepted between May and October for fixed 12-day volunteer stints that begin on Saturdays and end on Thursdays. No more than eight volunteers are accepted per group. Long-term volunteers may be accepted on a case-by-case basis.

Cost: The program fee is £645, it covers all meals and accommodations for 12 days. International airfare is not included in the program fee.

Getting Started: Prospective volunteers should send a brief resume with preferred dates for participation by postal mail or e-mail. Be sure to include your full address, contact telephone numbers, and e-mail address. Training is offered by team leaders and biologists at the beginning of the project.

Needed Skills and Specific Populations: This project is suitable for anyone who has normal physical health. Individuals with poor eyesight, problems with balance, respiratory problems, problems with walking, or problems with their weight will, however, experience difficulties in fully participating in this volunteer experience. The ability to swim is preferred but not necessary, as life jackets are provided and full safety regulations and training are undertaken. Volunteers must speak English fluently and be at least 18 years old. They should also be committed to nature conservation and animal protection and have a positive attitude toward living and working with a small group of enthusiastic people from different backgrounds and cultures. Smoking is not permitted on the research boat, in the work space, or within any room or communal space within the accommodation facilities that are provided.

Cheyenne River Youth Project

Billy Mills Youth Center, "The Main"
P.O. Box 410
Eagle Butte, SD 57625
(605) 964-8200; Fax: (605) 964-8201
E-mail: info@lakotayouth.org
Web site: www.lakotayouth.org

Project Type: Administrative; Community Development; Youth

Mission Statement Excerpt: "The Main is a youth drop-in center that is open seven days a week, providing alternative recreational activities along with sports, arts, and crafts, as well as other support services."

Year Founded: 1988

Funding Sources: The Cheyenne River Youth Project receives financial support through grants, private donations, and local fundraising.

The Work They Do: The Main is a multipurpose community youth facility that serves members of the Cheyenne River Sioux Tribe. Volunteers at the Main work directly with children aged 4 to 17 and provide support in all aspects of the center's work, such as project fundraising, community activities, and building maintenance. Volunteers are responsible for the implementation of planned activities, the development of recreational activities, arts and crafts, sports activities, and meal and snack preparation.

Project Location: The Main is located on the 1.4-million-acre Cheyenne River Indian Reservation, in north-central South Dakota.

Time Line: Volunteers are accepted for commitments of six weeks to two years.

Cost: Volunteers are provided housing and a small living stipend; volunteers may also be eligible to receive food through the Food Distribution Program to supplement their income. Volunteers must travel, at their own expense, to Pierre, South Dakota, by airplane or bus; the Main provides transportation from Pierre to the reservation upon the volunteer's arrival.

Getting Started: Prospective volunteers can complete an online application via the organization's Web site. To finalize the application, volunteers must also submit three letters of recommendation, a criminal history background check, and a $75 application fee, for which waivers are available. Once the application is complete, the Main will arrange a telephone interview.

Needed Skills and Specific Populations: All volunteers must have patience, compassion, energy, dedication, motivation, and commitment. Volunteers who have experience working with children are preferred. Volunteers must be willing to work long hours and view this experience as a full-time job.

Child Family Health International (CFHI)
995 Market, 11th Floor
San Francisco, CA 94103
415-957-9000; Fax: 415-840-0486
E-mail: students@cfhi.org
Web site: www.cfhi.org

Project Type: Medical/Health

Mission Statement Excerpt: "Child Family Health International (CFHI) builds and strengthens sustainable health care services for underserved communities worldwide."

Year Founded: 1992

Number of Volunteers Last Year: 500

Funding Sources: Individual donors

The Work They Do: CFHI achieves its mission by building health infrastructure at the community level, increasing access to and efficient use of medical supplies, and promoting cultural competency and awareness of international health issues. Volunteers participate in the collection and distribution of recovered medical supplies, do clinical rotations with local physicians in developing countries, and study medical Spanish and cultural norms as they relate to the health systems of developing countries.

Project Location: CFHI operates a total of 11 sites in the countries of Bolivia, Ecuador, India, Mexico, and South Africa. Volunteers live with host families (in most cases) and work in local health care clinics and hospitals during the day. Most host families provide two or more meals per day. Meals taken outside of the host-family home are generally at the volunteer's own expense. Some programs do not utilize host families, in which case volunteers stay in small hotels, hostels, guesthouses, and dorm-style accommodations.

Time Line: All CFHI programs are either four or eight weeks long, and they run year-round. All programs begin on the first Sunday of each month.

Cost: Program fees are approximately $1,650, but they vary from site to site. Program fees include a pre-departure copy of the organization's *Country Handbook and Program Guide*, accommodations, some meals, a cultural orientation workbook, Spanish language training (where applicable), health and medical evacuation insurance, and medical supplies to transport and donate to the volunteer's work site. Fifty percent of the program fees go directly to the host community.

Getting Started: All applications are processed online via CFHI's Web site. In addition to receiving the pre-departure materials, volunteers can participate in a pre-departure orientation as well as an in-country orientation, and CFHI holds weekly in-country meetings. Volunteers also receive debriefing materials to assist them in their return home.

Needed Skills and Specific Populations: Participants should have a strong interest in clinical health, and they should have completed pre-health course work. Thirty-five percent of CFHI's volunteers are premedical students, 22 percent are in their first or second year of medical school, and 34 percent are in their third or fourth year (or beyond) of medical school. The remaining 9 percent of the volunteers are composed of nurses, nursing students, students studying for a Master's of Public Health, physician's assistants, or others studying the allied health fields. Volunteers must be at least 21 years old. Senior volunteers are accepted, but the large majority of CFHI volunteers are in their twenties. Prospective volunteers with disabilities are welcomed to apply, but they should consult closely with CFHI's program staff to make sure that the selected site is accessible.

Cholsey and Wallingford Railway

P.O. Box 16, Wallingford
Oxon OX10 9YN
United Kingdom
01491 835067
E-mail: CWRail@yahoo.co.uk
Web site: www.cholsey-wallingford-railway.com

Project Type: Construction; Historic Preservation; Museum;
Natural Conservation (Land)
Year Founded: 1983
Number of Volunteers Last Year: 30
The Work They Do: Volunteers are involved with the restoration of a historic railway.
Project Location: The railway is located in Wallingford, Oxfordshire, in the United Kingdom. Volunteers are responsible for arranging their own lodging and food.
Time Line: Volunteers are welcomed at any time. There is no minimum or maximum stay required.
Cost: There is no program fee, but volunteers must pay for and arrange all of their own logistics, including flights, airport transfers, housing, and food.
Getting Started: Call or e-mail the railway to arrange for a start date of your volunteer experience. There is no application process. No formal orientation is given to volunteers, though some basic training may be available.
Needed Skills and Specific Populations: Volunteers must be at least 16 years old; there is no maximum age limit. The Railway cannot accommodate volunteers with disabilities.

Christian Peacemaker Teams (CPT)

P.O. Box 6508
Chicago, IL 60680
(773) 277-0253; Fax: (773) 277-0291
E-mail: delegations@cpt.org
Web site: www.cpt.org

Project Type: Human Rights; Political Action; Social Justice

Mission Statement Excerpt: "Christian Peacemaker Teams (CPT) offers an organized, nonviolent alternative to war and other forms of lethal intergroup conflict. CPT provides organizational support to persons committed to faith-based nonviolent alternatives in situations where lethal conflict is an immediate reality or is supported by public policy."

Year Founded: 1988

Number of Volunteers Last Year: 189

Funding Sources: Donations from church congregations and individuals, including a small percentage from church denominations. CPT also receives some small grants from private, church, or human rights-oriented foundations. CPT is an initiative of the Historic Peace Churches (Mennonites, Church of the Brethren, and Quakers) with support and membership from a range of Catholic and Protestant denominations.

The Work They Do: CPT focuses on violence deterrence, human rights observation and documentation, accompaniment of vulnerable individuals or groups in conflict areas, and service as a nonviolent public witness. Volunteers meet with local peacemakers and populations affected by violent conflict, engage in human rights documentation, and participate in nonviolent direct action. Volunteers also commit to sharing their experiences with a wider audience upon return to their home communities.

Project Location: As of this writing, volunteers work in Hebron (West Bank, Palestine), Iraq, Colombia, Kenora/Grassy Narrows (Ontario, Canada), and on the

Arizona-Mexico border, but this list changes as human rights situations change around the world. Volunteer teams stay in modest accommodations in the city, such as apartments or modest hotels or hostels with shared rooms, and they may travel to the countryside, where accommodations are similar to camping. Volunteers are housed together with at least two people (often more) per room. Depending on the location, volunteers may be required to walk over rough terrain, scramble over muddy riverbanks, or endure extreme heat or cold. Two meals per day are provided.

Time Line: The schedule changes yearly, but there are volunteer opportunities available throughout the year, though not always in every location. In general, all locations accept volunteer teams four to six times per year. Volunteers can work with CPT for ten days to two weeks.

Cost: Program fees run from $1,000 to $2,500, which covers all project expenses, including airfare.

Getting Started: Prospective volunteers should fill out an application for a "Short Term Delegation." These applications can be downloaded from the CPT Web site or are available from the Chicago office. CPT does not require any special training prior to delegation participation.

Needed Skills and Specific Populations: Volunteers should have experience or an interest in working for human rights and cross-cultural understanding, a commitment to non-violence, and a willingness to participate in nonviolent public witness, team worship, and reflection. The minimum age to volunteer with CPT is 18; many participants have been in their seventies, and a few have been age 80 and above. However, a degree of physical stamina, such as the ability to walk up to two or three miles over rough terrain, is required. CPT may not be able to accommodate persons with certain kinds of disabilities (for example, limited transportation options in the West Bank might preclude the acceptance of a volunteer who uses a wheelchair for that program).

All I Ask Is That I Not Become Indifferent

❖ By Elizabeth Redekopp ❖

Christian Peacemaker Teams (CPT)

The author, age 21, of Winnipeg, Manitoba, was part of a
delegation to Colombia in May 2003.

On Monday, May 26, 2003, more than 150 women, men,
and children gathered in the streets of a small neighborhood
in Barrancabermeja, Colombia, to walk, pray, and sing for
peace. This group action, which began as a discussion in
someone's living room, came alive as we were greeted by an
overwhelming crowd of Colombian partners and locals. One
hundred candles were passed out. Evening was upon us. We
began lighting the candles . . . one . . . two . . . three . . . until
the street was filled with light.

The first stop in our pilgrimage through this neighborhood was the house of a young man killed by paramilitaries
a few weeks earlier. We proclaimed these words of the
gospel, "Blessed are the poor in spirit for theirs is the kingdom of heaven. Blessed are those who mourn for they shall
be comforted." We prayed that in our grief we would be
touched by God's healing, and that in our emptiness we
would be filled with strength to be instruments of God's
peace.

We then processed to a place where the husband of a
woman we know was killed. Here, we again read two beati-
tudes and reflected on the message for us as a people of God.

We called for an end to all actions which diminish life, and for courage and power to continue hungering and thirsting for righteousness and peace. A young man, who was a relative of the man killed in this place, asked if he could play a traditional flute song in remembrance of his brother, who also loved music and art. We were then led in the song *Solo le Pido a Dios*, in English, "All I Ask of God, is that I do not become indifferent to death and suffering."

The next place we stopped was a place that has been used repeatedly for murdering humans. We remembered friends and loved ones who died in this place and prayed for hearts big enough to forgive. "Blessed are the merciful, for they shall obtain mercy. Blessed are the pure in heart, for they shall see God." As we gathered at the last site, the place of a horrible massacre, people began placing their candles along the road. One by one people added their lights to the row until we had a line of 100 illuminated candles, shining in the dark of the evening. At the end of journey we expressed our gratitude for having been able to participate in this pilgrimage together, and explained that we were a delegation of Christians from Canada and the United States who had come to learn about the violence in Colombia. We told our Colombian partners and the locals gathered that we were touched by the stories we had heard and that we would not forget them as we returned to our homes. The Colombians responded with applause, smiles, warm embraces, and kisses. Our prayers continue: "All I ask is that I do not become indifferent."

Citizens Network for Foreign Affairs (CNFA)

111 19th Street NW, Suite 900
Washington, DC 20036
(888) 872-2632 or (202) 296-3920; Fax: (202) 296-3948
E-mail: info@cnfa.org
Web site: www.cnfa.org

Project Type: Agriculture; Economic Development; Professional/Technical Assistance; Rural Development

Mission Statement Excerpt: "The Citizens Network for Foreign Affairs (CNFA) is . . . dedicated to stimulating economic growth around the world by nurturing entrepreneurship, private enterprise, and market linkage."

Year Founded: 1985

Number of Volunteers Last Year: 81

Funding Sources: USAID

The Work They Do: CNFA specializes in engaging private companies of all sizes in partnerships to expand economic activity and increase incomes. Through its volunteer program, CNFA helps people build a free market–based food and agricultural system. Since 1993, more than 600 volunteers have participated in this program. In order to achieve the greatest impact, CNFA sends multiple volunteers to long-term projects, with each volunteer assignment building upon previous ones. CNFA's long-term projects seek to develop private farmer associations, cooperatives, private agribusinesses, women's and young farmer's groups, and other organizations that can help people increase their incomes. Volunteers provide help to a wide variety of groups, including dairy processors and producers, beef cattle farmers, mushroom producers, honey producers, fruit growers, and greenhouse producers. The majority of volunteer hosts are democratically structured farmers' associations and cooperatives or small-scale agribusinesses. Typical assignments focus on strengthening associations, developing marketing skills, business planning, and developing financial management skills. Occasionally, CNFA will field a volunteer to train in crop production or processing for an individual farmer or agribusiness enterprise.

Project Location: CNFA volunteers work in the former Soviet states of the Ukraine, Belarus, and Moldova. Volunteer site locations vary from rural villages to capital cities. In cities, volunteers are provided an apartment, and they have full access to bathing and cooking facilities, as well as to laundry and cleaning services. In villages, each volunteer and a translator will stay with a host family. Although lodging conditions are modest, every effort is made to provide comfort for the volunteer during his or her stay. The host family also provides meals.

Time Line: Volunteers are accepted throughout the year, usually for three weeks at a time. The minimum volunteer stint is 16 days, and there is no maximum length of time for volunteers.

Cost: There is no program fee; all costs for volunteers are covered by CNFA.

Getting Started: Potential volunteers may submit an application and resume online. Other than a short briefing, volunteers receive no training. It is assumed that any appropriate volunteer will already have experience, so training should not be needed.

Needed Skills and Specific Populations: CNFA seeks experienced volunteers from a variety of specialties: farmers and ranchers, cooperative specialists, food processing professionals, agribusiness executives, extension agents, agricultural organization leaders, and others. Volunteers should have at least five years of experience in their fields, and senior citizens are encouraged to volunteer. Volunteers with disabilities are welcomed, but no special accommodations may be made. CNFA volunteers must be U.S. citizens or green card holders.

The Quest for Uniform Potatoes

❖ By William Wise ❖

Citizens Network for Foreign Affairs (CNFA)

The author is President and CEO of the Oregon Potato Commission.

"Moldova, where is that?" I wondered. I soon learned that it is an eastern European country, formerly part of the Soviet Union, which gained independence in 1991. I joined the Agribusiness Volunteer Program of CNFA and was sent to Moldova for the summer to see if I could help local growers and shippers with the arduous task of transitioning from collective farming to life in a market economy.

I did some research to learn more about Moldova than its location. Moldova is about the size of Maryland, or Belgium, and it is the poorest country in Europe. The population is only around 4.4 million, with a per capita income of $1,800. Agriculture accounts for 43 percent of the GDP (gross domestic product) and represents the number-one business in the country. The market in Moldova couldn't be more different from what I am used to working with in Oregon.

I arrived in Moldova and spent my first few days in the capital city of Chisinau. I visited several wholesale markets, checking out the potatoes (my specialty!) and onions, and noted that the price of the vegetables was completely independent of the quality of the vegetables. This disconnect is something you would not see in the United States. American growers are extremely quality conscious and understand that this factor is key to the successful marketing of their product. In Moldova, growers were used to a collective farming system under the Soviet regime (only recently had private farms become a reality) and quality had never been either an issue or a concern. After viewing the markets in the capital, I was ready to head out into the countryside.

I was driven north three hours to Donduseni, a farming village. There I encountered a different world from Chisinau. The Moldovan countryside was beautiful, with an abundance of crops including apples, corn, peaches, and sunflowers. Soon there were more horse-drawn carts than cars. Wells with buckets were in use in each town and village. I felt like we had stepped back in time, to an era lacking technology.

In Donduseni, I met with growers in an agricultural cooperative. We sketched out a plan for developing value-added products that the coop could sell in the Chisinau market. I introduced the idea of quality and uniformity of product, and explained the concept of packaging the product in an appealing manner.

We got right to work. We created a label for the coop. Next, we cut ½-kilo, 1-kilo, and 2-kilo bags from larger wholesale bags and had the coop's label hand sewn onto the bags. We culled the produce they had collected in the fields, picking high quality and uniform vegetables and filled up our sacks. Next, we headed to Chisinau and made contacts with distributors. One distributor sells to 28 grocery stores in the area. During our meetings it became apparent that the wholesale distributors really appreciated the cleanliness, uniformity, and quality of the produce and the package we showed them. The entire concept of meeting the demands of a potential customer was something startlingly new to the coop members and was a hard concept to grasp. Our plan was complete; the product created, the contacts made, the market

William Wise pauses by a roadside in Moldova as a farmer passes by transporting hay by use of a traditional horse-drawn cart. Working with rural farmers to increase produce quality and locate markets were challenging aspects to volunteering with CNFA in Moldova. *Photo courtesy of Citizens Network of Foreign Affairs*

obtained. Now all the villagers had to do was follow through. My time in Moldova was at an end.

Since returning home, I've heard from my friends in Moldova. They have moved ahead with the plan we put together and are selling to the grocery retail trade. They admitted to having some skepticism about how substantial this segment of the industry might be in Chisinau because most Moldovan people do not shop in grocery stores, but they have been pleasantly surprised to find there is a viable market for quality produce in grocery stores. The growers are increasing the amount of produce they send to Chisinau. It is my hope that they will soon explore additional buyers, perhaps even in neighboring Romania, as our plan suggested.

Back at my desk in Portland, Oregon, I have a new appreciation for the production and marketing skills that our growers possess. One take-home lesson for me is that we are pretty good at what we do in agriculture in the United States and we are fortunate to have a system that rewards the efforts we make to add quality and value to the supply chain for the benefit of our growers. My time in Moldova was beneficial to the coop in Donduseni, but it was just as valuable to me.

The Colorado Trail Foundation (CTF)

710 10th Street, #210
Golden, CO 80401
(303) 384-3729; Fax: (303) 384-3743
E-mail: ctf@coloradotrail.org
Web site: www.coloradotrail.org

Project Type: Natural Conservation (Land); Trail Building/Maintenance

Mission Statement Excerpt: "The mission of The Colorado Trail Foundation is to provide and to maintain, through voluntary and public involvement . . . a linear, nonmotorized, sustainable recreation trail between Denver and Durango, Colorado."

Year Founded: 1974

Number of Volunteers Last Year: 400

Funding Sources: Government and private donors

The Work They Do: CTF maintains the 470-mile, high-altitude, nonmotorized trail between Denver and Durango, Colorado. Volunteers rehabilitate sections of eroded trail, build bridges, create waterbars to divert water off the trail, install culverts, and reroute sections of the trail.

Project Location: Volunteers work in national forests along the spectacular Colorado Trail and camp in tents, which volunteers must provide. Campsites are reached by conventional vehicle, a four-wheel-drive vehicle, or backpacking. Elevations range from 6,000 to 11,000 feet. A description of each camp and work site is given with the crew registration materials. CTF provides the food for each volunteer crew.

Time Line: Volunteers are accepted in the months of June, July, and August. Volunteers work weekends, from Friday evening through Sunday afternoon, or for a full week, Saturday through Saturday.

Cost: Weekend crew members pay $25, and weeklong crew members pay $50. However, although volunteers may sign up for multiple weekend or weeklong crews, they pay the program fee only once per year. Obviously, for this low price, transportation costs to Colorado are not included in the program fee.

Getting Started: Prospective volunteers should contact CTF via phone, e-mail, or postal mail. Trail crew leaders conduct a crew orientation session, a trail building session, and a tool safety session on the first day.

Needed Skills and Specific Populations: Volunteers must be at least 16 years old; there is no maximum age limit. CTF cannot accommodate volunteers with disabilities.

Rolling Rocks

❖ By Rhiannon Mercer ❖

The Colorado Trail Foundation (CTF)

We gathered by a creek in the beautiful Collegiate Peaks Wilderness, a group of strangers from Colorado, Michigan, and New Mexico who soon became a team that was able to laugh while working hard to complete some necessary repair work on the great Colorado Trail. We spent a week together and managed to build a turnpike and a culvert.

The week began on Saturday. We strapped on our heavy packs and walked in the aromatic wake of the packhorses for four miles to our campsite. On reaching the campsite it was discovered that we failed to pack the poles for the kitchen tent, but with an ax and a handsaw we had it upright in no time. (The later discovery of missing dehydrated green beans from the supplies was not so easily remedied.) On Sunday, after a tour of the work site and a tool safety demonstration, the crew scattered into the hills for day hikes.

The work started on Monday. First we cleared out all the muck from a water-damaged trail. This involved much moving of mud with buckets. We had races to see who could move the most earth the fastest, to lighten our tasks and make us laugh. Everyone dove into the hard work and contributed all they could. Next, we scavenged the forest for rocks. We needed all sizes and rolled them (some quite a distance!) to their new resting spots at our work site. Logs were cut and peeled to act as a stabilizer for the turnpike, and soon, the open rock culvert materialized. Vegetation was reintroduced above the trail where the former slope was damaged. In the end, the completed project was a beautiful sight to behold.

Friday night, the crew celebrated the 30th anniversary of the Colorado Trail as well as the 40th anniversary of the Wilderness Act, candles and all! A Forest Service employee arrived with news that the fire ban for the area had been lifted. Enjoying our first and only campfire, we listened intently to a lengthy ghost story told by a volunteer. It was a lighthearted and fun evening to end a fantastic and productive week.

Conservation Volunteers Australia (CVA)

P.O. Box 423
Ballarat Vic 3353
Australia
(61) 3-5330-2600; Fax: (61) 3-5330-2922
E-mail: info@conservationvolunteers.com.au
Web site: www.conservationvolunteers.com.au

Project Type: Historic Preservation; Natural Conservation
(Land); Trail Building/Maintenance
Mission Statement: "To attract and manage a force of volunteers on practical conservation projects for the betterment
of the Australian environment."
Year Founded: 1982
Number of Volunteers Last Year: 5,000, including 2,000 international volunteers
Funding Sources: Government and private sources
The Work They Do: CVA takes on large-scale, critical environmental problems that can be addressed only through a significant amount of hands-on labor. CVA completes more
than 3,000 individual conservation projects each year.
Examples of projects include planting more than 750,000
trees annually; assisting with manual clearance of invasive
weeds, such as buffel grass in the beautiful surrounds of
Uluru (Ayers Rock); assisting with trail projects on Fraser
Island, the largest sand island in the world; surveying
endangered yellow-footed rock wallabies in the Flinders
Ranges of southern Australia; creating koala habitats; and
restoring historic buildings, including the first settlement
and gold rush–era properties. Volunteer activities are
hands-on, labor-intensive projects such as planting trees,
removing weeds, clearing trails, completing carpentry projects, and radio-tracking animals.
Project Location: Any at given time, up to 60 projects may be
occurring simultaneously across Australia. Volunteers
should be prepared to be outside all day, taking into

account the climate conditions and season when they are participating. CVA teams live together on or near the project site. Accommodations vary according to project and location. Typical accommodations can include caravans, hostels, bunkhouses, and camping, for which tents are provided. Volunteers should bring a sleeping mat as well as a sleeping bag. Volunteers are expected to help with the preparation of meals and the cleaning up of dishes, plus minor domestic duties, as required.

Time Line: Projects operate year-round. While individual projects can last from one day up to several weeks, volunteers must commit to a minimum of four weeks. There is a recommended maximum stay of twelve weeks; most volunteers stay for approximately six weeks.

Cost: The program fee for four weeks is A$ 815; the fee for six weeks is A$ 1,200. The program fees include all meals, accommodations, project-related travel within Australia, CVA membership, and a CVA T-shirt. Volunteers are responsible for their own airfare to Australia.

Getting Started: Prospective volunteers should contact CVA through its Web site, via e-mail, or by postal mail. Volunteers join a team with a maximum of ten volunteers and one CVA team leader. The team leader is responsible for managing the group's health and safety, for explaining the goals and aims of the project, and for providing on-site skills training to enable volunteers to safely and effectively complete the project. All volunteers complete a comprehensive orientation that includes an introduction to CVA, discussions on occupational health and safety, project details, and planned activities. Further orientation at the start of each individual conservation project outlines the reasons for and aims of the activity. Each day also has at least one safety briefing session.

Needed Skills and Specific Populations: All projects involve physical activity, so volunteers should be reasonably fit and healthy. Volunteers must listen carefully and comply with instructions from team leaders. International volunteers must be at least 18 years old, and senior citizens are "very welcome" to volunteer with CVA. CVA recommends that individuals with disabilities review the organization's Web site and judge for themselves whether this would be an appropriate activity. If so, please contact CVA to discuss your particular needs.

Coral Cay Conservation (CCC)

The Tower, 13th Floor, 125 High Street
London SW19 2JG
United Kingdom
+44 (0) 870 750 0668; Fax: +44 (0) 870 750 0667
E-mail: info@coralcay.org
Web site: www.coralcay.org

Project Type: Natural Conservation (Land); Natural Conservation (Sea); Scientific Research

Mission Statement Excerpt: "Providing resources to help sustain livelihoods and alleviate poverty through the protection, restoration, and management of coral reefs and tropical forests."

Year Founded: 1986

Number of Volunteers Last Year: More than 500

Funding Sources: No outside sources; self-funded

The Work They Do: CCC carries out tropical forest and coral reef conservation projects. Volunteers help collect scientific data, which is then used to form sustainable management recommendations. Volunteers can split their time between a marine expedition and a forest expedition.

Project Location: CCC volunteers work in remote, tropical environments in Fiji, Malaysia, Honduras, and the Philippines. Volunteers stay in fairly basic dormitories.

Time Line: Projects run year-round and have monthly start dates. The minimum stay is two weeks; there is no maximum stay.

Cost: Program fees for marine expeditions start at £700, and program fees for forest expeditions start at £550. Program fees include accommodations, food, and training. The costs of flights, insurance, and some equipment are not included.

Getting Started: Prospective volunteers can download an enrollment packet from CCC's Web site or contact the office to request that one be sent via postal mail. If required, science and scuba training can be provided on-site.

Needed Skills and Specific Populations: Volunteers do not need to have scientific or scuba training before volunteering. Volunteers must be at least 16 years old; there is no maximum age limit. CCC accepts volunteers from around the world. Volunteers with disabilities should contact CCC's office to discuss their particular situation.

Two Dives a Day in Paradise

❖ **By Mandy Hengeveld** ❖

Coral Cay Conservation (CCC)

"What is that thing moving in the shallows?" one of the volunteers exclaimed in surprise. It was a monitor lizard, out for a swim. I must confess, I never knew that these reptiles could swim. I guess it is not only humans that are enticed by the gorgeous turquoise blue waters that surround the Perhentian Islands! The waters here are truly incredible. They are an inviting 29°C (84°F) and extremely clear. From both the boats and the shore, one can make out the outlines of the fringing reefs and watch groups of damselfish dart around in the shallows. These damselfish are part of the seemingly endless assortment of fish, corals, algae, and invertebrates that, together, form a close-knit community consisting of tens of thousands of individual organisms.

After a brief orientation with CCC, we are now diving twice a day, surveying the reef and its inhabitants. On one of my first dives, I sat at the bottom and watched, enthralled by the interaction between the sand-dwelling gobies and their blind shrimp partners. While the goby stands guard at the mouth of its burrow, ready to alert the blind shrimp of any oncoming danger, the shrimp diligently digs out the subsurface home for both animals. Just one example of the many complex symbiotic relationships found between different types of organisms on coral reefs.

Although we are doing work while diving by surveying the reefs, each dive holds an element of surprise. You simply can't predict what you will witness during data collection.

A passing school of barracuda? A cryptic conch? A towering colony of dazzling blue coral? Coral reefs are like a massive box full of surprises. To the keen eye, each and every underwater visit holds a very special treat.

Unlike other coral reef sites I have visited in Southeast Asia, the reefs here appear to be relatively healthy. An interview with the head of marine parks here in the state of Terangganu revealed to me that the three biggest threats to reefs in this area are land-based pollution, fishing, and intensive use of the reef ecosystem—but not the extremely destructive dynamite or cyanide fishing practices I've witnessed in other areas. What a pleasant surprise!

There has been relatively little data collected in this area, so our research and surveying efforts are really important and will provide both the national and local governments with the information required to develop integrated management plans for the Perhentians. I feel honored to be able to make this contribution to protect the environment. And I'm thrilled that I get to do it by diving twice a day in paradise!

Cross-Cultural Solutions (CCS)

2 Clinton Place
New Rochelle, NY 10801
(800) 380-4777 or (914) 632-0022; Fax: (914) 632-8494
E-mail: info@crossculturalsolutions.org
Web site: www.crossculturalsolutions.org

Project Type: Community Development; Developmental Disabilities; Education; Medical/Health; Orphans; Women's Issues; Youth

Mission Statement Excerpt: "Our mission is to operate volunteer programs around the world in partnership with sustainable community initiatives, bringing people together to work side by side while sharing perspectives and fostering cultural understanding."

Year Founded: 1995

Number of Volunteers Last Year: Nearly 2,000

Funding Sources: Occasional funding from private donors, but mostly funded by program fees

The Work They Do: CCS operates extensive international programs that offer a wide range of volunteer opportunities. Volunteer placement is based on each individual's skills and interests. Each volunteer is required to fill out a skills and interest survey that helps CCS place the volunteer with a local partner program. Specific examples of volunteer positions available with CCS include: taking care of children in day-care centers and orphanages; teaching conversational English; conducting educational activities for teenagers; working with women's groups; caring for and developing activities for the elderly; observing and assisting with a local medical practice; taking care of people with mental and physical disabilities; and taking care of people living with HIV/AIDS. CCS is a recognized leader in the international volunteer field; it is in Special Consultative Status with the United Nations and in partnership with CARE, one of the world's largest international humanitarian organizations. CCS has been profiled in more than 300 news outlets.

Project Location: CCS volunteer programs are located in Brazil, China, Costa Rica, Ghana, Guatemala, India, Peru, Russia, Tanzania, and Thailand. All volunteers work in partnership with sustainable community initiatives in settings such as schools, orphanages, elderly homes, community homes, clinics, and offices. CCS provides a "home base" for all volunteers in each given country, which typically consists of a comfortable house in a local, middle-class neighborhood. Clean, modest accommodations with shared rooms are the standard. Accommodations always have basic amenities such as linens and running water. As part of the CCS program, staff cooks prepare and serve daily meals and snacks based on the regional cuisine.

Time Line: Volunteer programs are offered year-round, though start dates vary by program site. Volunteers stay for one to twelve weeks, though longer programs may be arranged on an individual basis.

Cost: CCS's program fee is $2,278 for two weeks and $259 for each additional week. Included in the program fee are all accommodations, meals, and in-country transportation; "Perspectives Programming," including excursions to nearby points of interest and special events; and in-country medical insurance. International airfare is not included in the program fee. Only 12 percent of CCS's program fee goes toward administrative expenses.

Getting Started: Prospective volunteers can join CCS through the "Enroll" section of the organization's Web site or by calling their toll-free phone number. Because CCS participants are from all over the world, the organization does not offer an orientation program prior to departure. However, all volunteers receive prepatory materials and pre-departure guidance, and once the volunteer arrives at the program site, there is an in-country orientation that is run by the local staff.

Needed Skills and Specific Populations: No specific skills, background, or experience are required to volunteer with CCS, though volunteers must have at least a basic knowledge of the English language. The minimum age for unaccompanied volunteers is usually 18, though some programs may accept 16- and 17-year-olds. The minimum age for a child traveling with a parent or guardian is 8. Senior volunteers are welcomed and are encouraged to join CCS. Volunteers with disabilities are also welcomed, and CCS has experience in placing volunteers with disabilities.

Mastering the Art of Building People

❖ By Justine (last name unavailable) ❖

Cross-Cultural Solutions (CCS)

I am in Costa Rica. It is taking 20 minutes to drive up this hill. Not because it's a far destination we're seeking, but because the road is congested with children, dogs, and an occasional broken-down jeep. Finally, our car takes a turn and we travel on a secondary road up to the blue-green building that sits on top of a hill. I walk in and there are children everywhere. As I step inside, not one of them looks up from their activities.

Standing in the middle of the room, the flurry of activity around me is slowed by my racing mind. First thought: why will they not look up at me? Second thought: will I be able to breach these cultural distances? Third thought: am I really capable of affecting 20 lives? A tug on my jeans brings the pace of my surroundings and the pace of my mind back to the room. Acknowledgment. Finally. A small boy holds up a yellow truck with three wheels. He does not say a word—he just smiles.

It has only taken a few days for the children to reach out to me. I feel a sense of relief when I walk into the little playroom now. It is definitely more welcoming than the bumpy ride up the hill. Today I've brought some string and lots of cut-up, colorful straws for the purpose of creating necklaces. Noel is so little. He must be about two and a half years old. He lets go of the blue straw and it slips down the string to meet his hand. He glances at me with the grin of accomplishment spread wide across his face and my heart skips a beat. His teeth are rotted out on top. I noticed a few days ago that there are toothbrushes above the communal sink, but they never come down. The rotted teeth behind his wondrous smile seem to epitomize a certain contradiction in his life. These children are so young, I think. They thrive under circumstances that we deem unlivable, and yet Noel smiles at me as if he is the happiest child on earth.

The drive is long again today. I want to arrive more quickly. I brought pictures of my family and friends. I sit down on the floor when I arrive and Flavia lies with her head in my lap. I play with her short brown hair and begin to sing. They gather around me and we all sit together. Joseph seems uninterested. He sits in the corner with his small dinosaurs. All of a sudden, as I am catching my breath, he starts to sing his own song. One voice turns into twenty and I am sitting in the middle of a chorus of expressive voices and clapping hands. Simple, honest joy.

One month has passed. The once bare walls of the room are covered in paintings and pictures. Joseph, Hazel, and I sing together every morning. Sammy does not build guns anymore with his clay. We've mastered the art of building people instead. My heart is aching right now. I cannot believe that I have to leave.

Cultural Destination Nepal (CDN)

G.P.O. Box #11535
Kathmandu, Nepal
+ (977) 1 437-7623 or + (977) 1 437-7696
Fax: + (977) 1 437-7696
E-mail: cdnnepal@wlink.com.np or
info@volunteernepal.org.np
Web site: www.volunteernepal.org.np

Project Type: Community Development; Developmental Disabilities; Education; Medical/Health; Rural Development; Youth

Mission Statement Excerpt: "Cultural Destination Nepal (CDN) aims to introduce the participant to Nepal's diverse geographical and cultural environment and to promote intercultural understanding through experiential learning in Nepal."

Year Founded: 1996

Number of Volunteers Last Year: 42

Funding Sources: Some funding is received from private donors

The Work They Do: Most volunteers teach English, social studies, mathematics, science, or environmental studies in Nepali schools. CDN also provides placement in nonprofit organizations that work in the areas of women's issues, the environment, disabled children, and other areas; however, volunteers in these more specialized fields must be qualified both through work or previous volunteer experiences and through their education. Volunteers also have the opportunity to participate in outdoor activities and excursions, as well as in cultural exchanges. Secondary projects may also be available at the placement site.

Project Location: All volunteers work in Nepal. During the two-week orientation, volunteers stay with a host family near CDN's offices; during the volunteer project, volunteers reside with a host family or in a hostel.

Time Line: Volunteers begin their volunteer experience as part of a group in February, April, June, August, or October. Volunteers commit to two- to four-month stints, with the average volunteer staying three to four months.

Cost: The program fee is $650. The fee includes a two-week orientation program (pre-service training); lodging with a host family; two meals a day (breakfast and dinner); a cultural orientation tour; cross-cultural orientation; a hiking day trip; lectures on Nepali religion, cultures, political system, history, and gender relations; guided meditation; cultural activities; volunteer placement; a village excursion; a jungle safari; white-water rafting; and in-country transportation. Expenses not included in the program fee are the volunteer's airfare to and from Nepal, insurance, personal expenses, visa fees, and entrance fees to tourist sites visited during training.

Getting Started: Contact CDN and request an application form, which must be returned by registered mail along with a resume, four copies of passport-sized photographs, and a nonrefundable application fee of $50. CDN offers what appears to be a very impressive two-week orientation program, which includes a general orientation to Nepali customs, language (taught by professional language teachers), and community interaction skills, all conducted while volunteers stay with host families. The cultural orientation includes discussions about Nepali history and a tour of historic cities within the Kathmandu Valley. Interestingly, it also includes a tour of basic service providers such as the post office, banks, and health clinics. The orientation also includes a one-day hiking trip outside of Kathmandu and lectures on religion, culture, history, politics, geography, necessary health precautions, women in Nepal, and various other topics that explain the diversity of Nepali life. Volunteers can also request lectures if they want to learn more about a particular topic during orientation.

Needed Skills and Specific Populations: Volunteers must be at least 18 years old and have a high school diploma. Senior volunteers are welcomed; the eldest CDN volunteer to date was 65 years old. Volunteers with disabilities are welcomed, but may not be able to participate in all of the planned activities.

Cultural Restoration Tourism Project (CRTP)

410 Paloma Avenue
Pacifica, CA 94044
(415) 563-7221
E-mail: info@crtp.net
Web site: www.crtp.net

Project Type: Agriculture; Archaeology; Community Develop-
ment; Construction; Economic Development; Historic
Preservation; Natural Conservation (Land); Social Justice;
Trail Building/Maintenance; Youth

Mission Statement Excerpt: "The mission of the Cultural
Restoration Tourism Project (CRTP) is to help communities
around the world restore artifacts of cultural importance,
promote responsible tourism, encourage cultural interaction, and provide a model of alternative funding for
other nonprofit organizations or grass-roots organizers."

Year Founded: 1998

Number of Volunteers Last Year: More than 100

Funding Sources: No outside funding sources

The Work They Do: CRTP is dedicated to the restoration of
culturally significant buildings and to community development around those buildings. Currently, it is restoring
monasteries in Nepal and Mongolia. Community development work, such as agricultural projects, education, and
cottage industry development, is carried out along with the
building projects. CRTP's volunteer opportunities consist of
a wide variety of construction tasks and community work,
including working in the garden and helping out in the
kitchen or on the construction site. Depending on volunteers' experiences and backgrounds, they may be handling
a shovel, a paintbrush, or a chisel.

Project Location: CRTP's current projects are located in rural,
remote areas of Mongolia and Nepal. Solar or hydroelec-
tric power and emergency communications are available.
Accommodations are in traditional housing for the area

and are shared with other travelers. The sites are environmentally beautiful, and living quarters are set up next to the work sites. Meals are prepared by the indigenous staff and are shared among the volunteers and locals.

Time Line: CRTP offers programs during many parts of the year. The average volunteer stay is two weeks.

Cost: The program fee to volunteer with CRTP is approximately $1,000 per week, which includes travel within the country, accommodations, and food while at the work site. Volunteers must also pay for their travel to the country of service.

Getting Started: Prospective volunteers should call or e-mail CRTP.

Needed Skills and Specific Populations: No previous skills or experience are required. To date, CRTP's youngest volunteer was 14 and the oldest was 76. Prospective volunteers with disabilities are encouraged to call the office and make an inquiry, but those with mobility difficulties will find the project sites to be inaccessible.

Dakshinayan

F–1169, Chittaranjan Park, First Floor
New Delhi—110019
India
+91 98242 74370; Fax: +91 94313 97178
E-mail: info@dakshinayan.org
Web site: www.dakshinayan.org

Project Type: Education; Rural Development; Youth
Mission Statement Excerpt: "Dakshinayan is a volunteer-based
organization providing education and health care to tribal
and other rural communities in India."
Year Founded: 1992
Number of Volunteers Last Year: 42
Funding Sources: None; self-funded
The Work They Do: Dakshinayan offers volunteers the opportunity to teach primary education classes to children in
remote villages in India. Volunteers help teach basic English, games, and art. Dakshinayan's objective is to provide
people who are concerned about development issues a
unique opportunity to observe and experience the culture
of rural India and to study the problems of communities
while gaining an in-depth perspective of the myth and reality of poverty in an economically developing nation. Dakshinayan's emphasis is not on work but rather on volunteer
participation in ongoing project activities and community
life. Therefore, work and activities are not organized especially for the volunteers.
Project Location: Dakshinayan's project is located in the Sun-
dar Pahari Block of Godda District in the new tribal state
of Jharkhand, India. Volunteers are usually placed on projects that are remote and that do not have electricity or
running water. Living conditions are basic, and food consists of simple vegetarian meals made from whatever vegetables are available locally.

Time Line: Volunteers are accepted year-round, but they must apply at least one month before they wish to depart, and they must arrive in New Delhi before the fifth of the month in which they wish to begin work. Volunteers must commit to at least one month of work.

Cost: Dakshinayan's program fee is $300 per month, which includes food and accommodation while at the project. Transportation costs to and from the project are not included.

Getting Started: Prospective volunteers should request, complete, and return a questionnaire by e-mail, which will then be screened. No orientation is given, though Dakshinayan provides some instructions and informal conversations before departure.

Needed Skills and Specific Populations: No special skills or certification are required, as most volunteers teach small children basic English or mathematics. A volunteer who cannot teach either subject may teach the children about the volunteer's own culture. Volunteers must be 18–30. Dakshinayan cannot accommodate volunteers with disabilities. Volunteers must be very culturally sensitive, as they are placed in rural villages that have had little exposure to other cultures.

DELPHIS

Island of Ischia, via Zaro n. 22
80075 Forio (NA)
Italy
+ 0039 081 989578
E-mail: info@delphismdc.org
Web site: www.delphismdc.org

Project Type: Natural Conservation (Sea); Scientific Research
Mission Statement Excerpt: "The conservation of cetaceans in
Mediterranean Sea, in particular the short-beaked common
dolphin."
Year Founded: 2000
Number of Volunteers Last Year: Approximately 80
Funding Sources: DELPHIS receives grants from a number of
international animal welfare funds, including the Humane
Society (United States), ASMS Ocean Care (Switzerland),
and the United Kingdom's RSPCA.
The Work They Do: DELPHIS's research is focused on conserving groups of cetaceans such as common, striped, bottlenose, and Risso's dolphins, as well as pilot, sperm, and
fin whales. The project examines the degree of residency of
cetaceans around the island of Ischia; estimates the population size; examines the social structure of the population
and assesses the production of calves; studies habitat use
and distribution; examines the dolphins' behavior; estimates the impact on animals of both fishery operations and
recreational vessel traffic; and studies the acoustic reper-
toire. Volunteers spend all day at sea, where they help
researchers study dolphins by spotting, observing, and noting dolphin behavior. Volunteers also help sail the boats,
and they are treated to lectures on cetology. In the
evenings, volunteers can help transfer data into the main
computer and have an opportunity to learn more about
techniques and research topics from the DELPHIS staff. It
is expected that all volunteers also help with the daily

duties, including cleaning the boat, shopping, cooking, and washing the dishes. At the end of the week, all participants are expected to help with the general cleaning of the boat before leaving.

Project Location: Near the islands of Ischia, Procida, and Vivara off the Italian coast in the Gulf of Naples. Volunteers live on board the *Jean Gab*, a 17.7-meter (58-foot) sailing laboratory that was built in 1930. The boat includes a kitchen, sleeping quarters for six people, restrooms, and a changing room. Volunteers should be aware of the possibility of mixed-sex sleeping arrangements. The shower is on deck, and it features solar-powered hot water. Life on board the ship is simple and communal.

Time Line: Volunteers are accepted between May and October, for a maximum of three weeks. Volunteers commit to at least one week on the boat.

Cost: The program fee runs between $720 and $820 per week, depending on the week selected; the most expensive weeks are in late July and early to mid-August. The program fee includes all meals and lodging on board, insurance, membership in DELPHIS, and fuel and port fees. Not included is transportation to Ischia and the first night's dinner on shore. Lunch and dinner are important social events on board, and they are served outside on a splendid table with a view of the sea and often dolphins. If crew members all agree, some dinners are consumed in local taverns, which allows volunteers to experience the local culture.

Getting Started: Prospective volunteers should download the application form found on DELPHIS's Web site, complete it, and fax or e-mail it to them. DELPHIS does not offer training or orientation.

Needed Skills and Specific Populations: Volunteers must be in good physical condition, speak English or Italian, and be at least 16 years old or accompanied by an adult. Senior volunteers are welcomed as long as they understand and accept that conditions are rugged. Prospective volunteers with disabilities are also welcomed, though evaluations will be made on a case-by-case basis to determine the feasibility of volunteering with DELPHIS. Volunteers with vision, hearing, balance, or locomotive difficulties will face particular challenges with living on a boat. All volunteers should be aware of the challenges inherent in living and working in close quarters and approach the project with flexibility and a sense of humor.

Dolphin Research Center (DRC)

58901 Overseas Highway
Grassy Key, FL 33050
(305) 289-1121 x230; Fax: (305) 743-7627
E-mail: drc-vr@dolphins.org
Web site: www.dolphins.org

Project Type: Developmental Disabilities; Natural Conservation
(Land); Natural Conservation (Sea); Scientific Research
Mission Statement Excerpt: "The Dolphin Research Center
(DRC) exists to provide the very best care humanly possible to the animals who call this place home. Following
that, DRC conducts research to increase knowledge about
dolphins, their needs, and their capabilities, and educates
through a variety of methods, especially through experiential programs that bring people into close contact with dolphins, creating bonds that encourage students and guests to
become ambassadors for dolphins and the environment we
share."
Year Founded: 1984
Number of Volunteers Last Year: 75
Funding Sources: Private donors
The Work They Do: DRC is an education and research facility
dedicated to educating the general population on the value
of marine life in the world and to promoting conservation.
It provides interactive programs, such as swimming and
playing with dolphins, participating in conservation workshops, recycling office supplies, participating in educational
outreach, and participating in a manatee rescue program.
Volunteers serve as the primary caregivers to DRC's exotic
bird population, assist guests in public programs, act as
docents for DRC activities, assist in preparation and
cleanup of dolphins' meals, assist the medical staff with
capturing dolphins, and provide general facility support.

Project Location: All volunteer projects take place outdoors at DRC's facility in the Florida Keys. Volunteers must provide their own accommodations.

Time Line: First-time volunteers from out of town must commit to a minimum of four weeks, though subsequent volunteer trips to DRC can be shorter. DRC also accepts interns for 12 to 18 weeks.

Cost: There is no program fee, but DRC asks that volunteers purchase one shirt with the DRC logo for $10. Volunteers are responsible for all of their own expenses, including housing, food, and travel. Volunteers should expect to spend $750 to $1,000 per month on living expenses in the summer and fall, and $1,500 to $2,000 per month in the winter and spring, when prices in the Florida Keys rise dramatically.

Getting Started: Applications for prospective volunteers are available on DRC's Web site. This can be printed, completed, and mailed or faxed to DRC's office. DRC provides one day of orientation and two days of training, all on-site, for new volunteers.

Needed Skills and Specific Populations: Volunteers must be at least 18 years old. Several senior volunteers have been mainstays of the DRC's staff during the winter months, and DRC welcomes other senior volunteers. DRC will work with volunteers with disabilities to find appropriate positions for them. Volunteers must be able to speak and understand English.

Earthwatch Institute

3 Clock Tower Place
Maynard, MA 01754
(800) 776-0188; Fax: (978) 461-2332
E-mail: info@earthwatch.org
Web site: www.earthwatch.org

Project Type: Archaeology; Community Development; Historic
Preservation; Natural Conservation (Land); Natural Conservation (Sea); Scientific Research
Mission Statement Excerpt: "Earthwatch Institute engages
people worldwide in scientific field research and education
to promote the understanding and action necessary for a
sustainable environment."
Year Founded: 1971
Number of Volunteers Last Year: 4,000
Funding Sources: Some money from private sources
The Work They Do: Earthwatch Institute expeditions are
short-term volunteer opportunities to directly assist qualified and respected scientists in their field research and to
work on critical and current issues. Research topics span a
wide range of scientific study and include ecology, zoology,
and archaeology. The range of tasks on Earthwatch Institute expeditions is enormous, from using dental picks to
coax free a dinosaur bone to freeing a bird from a mist net.
Other examples of possible volunteer activities include
counting fish on a coral reef, recording the mating rituals
of monkeys, interviewing poor farmers or homeless
women, and utilizing scientific instruments (from a gravity
meter to a satellite tracking system to a pair of tweezers
and a magnifying glass). Other volunteers might whisk the
dust off of a bowl that was last seen by a Roman soldier in
the first century A.D. or dig up the remains of ancient
hominids in Olduvai Gorge.
Project Location: Volunteer projects are carried out in 49
countries around the world, from the United States to

Tanzania to Mongolia. Much of Earthwatch Institute's work takes place in wildlife reserves, at important historical sites, and in national parks. In some cases, volunteers work in areas that are inaccessible to tourists, in pristine regions that only researchers are allowed to enter. Accommodations and food arrangements vary widely and might take the form of hammocks, dorm rooms, country inns, formal hotels, or condos, and they may or may not include electricity or running water. Food ranges from spaghetti cooked over a fire to four-course meals in a safari camp. Earthwatch Institute's online project descriptions provide specific details for each trip.

Time Line: Projects are offered year-round, though each project takes place in a specific time frame. Most projects are 10 to 14 days long, but there are also one-week, three-week, and weekend opportunities available. The shortest projects take place over a weekend, and the longest projects run 22 days.

Cost: Program fees range from $400 to $4,000, with the average being about $2,000. The program fee includes accommodations and food, travel during the expedition, and any permits that are needed. Only 12 percent of the program fees go to administrative overhead costs; the remainder goes toward paying for the volunteer's expenses and for the scientific research project. Volunteers must provide their own airfare to the work site, and pay for other personal expenses. Earthwatch Institute estimates that the average volunteer spends about $750 on airfare and $250 on other expenses.

Getting Started: Prospective volunteers can sign up for an expedition online, over the phone, or through the mail. Volunteers then receive an expedition briefing that includes all of the necessary program details. In the field, volunteers are given one or more training sessions that cover all needed skills with the exception of scuba certification, which is required by one or more projects. Some projects require volunteers to have extensive backpacking and camping experience before their arrival.

Needed Skills and Specific Populations: All projects have a minimum age requirement of either 16 or 18. Senior volunteers are encouraged to work with Earthwatch Institute. Volunteers with disabilities are welcomed provided that the type and level of disability can be accommodated by the specific project. Expeditions that require a high level of fitness or scuba certification are clearly identified in their online descriptions.

Shards, Obsidian, and Lower Blood Pressure

❖ **By Ladnor Geissinger** ❖

Earthwatch Institute

My adventure began while standing in line at Starbucks, waiting for my cup of coffee; I picked up a brochure and was introduced to Earthwatch Institute (for once my addiction to caffeine paid off). Soon their expedition guide arrived, and what caught my eye was the opportunity to join an archaeological dig at an ancient Mayan site in Guatemala. I was instantly hooked. For at least 40 years I've been interested in Central America, the Maya, and archaeology. As a math professor, I don't get many opportunities to check out some ancient history or dig for buried treasure in a foreign country. Here was my chance to finally pursue a lifelong dream.

So for two weeks a dozen of us from all over America (and one from London) volunteered in the small Mayan town of Chocola', which sits in the middle of a large pre-classic Maya site. Our team included schoolteachers, a couple who own a marketing survey company, a venture capitalist, an architect, a retired business professor, and an accountant (these last two had each been on three earlier Earthwatch expeditions). Each of us felt drawn to this project and were excited for a new experience.

Chocola' is located about 40 miles from the Pacific coast, at the foot of a line of volcanoes which form the southern border of beautiful Lake Atitlan. In the time of the ancient

Maya the principal crop grown here was cacao, the source of chocolate, and this formed the basis for their trade with other peoples. By the late 1800s Chocola' was part of a huge German-owned coffee plantation which the Guatemalan government expropriated in 1946. Because of the existence of the plantation, the town has a good water system, a town hall, and a water-powered machine shop and coffee mill that are still in use, in addition to the old plantation house and guesthouse. Everywhere that anyone digs in Chocola', for a house or to fix broken water pipes or for street work, Mayan artifacts are unearthed. We dug at two mounds right outside the town, in small clearings among the coffee bushes (kind of karmic to end up right where this adventure started—with coffee).

Over the course of two weeks we learned how to do field archaeology. Using sophisticated GPS (Global Positioning System) equipment, we laid out grids to help with surveying mounds and terraces. Once we had our plots marked off, the manual labor started. We dug up and carted off *tons* of dirt, uncovering walls and house foundations and exposing an extensive system of channels that was used to distribute water. We sifted through the dirt and were rewarded by finding shards, obsidian, bits of charcoal, a figurine, and ceremonial bowls. Lastly, we cleaned what we found. It was exciting to uncover a bit of the history of the Mayas, to hold it in our hands.

When we weren't digging at the site, we would take short field trips. Everything was fun and fascinating to explore. One day we visited another large ancient Mayan site, Takalik Abaj, which has had ongoing excavations and restoration for more than 25 years and is now a national park and popular tourist site. In May 2004 *National Geographic Magazine* had an article on unearthing a royal tomb there. We imagine that some day the Chocola' site will look a lot like that. One weekend we visited Lake Atitlan and the resort of Panajachel. Another time we took a long hike through the wild tangled mountain area above the town, along small streams in steep-sided valleys with dense vegetation, many birds, and awesome trees. Occasionally we came across small fields of corn, beans, coffee, and squash, as well as fruit trees. A short bus trip took us to a nearby town to wander and shop in the open market, where it seemed they had everything.

There was also time to spend in town. One afternoon I sat under some palm trees watching a soccer match played on the top of a shaved mound with the volcanoes above, the green coastal plain below, and, far off, the Pacific Ocean. With the sun going down and the light changing in the lush, green valley below, it was hard to remember the stress and busyness of life back home. One of our last nights in Guatemala, we threw a party and some of the town folk came out and joined us because we hired the local marimba band. They were terrific! Quite a festive closure to a two-week crash course in field archaeology.

I came away from my time with Earthwatch not only with an education in field archaeology, but also more knowledgeable about the opportunities (volunteer and otherwise) that are opening up to me in the future as I consider retiring. Volunteering gave me a chance to experience something new on a short-term basis. I highly recommend this opportunity to anyone who is nearing retirement or thinking of a career change.

One final note from a 66-year-old volunteer: the day following my return to the States, I had a regular doctor's appointment. My blood pressure was lower than ever before. Do you suppose there is a connection? I certainly think so. And it bodes well for me to have a long and healthy future full of exciting volunteer adventures! I wish you the same.

Eco-Center Caput Insulae—Beli (ECCIB)

Beli 4, 51559 Beli
Island of Cres
Croatia
+385 51840525
E-mail: caput.insulae@ri.htnet.hr
Web site: www.caput-insulae.com

Project Type: Archaeology; Community Development; Historic
  Preservation; Natural Conservation (Land); Rural Development; Scientific Research
Mission Statement Excerpt: "Protect and preserve natural
  diversity and work toward the protection of original values
  and cultural-historical heritages."
Year Founded: 1993
Number of Volunteers Last Year: 350
Funding Sources: Government and private funding
The Work They Do: Eco-centre Caput Insulae—Beli (ECCIB)
  works to protect Eurasian griffon vultures and the natural
  and historical heritage of the island of Cres in Croatia. Volunteers help conduct observations of griffon vultures, learn
  about and maintain historic stone walls, assist with trail
  maintenance, build labyrinths, and staff and maintain a
  historical interpretation center.
Project Location: Volunteers live and work in the village of
  Beli, to the north of the Adriatic island of Cres, in Croatia.
  The village dates back to 4,000 B.C.E., when it was a
  Roman settlement. Volunteers stay in dormitories that have
  shower and kitchen facilities, and cooking tends to be
  communal.
Time Line: Volunteers are accepted from mid-January through
  mid-December. Volunteers must stay at least one week, and
  the maximum volunteer stint is six months. The average
  volunteer stays for three or four weeks.
Cost: One-week projects cost between $98 and $149, while
  two-week projects cost between $122 and $271. Every

extra day costs $10. The program fee includes travel from the town of Cres to the village of Beli, accommodation, and training; it does not include travel to Cres, insurance, visas, or meals.

Getting Started: Prospective volunteers should contact ECCIB by e-mail or phone. On the first day after arrival, volunteers are given an introductory lecture that includes information on the Eurasian griffon vulture and the surrounding area. For the first few days, volunteers accompany a coordinator or an ecocenter staff member to learn more about the work done at the center. Later during their stay, volunteers take a day-long hike along the ecotrails in the area and have the opportunity to explore the island of Cres.

Needed Skills and Specific Populations: Volunteers must be at least 16 years old, speak English, Croatian, or Polish, and be in good physical condition, which includes the ability to swim. Senior citizens are welcome to volunteer with ECCIB, as are volunteers with disabilities who meet the physical requirements.

Ecovolunteer Program

Meijersweg 29, 7553 AX
Hengelo
The Netherlands
(31) 74-2508250; Fax: (31) 74-2506572
E-mail: info@ecovolunteer.org
Web site: www.ecovolunteer.org

Project Type: Natural Conservation (Land); Natural Conservation (Sea); Scientific Research
Year Founded: 1992 as a part of a larger organization; became an independent organization in 1998
Number of Volunteers Last Year: Approximately 500
Funding Sources: None; self-supported
The Work They Do: The Ecovolunteer Program offers a large number of diverse volunteer opportunities in wildlife conservation, animal rescue, and fieldwork. Sample projects include: giant otter research in Bolivia, Tucuxi dolphin research in Brazil, river otter research in Brazil; humpback whale research in Brazil; conservation of rare breeds of horses, sheep, and livestock-guarding dogs in Bulgaria; wolf research in Bulgaria; whale research in Canada; tropical rainforest research in Colombia; griffon vulture research in Croatia; Andean bear research in Ecuador; bottlenose dolphin research in Italy; Przewalski horse reintroduction in Mongolia; beaver research in Poland; wolf research in Portugal; wolf research in Russia; bottlenose dolphin research in Scotland; rhino conservation in Swaziland; gibbon center maintenance in Thailand; wildlife center maintenance in Thailand; elephant camp maintenance in Thailand; marine turtle conservation in Thailand; Monkseal Project participation in Turkey; and African wild dog research in Zimbabwe. In all of these projects, volunteers participate as hands-on assistants. All projects are conducted by local nongovernmental organizations according to local standards. A high level of adaptability and flexibility is sometimes required of volunteers to cope with different organizations around the world.

Project Location: The Ecovolunteer Program runs approximately 30 projects per year in North America, South America, Asia, Africa, Oceania, and Europe. Work sites vary from jungle-based to boat-based; accommodations vary from tented camps to small bungalows, and from a field station to a small local hotel. The level of conditions is usually fairly basic, and volunteers should not expect luxury.

Time Line: There are always projects available throughout the year, though not all projects are available at all times. While some specific projects run year-round, others are seasonal, depending on, for example, the migratory patterns of birds. Lengths of projects vary, but volunteers can set their own dates of arrival and departure. In general, the Ecovolunteer Program expects a minimum of a week-long commitment and a maximum commitment of six months.

Cost: Program fees range from approximately $500 to $1,500 for a two-week project, but they vary based on the project and the length of the volunteer experience. Included in the program fees are lodging and, usually, food; when food is not included, it is almost always available nearby and is quite inexpensive. Not included in the program fee are transportation costs, travel insurance, and any visa expenses. Approximately 80 percent of the program fee is used to administer the volunteer experience itself, with most of the rest going into program overhead.

Getting Started: Prospective volunteers should apply via the program's Web site. Projects usually include on-the-job training, and some also offer an introductory day or lectures.

Needed Skills and Specific Populations: Most projects require participants to be at least 18 years old, though a few mandate that volunteers be at least 20 or 21 years old. Similarly, most projects do not have a maximum age, though there are a few exceptions to this. Most of Ecovolunteer Program's projects are not suitable for volunteers with disabilities, but final decisions will be made on a case-by-case basis by the project manager, who will review the applicant's file.

El Porvenir

48 Clifford Terrace
San Francisco, CA 94117
(303) 520-0093; Fax: (413) 618-4048
E-mail: info@elporvenir.org
Web site: www.elporvenir.org

Project Type: Community Development; Construction; Rural Development

Mission Statement Excerpt: "Through sustainable water, sanitation, and reforestation projects, El Porvenir works to improve the standard of living of poor people in rural Nicaragua."

Year Founded: 1990

Number of Volunteers Last Year: 72

Funding Sources: Faith-based and private sources

The Work They Do: El Porvenir works with villagers to build wells, latrines, communal wash facilities for bathing and washing clothes, efficient wood-burning stoves, and community tree nurseries. Water and sanitation projects may include building a communal washing facility near the village well, which will relieve women of the burden of carrying water long distances to wash clothes; rehabilitating a well to ensure that the community has access to safe drinking water; and building latrines to prevent the spread of disease and to protect the water source. Reforestation projects include clearing brush areas, planting seedlings, fencing areas, and building efficient wood-burning stoves. Villagers who are assisted by this project live in adobe or brick homes with dirt floors, and they rarely have electricity. The conditions are poor, but the villagers are committed to improving their lives and they welcome the volunteers to their communities. Volunteers work alongside villagers mixing cement, laying bricks, cutting and tying wire, sifting sand, and filling bags for planting trees. The tasks range from easy to difficult, and the volunteers decide which tasks they will perform. All of El Porvenir's projects are initiated, built, and maintained by the villagers, and El Porvenir supports locally owned businesses whenever possible.

Project Location: Projects are carried out in central Nicaragua in the small villages near the towns of El Sauce, Camoapa, and Ciudad Dario. Volunteers stay in modest hotels in nearby towns and travel daily via four-wheel drive trucks to the work sites in small villages. Most meals are eaten in restaurants, though some are eaten in the host communities.

Time Line: Trips are offered throughout the year, usually in January, February, March, June, July, August, September, and November, and they are one to two weeks in length.

Cost: A two-week trip with El Porvenir costs between $800 and $1,050. The program fee includes food, lodging, all in-country transportation, two bilingual guides, travel and health insurance, and activity fees. Volunteers are responsible for their own transportation to and from Nicaragua. Two hundred dollars of the program fee goes directly to the population being served.

Getting Started: Prospective volunteers should contact El Porvenir via e-mail or phone to request an information form. Orientation and a brief history of Nicaragua are provided to volunteers upon arrival.

Needed Skills and Specific Populations: A parent must accompany volunteers who are younger than 18. El Porvenir offers two elderhostel trips per year for volunteers over 55 years old. Volunteers with disabilities are welcomed as long as they can climb in and out of a four-wheel drive truck, climb steps, and exist comfortably in a tropical climate. Refrigeration is available for medications. Volunteers from outside the United States should check Nicaragua's visa regulations before applying.

Explorations in Travel (ET)

2458 River Road
Guilford, VT 05301
(802) 257-0152; Fax: (802) 257-2784
E-mail: explore@volunteertravel.com
Web site: www.volunteertravel.com

Project Type: Education; Natural Conservation (Land); Trail Building/Maintenance

Mission Statement Excerpt: "To provide qualified volunteers for grassroots organizations working to protect environments, develop sustainable industries, and animal welfare and rehabilitation."

Year Founded: 1991

Number of Volunteers Last Year: 15

Funding Sources: None; self-funded

The Work They Do: ET assists independent organizations in locating volunteers in the areas of education, animal welfare, wildlife rehabilitation, and conservation.

Project Location: ET operates programs in Costa Rica, Puerto Rico, Ecuador, Belize, and Guatemala. Most work sites are in rural, less developed locations. Some work may be physical; it can be hot and humid, and there will be insects. Actual physical conditions vary from site to site. In some cases volunteers live with local host families in a rural setting; in other cases they share housing with other volunteers. ET arranges for housing.

Time Line: Projects go on throughout the year. Most sites prefer that volunteers stay for a minimum of one month.

Cost: There is a $35 application fee and a $975 program fee. Additionally, volunteers make a $100 donation to their host organization.

Getting Started: Prospective volunteers should e-mail ET for an application. The volunteer's supervisor provides orientation on-site.

Needed Skills and Specific Populations: Volunteers must be at least 18 years old. Senior citizens are welcomed. Some sites may be accessible to volunteers with disabilities. ET places volunteers from all over the world, but it does not assist with obtaining visas. ET requests volunteers who are "mature and self-motivated."

Farm Sanctuary

P.O. Box 150
Watkins Glen, NY 14891
(607) 583-2225; Fax: (607) 583-2041
E-mail: intern@farmsanctuary.org
Web site: www.farmsanctuary.org

Project Type: Administrative; Agriculture; Political Action
Mission Statement Excerpt: "Farm Sanctuary is working to change the way society views and treats animals used for food production."
Year Founded: 1986
The Work They Do: Farm Sanctuary volunteers help take care of and feed hundreds of animals and run the organization's two farms. Volunteer tasks include general farm chores such as barn cleaning, animal care, and feeding, as well as staffing the organization's visitor centers, running educational tours, and helping with administrative projects. Volunteers who choose to live at the shelter also assist with shelter security, which includes being on-call two to three nights during the week in case of emergency. Volunteers are also required to share in household cleaning chores and to keep community areas clean. In addition to their regular duties, many of Farm Sanctuary's volunteers choose to help with extra programs, such as animal health care and grooming, research, and activist campaigns.
Project Location: Farm Sanctuary owns two farms: a 175-acre shelter in upstate New York, near Ithaca, and a 300-acre shelter in northern California, 30 miles west of Chico. These farms house more than 1,000 rescued cows, pigs, chickens, turkeys, sheep, goats, rabbits, ducks, and geese. On-site housing is offered to all Farm Sanctuary volunteers, and it includes shared bedrooms, bathrooms, and kitchen facilities.
Time Line: Farm Sanctuary internships are available year-round. Positions are filled on an ongoing basis as

applications are received; summer months are the most popular for volunteers, so prospective summer volunteers are well advised to apply early. Volunteer positions begin on the first day of every month. Volunteers must commit to at least one month of service, though Farm Sanctuary prefers that volunteers stay two or three months. All volunteers work a full-time, 40-hour-per-week schedule. The shelters are open seven days a week, so volunteer schedules generally include weekends and holidays.

Cost: There is no program fee to volunteer with Farm Sanctuary, and housing is provided at no charge. Volunteers must provide their own transportation to the work site and are responsible for buying and preparing their own food. Weekly trips to the grocery store are provided for volunteers without vehicles.

Getting Started: Prospective volunteers can complete an online application, available at Farm Sanctuary's Web site, or can call to request an internship application. Applicants are asked to submit two letters of recommendation on their behalf.

Needed Skills and Specific Populations: Volunteers must be at least 16 years old. They must have a strong commitment to animal rights and a personal commitment to vegetarianism or veganism. All staff members and volunteers are required to follow vegan practices while on Farm Sanctuary premises, which includes diet (no meat, dairy products, eggs, honey, or other animal byproducts), personal care items (cruelty-free and nonanimal by-products), and clothing (no leather, silk, or wool).

Foundation for Sustainable Development (FSD)

870 Market Street, Suite 321
San Francisco, CA 94102
(415) 283-4873
E-mail: info@fsdinternational.org
Web site: www.fsdinternational.org

Project Type: Administrative; Agriculture; Community Development; Construction; Developmental Disabilities; Economic Development; Education; Human Rights; Legal; Medical/Health; Natural Conservation (Land); Orphans; Professional/Technical Assistance; Social Justice; Rural Development; Trail Building/Maintenance; Women's Issues; Youth

Teaching is a key part of sustainable development—sharing your skills with another, so they can carry on teaching after you return home. A student at the University of North Carolina volunteered with FSD in Dar Es Salaam, Tanzania. Although he was placed in the area of youth education and worked primarily in an elementary school, he also developed an English literacy class for adults when he saw the need in the community. *Photo courtesy of Foundation for Sustainable Development*

Mission Statement Excerpt: "The Foundation for Sustainable Development (FSD) supports the efforts of grassroots development organizations in the developing world that are working to better their communities, environments, and the economic opportunities around them."

Year Founded: 1995

Number of Volunteers Last Year: More than 100

Funding Sources: Private donors and grants

The Work They Do: FSD offers a number of types of volunteer experiences, including eight-week or longer internships, short-term volunteer placements that last from one to six weeks, "enrichment trips" for self-formed groups, "alternative spring breaks" for college students, the ProCorps program for experienced professionals and retirees, and the longer-term GradCorps for recent college graduates. The work done by volunteers depends on the program and place selected. Examples of internships include teaching in an elementary or secondary school, creating a Web site and a marketing plan for a women's sewing cooperative, conducting a health survey in a rural village, developing a tree nursery as an income-generating activity for a community group, creating finance and business training courses for microfinance clients, preparing workshops on topics such as health and hygiene, giving environment and conservation talks at schools, and writing grants and proposals for funding development projects.

Project Location: Projects take place in Argentina, Bolivia, Ecuador, India, Kenya, Nicaragua, Peru, Tanzania, and Uganda. Both rural and urban placements are available. Living conditions can be pretty basic, but almost all sites have running water and electricity. Program participants usually stay with host families, but some of the study tours and trips also involve hostels and hotels.

Time Line: Volunteer opportunities are available year-round (some summer programs begin in May or June and run for eight to ten weeks). Volunteers must commit to one week of service, but they can volunteer for up to a year. The average volunteer stays two to four months.

Cost: Program fees vary by country, but they range from about $500 to $3,000. The program fees cover all in-country expenses including room, board, transportation, training materials, communications, a host organization grant or a service project grant, a group leader, translation, logistical support, health insurance and emergency evacuation coverage, orientation and debriefing sessions, and program support. It does not include airfare to and from the country of service.

Getting Started: Prospective volunteers can download an application from FSD's Web site. FSD provides an information packet prior to departure, as well as an in-country orientation and training that can last from one day to one week, depending on the country and the program.

Needed Skills and Specific Populations: Volunteers should have a demonstrated interest in international development. Spanish is required for volunteering with the Latin American internship program. Volunteers must be at least 18 years old; senior citizens are welcomed. FSD is able to accommodate some volunteers with disabilities.

Friends of the Cumbres and Toltec Scenic Railroad

6005 Osuna Road, NE
Albuquerque, NM 87109
(505) 880-1311; Fax: (505) 856-7543
E-mail: nanclark@cumbrestoltec.org
Web site: www.cumbrestoltec.org

Project Type: Archaeology; Construction; Historic Preservation; Museum; Natural Conservation (Land)

Mission Statement Excerpt: "The Friends is organized to serve a public purpose—the historic preservation of the Cumbres and Toltec Scenic Railroad."

Year Founded: 1988

Number of Volunteers Last Year: 420

Funding Sources: Some funding from private sources; membership dues

The Work They Do: The Friends is in charge of interpretation, preservation, and restoration of this historic railroad, including rolling stock and structures. This work includes repairs, reconstruction, painting, car lettering, rail line clearing, interior repairs to locomotive cabs, landscaping, archaeological study of previously existing structures, and a docent program. Most volunteers help with woodworking, painting, electrical work, carpentry and construction, and landscaping and gardening. Other volunteers help to document historic restoration work, serve as docents, or work on archaeological studies.

Project Location: Volunteers work in northern New Mexico and southern Colorado along the 64-mile railroad line, which is at high elevations that range from 7,800 to 10,000 feet above sea level. Volunteers are responsible for their own accommodations; a large percentage stay in one of three local campgrounds, and the remainder stay in bed-and-breakfasts or motels.

Time Line: Volunteers are accepted for two weeks in each of the months of May, June, and August. Volunteers must commit to at least one five-day work week, Monday to Friday, though many volunteers stay for two consecutive weeks. The exception to this is docents, who are utilized from Memorial Day through mid-October.

Cost: The program fee is $40 per week, plus a one-time insurance charge of $15 per year. The $40 fee covers a daily sack lunch and daily snacks and drinks. Volunteers must provide for their own transportation, lodging, breakfasts, and dinners.

Getting Started: Prospective volunteers should download registration materials from the Friends' Web site or request them from the main office. People must join the organization before participating as volunteers. Volunteers select up to three preferred assignments from the list of scheduled work session projects; these choices are submitted along with the registration materials. Every effort is made to assign volunteers to a requested project, and volunteers are notified ahead of time of their assignment. Each Monday a safety meeting is held, after which volunteers meet with their team leaders and the rest of their volunteer groups for a project-specific orientation prior to beginning their work.

Needed Skills and Specific Populations: Volunteers should come into this experience with skills already in place; they should not expect to be trained in these areas. Volunteers for the regular programs must be at least 13 years old; though there is a junior volunteer program for youth aged 10–12, who may take on limited, supervised responsibilities. Senior volunteers are welcomed and may request "light duty" if there are health issues or limitations. However, volunteers should remember that the work is all at high elevation and in a remote area with limited medical facilities. Volunteers with disabilities may find access around the railroad yard difficult because of the railroad tracks. In addition, support cars for volunteers are actually boxcars, and volunteers are required to enter them via freestanding stairs. The Friends welcome any volunteers with disabilities who can work within those limitations.

Friends of the Great Baikal Trail (FGBT)

2638 Warring Street, Suite C
Berkeley, CA 94704
(415) 788-3666, x109; Fax: (415) 788-7324
E-mail: baikalwatch@igc.org
Web site:
www.earthisland.org/ecotours/volunteer/eurasia/baikal/
gbt_brochure.html

Project Type: Community Development; Economic Development; Historic Preservation; Natural Conservation (Land);
Natural Conservation (Sea); Trail Building/Maintenance

Mission Statement Excerpt: "The FGBT promotes sustainable
economies in eastern Russia, first and foremost by encouraging the development of ecotourism in the region."

Year Founded: 1991

Number of Volunteers Last Year: 348

Funding Sources: Government and private sources

The Work They Do: FGBT helps to recruit and organize teams
of international volunteers to work on any of dozens of
trail-building projects that occur each summer in the parks
and nature reserves around Lake Baikal, the largest and
deepest lake in the world. Most of the volunteers work
alongside local people to build the Great Baikal Trail as a
way to promote low-impact tourism to the region. In some
instances, volunteers help with design, interpretation (both
language and natural), and other less manual aspects of
FGBT's work. However, most of the work involves digging,
leveling, and the construction of campsites and other
wooden structures along the trail. Half of the members of
volunteer groups are Russians from local towns and cities,
and half are non-Russian citizens.

Project Location: Volunteers work at one of several dozen
work sites along the shores of Lake Baikal in Russia. Most
work sites are within one or more of the national parks
around the lake. Several of the project areas run into the

mountain ranges that surround the lake. Most work sites are located in wilderness areas and are often not easy to access by roads or other public transport, although most are accessible by boat. Accommodation is almost always in tents, which are provided by FGBT. Food, which is also provided by FGBT, is prepared at campsites. Most trail-building sites are located within walking distance of the lake, where volunteers can swim and hang out on the shore. The national parks approve each work site, along with the trails themselves, to make sure that environmental impact is minimal.

Time Line: Projects run from June to September, and each lasts two weeks. Volunteers can work on two consecutive projects, and volunteers with extensive trail-building experience may sign up for more than that.

Cost: Volunteers pay a program fee of $250 for two weeks, which covers all of the on-site program costs, including food and lodging in tents, language interpretation, and training. Volunteers are responsible for their travel to Irkutsk via Moscow (which involves traveling by either air or train), as well as to the project site from Irkutsk. Volunteers may elect to pay an additional $100 to work at a second project site. Volunteers are also responsible for any visa fees.

Getting Started: Prospective volunteers should send an e-mail requesting an application and a list of project dates and locations. Orientation and training take place on the first full day of each project and include cultural pointers. Training in the proper and safe use of tools is also given on the first day, with "reminder training" given daily. Prospective volunteers should be aware that passport holders from some nations, particularly African ones, may have problems obtaining visas to enter Russia.

Needed Skills and Specific Populations: No trail-building or Russian language skills are required, though FGBT encourages people who possess these skills to apply. Volunteers must be in good health and have both a sense of adventure and a willingness to work hard. Volunteers must be at least 18 years old (though exceptions to this rule can be made for volunteers traveling as part of a school group led by teachers or parents). Senior volunteers who are physically capable of the hard work and wilderness living are also welcomed. Volunteers with disabilities may be able to volunteer with FGBT in the future, once a fully accessible portion of the Great Baikal Trail is completed.

The Deepest Lake in the World

❖ By Josh Brann ❖

Friends of the Great Baikal Trail (FGBT)

The Great Baikal Trail (GBT) project is a very ambitious, if not a little bit crazy, idea to build a hiking trail all the way around the world's deepest lake, Lake Baikal in Siberia. Even when the project is finished—in approximately 30 years—who is actually going to hike the full 2,000 km (1,243 miles) around the lake? Probably a lot more people than one might expect. Although the GBT is the first such mega-trail project in Russia, other long-distance trails, such as the Appalachian and Pacific Crest Trails in the United States, have proven the "lengths" that dedicated backpackers are willing to go for a true wilderness experience.

Although grandiose in objective, the GBT has smaller benefits as well. Communities around Lake Baikal, which currently have few livelihood options, will have greater potential to attract tourists for fishing, kayaking, horseback riding, mountain biking, and other outdoor activities—activities that will increase income for local communities. Lake Baikal is well positioned to become the outdoor-sports capital of the Far East.

In July of 2003, I spent two weeks sweating and smiling as part of a work party on the GBT. There were two Americans, five Germans, and six Russians. The schedule was arduous: up at 8:00 A.M., to work by 9:00 A.M., lunch at 1:00 P.M., and back on the trail for three more hours of work in

The goal of the Great Baikal Trail Project is to create a comfortable trail—one that, it is hoped, will entice tourists—around the perimeter of the deepest lake in the world. Volunteers work to build the trail between towns; this photograph shows volunteers working near Severobaikalsk, a city on the northern part of Lake Baikal in Siberia. *Photo courtesy of Anya Skitnewskaya, of Friends of the Great Baikal Trail*

the late afternoon. Seven hours of labor in the surprisingly hot Siberian sun was more than enough for us. Fortunately, ice-cold Lake Baikal was waiting each time we arrived back in camp.

Our particular project was to build a switchback trail up the side of a small mountain. Though it was difficult work, it was especially rewarding, as our section connected the primary trail from Listvyanka, the main port town, to the northwest shore of the lake—a key link in the early stages of the GBT. Now that "the longest switchback in Russia" is completed, hikers can avoid the dangerous lakeside section of trail that skirts the short cliffs which drop to the lake at the foot of steep forested slopes.

There were many memorable aspects of this trip. Getting to know my fellow volunteers through timid attempts at Russian, German, and English was one. The food, for its highs and its lows, was another. The ants in my underwear and the snake in my backpack won't soon be forgotten. The opportunity to spend ten days in the woods working with my father was very special, in addition to creating something lasting that facilitates others' enjoyment of the beauty of Siberia. Experiencing the majesty and beauty of Baikal is an opportunity not to be missed.

Friends Workcamp Program, Philadelphia Yearly Meeting (FWP)

1515 Cherry Street
Philadelphia, PA 19102
(215) 241-7236
E-mail: arinh@pym.org for Philadelphia work camps;
chinaworkcamp@pym.org for the China program
Web site: www.pym.org/workcamp/index.html

Project Type: Community Development; Construction; Economic Development; Social Justice

Mission Statement Excerpt: "Friends Workcamp of PYM invites Quakers and non-Quakers to a spiritually based experience in low-income communities to increase awareness of economic, racial, and cultural differences and inequalities. We seek to recognize 'that of God' in everyone. Through small group service experiences in the Philadelphia Yearly Meeting region and beyond, Workcamp participants repair homes and accomplish other community services while building relationships and promoting mutual respect." (Note: this is an excerpt of a draft of the organization's mission statement, which has not been finalized.)

Year Founded: 1945

Funding Sources: Faith-based sponsors, mostly from the Religious Society of Friends (Quakers)

The Work They Do: FWP offers spiritually based group volunteer experiences in low-income communities to increase awareness of economic, racial, and cultural differences and inequalities, as well as the discovery of similarities. Volunteers perform a wide variety of activities, from preparing meals and taking care of children at a shelter for homeless women to visiting the elderly and helping people repair their homes. FWP combines hands-on volunteerism, community building, reflection, and history in a faith-based environment. In China, FWP volunteers tutor local people, experience and understand rural living, and build community across cultures.

Project Location: Most of FWP's programs take place in Philadelphia; there is one program in China each year. Most of the volunteer projects take place at FWP's center in West Philadelphia.

Time Line: Philadelphia-based FWP projects take place over weekends that are scheduled throughout the year. Volunteers arrive on a Friday at 6:00 P.M. and depart the following Sunday at 2:00 P.M. Most of the volunteer work takes place on Saturday; Sunday is devoted to worship and a tour of West Philadelphia. FWP's China program lasts about four weeks and takes place during the summer.

Cost: The program fee for weekend work camps is $45, which includes food and accommodations for the weekend. Housing is usually basic, and volunteers must bring a sleeping bag. Transportation is not included in the program fee. The program fee for the China program is $2,200, which includes all accommodations, food, and international travel.

Getting Started: Prospective volunteers should visit FWP's Web site for a schedule of weekend work camps, then call or e-mail the FWP office to find out if there is space available during the desired weekend. A one-page registration form, available on the Web site, should be sent to the office, along with a check for the program fee. Applications for the China program are due in March and require an interview.

Needed Skills and Specific Populations: Volunteers under age 18 must have a signed parental permission form to attend a work camp. For the China program, volunteers must be at least 16 years old. FWP is very friendly toward volunteers with disabilities, noting, for example, that ASL (American Sign Language) interpretation is available. Youth-specific work camps are also available.

Frontier

50-52 Rivington Street
London, EC2A 3QP
United Kingdom
+44 (0) 20 7613 2422; Fax: +44 (0) 20 7613 2992
E-mail: info@frontier.ac.uk
Web site: www.frontier.ac.uk

Project Type: Natural Conservation (Land); Natural Conservation (Sea); Scientific Research

Mission Statement Excerpt: "To promote and advance tropical field research and to implement practical projects contributing to the conservation of natural resources and the development of sustainable livelihoods."

Year Founded: 1989

Number of Volunteers Last Year: 270

Funding Sources: Government and private donors

The Work They Do: Frontier runs conservation and development projects in tropical developing countries, carrying out baseline biodiversity assessments of previously unmapped areas. Frontier's research helps shape environmental policy in their host countries; for example, national parks have been established in Tanzania, Madagascar, and Mozambique as a result of Frontier's work. Environmental education, income generation, and capacity building are also part of their work. Volunteers assist with scientific research by carrying out biodiversity surveys. Work includes small mammal trapping, butterfly netting, bird walks, GPS mapping, mist netting for bats, coastal work, mammal and turtle observations, and scuba surveying of marine projects.

Project Location: Frontier currently operates projects in Cambodia, Nicaragua, Tanzania, and Madagascar. Lodging is provided in communal tents or huts; food is cooked by the group and mostly consists of local produce, beans, and rice.

Time Line: Frontier's projects begin in January, April, July, and October. Volunteers can join projects for four, eight, ten, or twenty weeks.

Cost: Program fees are as follows: £1,400 for four weeks; £1,900 for eight weeks; £2,250 for ten weeks; and £3,350 for twenty weeks. The program fees include an orientation session in the United Kingdom, accommodation, transfers, food, group expedition equipment, and—for U.K. residents only—insurance and visa. Volunteers are responsible for their flights and personal equipment.

Getting Started: Prospective volunteers can apply online or request a paper application by postal mail. All volunteers must complete a short telephone interview. An optional weekend orientation program takes place in the United Kingdom six weeks before departure. Health and safety, scientific, and (as needed) scuba training are provided upon arrival.

Needed Skills and Specific Populations: Volunteers must be at least 17 years old; senior volunteers are not encouraged to volunteer with Frontier. Given the physical demands of Frontier's remote projects and locations, many volunteers with disabilities may not be able to work with this organization.

Gibbon Conservation Center (GCC)

P.O. Box 800249
Santa Clarita, CA 91380
(661) 296-2737; Fax: (661) 296-1237
E-mail: gibboncenter@earthlink.net;
volunteer@gibboncenter.org
Web site: www.gibboncenter.org

Project Type: Natural Conservation (Land); Scientific Research

Mission Statement Excerpt: "The mission of the Gibbon Conservation Center is to prevent the extinction of this small Southeast Asian ape and to advance its study, propagation, and conservation by establishing secure captive gene pools in case attempts to preserve species or subspecies in the wild fail . . . . We educate the public, assist zoos and rescue centers in better captive management, encourage noninvasive behavioral studies, and support ongoing field conservation projects."

Year Founded: 1976

Number of Volunteers Last Year: Approximately 180, including 17 live-in volunteers (most of the rest were in groups)

Funding Sources: Private donors and grants from foundations

The Work They Do: GCC is the only facility in the world devoted exclusively to the conversation, propagation, and study of gibbons, an increasingly rare ape. GCC houses nearly 40 gibbons, among them 6 of the 13 living species, including the only Javan gibbon in captivity in the United States. GCC specializes in behavioral studies on gibbons that are conducted by students, scientists, and volunteers working at the center, and it also has the largest gibbon library in the world. Volunteers have three work options. Primate keepers work directly with the care of gibbons, including feeding, cleaning, and changing water. This role may also include administering medication, doing behavioral observations, and assisting with administrative duties. Most resident volunteers are primate keepers, and they work 10–12 hours per day, beginning in the early morning, seven days per week. Center assistants may do maintenance work, take behavioral observations, clean, and help with administrative tasks; they also keep a minimum distance of six feet from all enclosures. Clerical assistants help with administrative tasks and may do behavioral observations.

Project Location: All volunteers work at the GCC site, which is located about one hour north of Los Angeles. GCC occupies five acres in a rural canyon area on the outskirts of a medium-sized city and is in a desert area. Weather conditions can be extreme, reaching from a high of 105 degrees in summer months to a low of 35 degrees at night in the winter. GCC provides free lodging to resident volunteers in an older, basic travel trailer with free access to bathroom, kitchen, and laundry facilities. Volunteers are responsible for providing their own food and personal items.

Time Line: Volunteers are welcome seven days a week, year-round. Resident volunteers must commit to a minimum of one month; there is no stated maximum stay. Many volunteers stay for several months, with the average being two months. Resident volunteers who have completed at least one month in the past may volunteer again for less than one month.

Cost: There is no program fee to volunteer at GCC, but volunteers are responsible for their own transportation to and from the work site, as well as for personal expenses incurred during the volunteer experience. GCC also requires a number of medical exams and inoculations before volunteers may enter the facility. Volunteers must have valid health insurance coverage.

Getting Started: Prospective volunteers may download an application from the GCC Web site or contact the office to receive an application. Applications must include a resume, a cover letter, and two letters of recommendation. A one-week training session is required, and it covers mandated procedures and GCC's own goals of cleanliness, welfare, breeding, and safety. The training is conducted by an experienced primate keeper.

Needed Skills and Specific Populations: GCC wants volunteers who are self-motivated and have a love for animals. No smoking is allowed at the center. All volunteers must be at least 18 years old, and resident volunteers must be at least 20 years old. There is no maximum age for volunteers, as long as they are capable of undertaking strenuous work. Volunteers who serve as primate keepers must be physically fit. Volunteers with disabilities will be considered on an individual basis.

Gaga for Gibbons

❖ By Lisa G. Thorpe ❖

Gibbon Conservation Center (GCC)

In March 2003, I took a personal leave of absence from my full-time job because I needed to scratch the itch that I'd had for years; I needed to pursue my interest in primates. It took guts to put my whole life on hold to volunteer for a month. I didn't know if I was crazy to pursue my interests or not, though I knew they weren't fleeting. As a cultural anthropology major at Hobart and William Smith, I had studied abroad in Mexico as well as taken a course called Primate Behavior during my senior year. These were the foundations for my interest in primates. So I did it. I left my job, my home, my house, and went to California to volunteer for a month at the Gibbon Conservation Center.

And I'm so glad I did. Within that month, I gained a wealth of knowledge about the small southeast Asian apes housed there. There are nearly 40 gibbons at the center, representing six species: Javan, Pileated, Agile, White-Cheeked, Hoolock, and Siamang. As a resident primate keeper, my daily duties included preparing food, feeding the gibbons, maintaining the grounds, as well as reporting deviations from normal food consumption, unusual behavior, and any unsafe conditions in the enclosures.

Volunteering at the center was an amazing experience. Every day I woke up to wonderful vocalizations at about 5:30 A.M. My workday actually started at 6:45 A.M., when I prepared the first feeding of the day: apples and monkey chow, followed by the big vegetable feed, then nut treats. In the afternoon the gibbons would be fed more apples and bananas, then receive a lettuce treat at the end of the day. I also had to change the water in the enclosures before 4:00 P.M., as that was the time they went to sleep. This was a seven-day-a-week job, which was sometimes strenuous, but always rewarding.

As the days went by, I learned the different personalities of each gibbon, what their favorite food was, who liked to intimidate, and who was moody. Their behavior was remarkable to observe because this is exactly how we humans are. I also was lucky to be present at the birth of a baby Agile gibbon named Chioma.

I am delighted that I made the time and space in my life to volunteer at the center. Who knows? Maybe there is a possible career change ahead of me!

Global Citizens Network (GCN)

130 North Howell Street
St. Paul, MN 55104
(651) 644-096 or (800) 644-9292; Fax: (651) 646-6176
E-mail: info@globalcitizens.org
Web site: www.globalcitizens.org

Project Type: Community Development; Education; Rural
Development; Social Justice

Mission Statement Excerpt: "Global Citizens Network sends
short-term teams of volunteers to communities in other cultures, where participants immerse themselves in the culture
and daily life of the community. Each volunteer team is
partnered with a local grassroots organization active in
meeting local needs."

Year Founded: 1992

Number of Volunteers Last Year: More than 100

Funding Sources: Individual private donors

The Work They Do: GCN carries out community development
and cultural immersion programs. Participants stay with
local families or at other facilities within the community
while working on site-directed development projects.
Examples of volunteer projects include building health clinics, renovating a youth center, and teaching in a primary
school.

Project Location: Projects take place in the United States (Arizona, New Mexico, and Washington) as well as internationally in Kenya, Tanzania, Nepal, Mexico, Peru,
Thailand, and Guatemala.

Time Line: Projects take place throughout the year and last
from one to three weeks.

Cost: Costs vary according to the length and location of the
project, but they range from $650 for sites in the United
States to $1,950 for international programs. Program fees
include food and lodging, a donation to the project, training materials, emergency medical and evacuation insurance

(for non-U.S. sites), and a T-shirt. A portion of the fees go to cover GCN program costs. Volunteers are responsible for their own transportation costs. Discounts are available for returning volunteers, children, groups, and those who register early.

Getting Started: Prospective volunteers can download an application from GCN's Web site or call or e-mail to request an application. Pre-departure orientation is provided to volunteers by the team leader via e-mail or telephone. During the first evening of the volunteer experience, all teams hold an orientation meeting; daily team meetings are held for the duration of the project.

Needed Skills and Specific Populations: Volunteers need only a willingness to experience and accept a new culture. No specific physical or occupational skills are required. Volunteers must be at least 8 years old, and participants under the age of 18 must be accompanied by an adult. Senior citizens are "absolutely!" encouraged to volunteer with GCN. Prospective volunteers with disabilities should confer with GCN before applying to ensure that accommodations will be available.

We Shared More than Hammers

❖ By Andrew Rippeon ❖

Global Citizens Network (GCN)

I remember the flea market in Gallup, the western border town between white America and the "native" world, our first Saturday of our Global Citizens Network experience. We were anxious to work and yet were given this day off. Perhaps this was the best initiation to the Navajo world we could have had, walking in the market among those to whom this culture belonged.

In some places, entire families sat behind folding tables, dark-headed children behind them throwing gravel into mud puddles. The middle generation stood at the tables speaking broken Dine—not broken English—to potential buyers of used engine parts or plastic bows and arrows or melting candy bought in the city. The elders sat unseeing (eyes far away behind cataracts) and silent but for the occasional comment in the traditional language, Dine, which their grown children barely understood. If the talk was in English, I heard about the 10-year drought, how the cattle had to be driven to the mountains earlier and earlier as the dry years passed and the rain never came, how herds were sold for less than their purchase price. I heard of a more pressing drought, of the increasing lack of interest on the behalf of the younger generations of anything Dine, and, as concerned as these men were about when the last of the water would disappear, their greater worry was when their culture might dry up. How far

A volunteer works side by side with a farmer in Kenya to harvest a local crop of tea leaves. These will be used both as a drink and, more importantly, as a cash crop. *Photo courtesy of Global Citizens Network*

we journeyed together over the course of a week from that first wide-eyed day in New Mexico!

Our week was spent working beside the teenagers of the Tohatchi Boys and Girls Club on a variety of projects. We saw their efforts to live in two cultures. They struggled to teach us bits of a language they were struggling to remember while we worked to repair a large storage shed that belonged to the club. We shared more than hammers putting up a new roof. Awkwardness dissolved with the steadying of a ladder, in the passing of handfuls of nails, with arms out to guard each other at the edges of the new roof when we rolled out the tar paper. We saw farther than the horizon when we stood on top of our finished work at the end of the day.

Our next project was doing repair work on a sheep ranch run by Anne and Eugene, who were each more than 80 years old. We shoveled the dung and drifted sand out of the pony stalls, fed the sheep and goats and moved them to greener pastures, and fixed the fences to the lamb and ewe pens. After a long day's work, Eugene approached us slowly on his crutches and said to me in a very clipped but smiling way, "Yu du goot werk." I said back nearly my entire Dine vocabulary. "Ee-yahii, sh'cha. Ee-yahii." Thank you, my grandfather. Thank you. At the door of the house, Anne was speaking in Dine to a semicircle of volunteers and club members and her eyes were welling up with tears. Our interpreter translated blessing after blessing, thanks upon thanks, and here the volunteers and the club members, at mid-week, became a single group, rather than two groups working together. The week passed. Dinners together, traveling to places the club had decided it wanted us to see, and always, there was that mix of things modern and things historical. We saw Window Rock, the natural arch through which, the Dine people's oral history tells them, they were born. Our week as volunteers ended, and our group splintered and drifted home.

Sitting in the club house, ready to leave in less than an hour, I realized it wasn't the "help" we'd given that was important, it was the time we'd spent, and that perhaps the import wasn't with what we'd left, but what we'd taken away.

Global Crossroad

8738 Quarters Lake Road
Baton Rouge, LA 70809
(800) 413-2008; Fax: (225) 922-9114
E-mail: info@globalcrossroad.com
Web site: www.globalcrossroad.com

Project Type: Agriculture; Community Development; Developmental Disabilities; Economic Development; Education; Human Rights; Medical/Health; Natural Conservation (Land); Natural Conservation (Sea); Orphans; Rural Development; Social Justice; Trail Building/Maintenance; Women's Issues; Youth

Mission Statement Excerpt: "Global Crossroad brings together volunteers who want to help others with people and communities in developing nations who need assistance."

Year Founded: 2002

Number of Volunteers Last Year: More than 600

Funding Sources: None; Global Crossroad is self-funded

The Work They Do: Global Crossroad offers volunteer placements in a variety of projects. In each host country, Global Crossroad has developed a project working with disadvantaged children and teaching English; additional projects vary depending on the country. Conservation projects range from maintaining trails in national parks to supporting reforestation, from sea turtle conservation on the Pacific coast to bird conservation in Africa. Community development projects include working with local women's groups on microcredit development in India, assisting the elderly in a nursing home in Costa Rica, working on a community organic fertilizer farm, and even assisting with a variety of projects in a single community. Volunteers may help care for children in an orphanage, teaching them English, leading them in games and activities, helping to cook and distribute food at mealtime, and mentoring the children. Volunteers in health care projects assist a local doctor or nurse in a health clinic or hospital to the extent that their skills and experiences allow. Conservation projects offer the widest variety of activities for volunteers, from the physical labor of maintaining trails through national parks to the tracking of native birds through the Kereita Forest in Kenya as part of a research project.

Project Location: Global Crossroad currently operates in China, India, Nepal, Tibet, Thailand, Sri Lanka, Mongolia, Ghana, Kenya, Tanzania, South Africa, Costa Rica, Guatemala, Honduras, Ecuador, and Peru. Because of the enormous variety of projects and host countries, the work settings vary tremendously. Projects involving children are usually indoor projects and are usually set in an orphanage, children's home, or school. Conservation projects are usually outdoors, and they often involve considerable physical labor. Depending on the exact placement, lodging may be with a host family, at a hostel, or at a lodge. Most lodging is with host families, especially in Africa and Latin America. Food is included as part of the placements and is usually provided by the host family; volunteers staying at hostels or hotels may eat there or at local restaurants.

Time Line: Projects begin on the first and third Mondays of each month. The minimum volunteer stint is two weeks, and the maximum is usually twelve weeks (this can sometimes be extended to 24 weeks, depending on the country's visa regulations). The average volunteer works for Global Crossroad for about six weeks.

Cost: Global Crossroad's program fees run from $800 to about $2,500, averaging about $1,500. The program fee includes all housing, meals, comprehensive travel insurance, and airport transfers. The program fee does not include airfare to the host country, visa and airport fees, or immunizations.

Getting Started: Prospective volunteers can apply online through Global Crossroad's Web site or by completing and submitting an application form, which can be downloaded from the Web site or requested from the head office. On the first day of their projects, volunteers receive a pre-departure orientation package and a one-day orientation session that covers safety, health, culture and customs, general information on the country, and an introduction to the project, host family, and living conditions. A two-week language and cultural orientation course is offered as an optional beginning for the volunteer trip.

Needed Skills and Specific Populations: Health care placements require that the volunteer have a health care background, such as being a medical student, nurse, therapist, or having extensive volunteer experience in a hospital. Teaching positions in China and Thailand require that the applicant be a native English speaker; positions in Thailand also require a bachelor's degree. Volunteers aged 15 and under must be accompanied by a parent or close adult relative; volunteers aged 16 and 17 may volunteer unaccompanied, but must have a permission letter from their parents. Senior volunteers in good health are welcome to volunteer. Volunteers with disabilities should contact Global Crossroad's office to discuss their specific needs; Global Crossroad has previously placed a volunteer in a wheelchair at a site in Nepal.

Global Eco-Spiritual Tours (GEST)

250 South Ocean Boulevard, Suite 266
Delray Beach, FL 33483
(561) 266-0096; Fax: (561) 266-0092
E-mail: global@paradista.net
Web site: www.globalecospiritualtours.org

Project Type: Agriculture; Community Development; Natural
Conservation (Land); Social Justice

Mission Statement Excerpt: "Our primary goals are to make
contributions to the educational and health care needs of
impoverished children through our member donations; to
improve the environment in our tour region with simple
sustainable development projects through our member
work; [and to] introduce and educate our members to
expand their perspective of other cultures and religions in
our tour region."

Year Founded: 2001

Number of Volunteers Last Year: 10

Funding Sources: Self-funded through program fees

The Work They Do: GEST offers trips that combine ecotourism and spiritual awareness. As a part of the ecotourism aspect of the trip, volunteers undertake ecological
volunteer projects such as planting sapling trees, installing
solar panels on remote homes, cleaning up littered campsites along mountain trails, participating in summer harvest
festivals at watermills, locating and identifying endangered
species for scientists, bottling pure mountain spring water
for local charities, and marking glacial retreats during the
summer melt. Volunteers also participate in local religious
life by visiting and exploring monasteries, attending meditation and prayer sessions, and constructing religious
artifacts.

Project Location: GEST operates its tours in the Himalayan
Mountains, a wonderful site for people who wish to investigate questions of ecology and spirituality. Volunteers stay
in hotels and tents during their tours.

Time Line: GEST's tours usually run in August. They offer a 12-day, set itinerary that the group follows together.

Cost: The program fee of $2,500 includes accommodations and all meals. Twenty percent of the program fee is donated to schools and health clinics in the tour area; 60 percent goes toward the cost of running the program; and the remaining 20 percent is used for administrative costs. The program fee does not include international airfare, but it does include in-country transportation costs.

Getting Started: Prospective volunteers can register online via GEST's Web site or by calling the office. A $750 deposit, which may be partially refundable, is required at the time of registration. A full application, physician-signed health statement, and the balance of the program fee are due at least 30 days before departure. GEST limits its tours to 10 volunteers per group, and volunteers are selected, for the most part, on a first-come, first-served basis. Generally, GEST plans to send just one group per year, but it can plan a second group if there is sufficient demand.

Needed Skills and Specific Populations: Given the project's location in the Himalayan Mountains, volunteers should expect to work at high elevations. Volunteers must be in good physical condition and be capable of walking or hiking one to five miles per day.

Global Routes

1 Short Street
Northampton, MA 01060
(413) 585-8895; Fax: (413) 585-8810
E-mail: mail@globalroutes.org
Web site: www.globalroutes.org

Project Type: Community Development; Construction; Education; Natural Conservation (Land); Natural Conservation (Sea); Orphans; Rural Development; Trail Building/Maintenance; Youth

Mission Statement Excerpt: "Global Routes . . . [sends] high school students all over the world to participate in community service projects."

Year Founded: 1985

Number of Volunteers Last Year: 300

Funding Sources: None; self-funded

The Work They Do: Global Routes volunteers participate in projects focused on construction, working with children, and environmental conservation. Working in groups, volunteers build community centers, schoolhouses, playgrounds, and health clinics in rural communities. Volunteers can also teach English and work with youth to create summer camps, soccer camps, and other youth-focused activities.

Project Location: Projects take place in Belize, Costa Rica, the Dominican Republic, Ecuador, China, Ghana, Mexico, Guadeloupe, St. Lucia, Thailand, Vietnam, New Zealand, and Puerto Rico. Accommodations are host-family homes or group living quarters, and food is provided at these.

Time Line: High school programs run three to five weeks in the summer; college programs run seven weeks in the summer and twelve weeks in the fall, winter, and spring.

Cost: Program fees range from $3,350 to $5,550. All fees include accommodation, food, and all in-country costs other than personal expenses. Volunteers must provide their own airfare.

Getting Started: Applications are available on Global Routes's Web site. The in-country orientation lasts from four to ten days.

Needed Skills and Specific Populations: Volunteers must be at least 14 years old; all programs are designed for high school and college students. Volunteers with disabilities cannot be accommodated.

Global Service Corps (GSC)

300 Broadway, Suite 28
San Francisco, CA 94133
(415) 788-3666 x128; Fax: (415) 788-7324
E-mail: gsc@igc.org
Web site: www.globalservicecorps.org

Project Type: Agriculture; Community Development; Developmental Disabilities; Education; Medical/Health; Orphans; Professional/Technical Assistance; Rural Development; Youth

Mission Statement Excerpt: "Global Service Corps (GSC) creates opportunities for adult participants to live in developing nations and work on projects that serve Earth's people and her environment. These projects emphasize grassroots collaboration on the local level, promote mutual transfer of skills, and foster cross-cultural understanding."

Year Founded: 1992

Number of Volunteers Last Year: 128

Funding Sources: No outside funding; GSC is self-supporting

The Work They Do: GSC is a nonprofit international volunteer organization that provides volunteer opportunities for people to live and work in Thailand or Tanzania. In Thailand, volunteers work on health, education, and Buddhism projects. Specifically, volunteers teach in primary or secondary schools, monasteries, or orphanages; observe in hospitals; and teach in a monastery, where they learn firsthand about Buddhist practices. Programs available in Tanzania involve health, sustainable agriculture, and HIV/AIDS prevention. For example, volunteers can assist with demonstration plots, help teach about sustainable agriculture, or provide HIV/AIDS awareness talks and seminars.

Project Location: GSC's projects in Thailand are located in Kanchanaburi and Nonthanaburi; in Tanzania, projects are located in Arusha. Volunteers are immersed in the cultures in which they work. Volunteers stay in homes that are "comfortable by Western standards." All meals and project-related transportation are provided by host

Three colorfully garbed volunteers joyfully celebrate the implementation of a sustainable agriculture program with a group of Tanzanian farmers. *Photo courtesy of Global Service Corps*

families, and host families often include their volunteer guests in outings and activities and teach them about culture, lifestyles, and family customs. Each volunteer has his or her own furnished room, and GSC can arrange for friends or couples to stay together. Volunteers in Thailand have the option of staying in a guesthouse or hostel if they so wish.

Time Line: Projects are carried out year-round. Applications are accepted on a rolling basis. Participants must volunteer for at least two weeks, with a maximum of six months; the average volunteer stays for one month.

Cost: Program fees begin at $2,075. The program fees include airport pickup and project transportation, hotel, hostel or home-stay accommodation, all meals, weekend excursions, project administration, and support. International airfare is not included in the program fee.

Getting Started: Prospective volunteers can download a copy of the application form from the Web site. The completed application form should be sent in with a resume, a personal statement and a $150 refundable deposit. Upon signing up for a project, volunteers receive an orientation manual with information about the country and the program, a reading list, a packing list, and health and travel tips. Volunteers also receive an on-site orientation, which is conducted by the in-country coordinators.

Global Volunteer Network (GVN)

P.O. Box 2231
Wellington, New Zealand, 6001
+ (800) 963-1198
E-mail: info@volunteer.org.nz
Web site: www.volunteer.org.nz

Project Type: Agriculture; Community Development; Construction; Economic Development; Education; Human Rights; Medical/Health; Natural Conservation (Land); Orphans; Scientific Research; Social Justice; Trail Building/Maintenance; Youth

Mission Statement Excerpt: "Our vision is to connect people with communities in need. We do this by supporting the work of local community organizations through the placement of international volunteers."

Year Founded: 2001

Number of Volunteers Last Year: 1,500

Funding Sources: No outside sources

The Work They Do: GVN offers volunteer opportunities in areas of teaching, environmental work, wildlife care, orphanages, disabled children, medicine, HIV/AIDS education, and economic sustainability. Working with partner organizations, volunteers may teach in a school in Ghana, help in an orphanage with disabled children in Romania, work with mistreated wildlife in Thailand, and participate in reforestation projects on the Galápagos Islands.

Project Location: GVN runs projects in Alaska, China, Ecuador, El Salvador, Ghana (two projects), Nepal, New Zealand, Romania, Russia, South Africa, Thailand, Uganda, and Vietnam. Volunteers generally live and work in the same conditions as members of the host community.

Time Line: Projects are available throughout the year and range from two weeks to six months in length. The average volunteer project is about six weeks long.

A volunteer amid a sea of Ghanaian faces. Her projects included teaching, education, and school support. *Photo courtesy of Jono Ryan, of Global Volunteer Network*

Cost: All volunteers pay an application fee of $350, which allows them to participate in as many projects as the volunteer wishes for two years. Program fees vary by project, but they average about $800 for six weeks. Each program fee covers accommodation, meals, and most in-country costs; volunteers are responsible for airfare, insurance, and visas.

Getting Started: Volunteer application forms are available on GVN's Web site. Partner organizations provide training and orientation programs.

Needed Skills and Specific Populations: Most projects require volunteers to be at least 18 years old. Senior volunteers are welcomed, but are advised that some project sites are more physically strenuous than others. Prospective volunteers with disabilities will be considered on a case-by-case basis.

Global Volunteers (GV)

375 East Little Canada Road
St. Paul, MN 55117
(800) 487-1047
E-mail: e-mail@globalvolunteers.org
Web site: www.globalvolunteers.org

Project Type: Community Development; Construction; Developmental Disabilities; Economic Development; Education; Medical/Health; Natural Conservation (Land); Orphans; Professional/Technical Assistance; Rural Development; Youth

Mission Statement Excerpt: "Global Volunteers's goal is to help establish a foundation for peace through mutual international, cross-cultural understanding."

Year Founded: 1984

Number of Volunteers Last Year: 1,600

Funding Sources: GV receives a small number of private donations, mostly from individuals.

The Work They Do: GV works on locally initiated projects that include teaching conversational English, caring for at-risk children, constructing and repairing community buildings and facilities, working to develop and promote natural resource conservation, and assisting with medical care. Working in cooperation with local people, past GV volunteers have built schools in Tanzania and China; constructed community centers in Costa Rican and Jamaican villages; built new homes in Appalachia; created adaptive furniture for Ecuadorian children with disabilities; taught English to future leaders of China, eastern Poland, southern Italy, Ukraine, Hungary, Tanzania, Ghana, and Greece; and provided care to vulnerable babies in Romania and orphans in southern India. Volunteers serve as part of teams, which are led by experienced team leaders who have undergone extensive training; most team leaders are citizens of the host community.

A volunteer serves as the support system (both physical and emotional) for a two-layer-thick wall of babies in a Romanian orphanage. *Photo courtesy of Global Volunteers*

Project Location: GV carries out projects in Australia, China, the Cook Islands, the United States (including Hawaii), India, Tanzania, Ghana, Ukraine, Hungary, Romania, Poland, Greece, Ireland, Italy, Costa Rica, Mexico, Jamaica, Ecuador, and Indonesia. (Please note that, as of this writing, the Indonesia program is temporarily suspended.) Accommodations vary by site, and they range from tourist hotels to "indoor camping" on community center floors. GV arranges for all lodging and meals.

Time Line: Programs are available year-round at most sites, and there are more than 150 programs on the calendar each year. There is a minimum one-week commitment, and the longest volunteer program offered by GV is three weeks.

Cost: Program fees range from $750 for one week in the continental United States to $2,650 for three weeks in Australia. Each fee includes all meals and accommodations, as well as ground transportation in the host country. Volunteers must also pay for their airfare to the work site. Only 16 percent of GV's program fee goes toward administrative overhead. Discounts are available for groups, students, and people who apply online.

Getting Started: An online application is available at GV's Web site; prospective volunteers can also call the office to speak with a volunteer coordinator, who can give advice on which programs might be the most suitable. Applicants must provide character references and complete a health and skills questionnaire. Volunteers receive pre-departure orientation materials that outline GV's procedures and philosophy as well as project and country information. The first few days of each program are devoted to extensive orientation sessions, team-building exercises, and community introductions, as well as to basic language instruction.

Needed Skills and Specific Populations: GV has one of the lowest minimum age requirements; it accepts volunteers as young as 8 for some programs, and as young as 11 for others. Senior volunteers are encouraged to volunteer with GV. Volunteers with disabilities may be able to serve with GV, depending on project size and logistics; specifics should be discussed with a volunteer coordinator. Volunteers who wish to teach English must be native speakers.

Global Works

1113 South Allen Street
State College, PA 16801
(814) 867-7000; Fax: (814) 867-2717
E-mail: info@globalworksinc.com
Web site: www.globalworksinc.com

Project Type: Agriculture; Archaeology; Community Development; Construction; Historic Preservation; Natural Conservation (Land); Natural Conservation (Sea); Rural Development; Trail Building/Maintenance; Youth

Mission Statement Excerpt: "Global Works strives to provide rewarding community service and adventure travel programs for high school students that foster personal growth and promote social and cultural awareness."

Year Founded: 1990

Number of Volunteers Last Year: 440

Funding Sources: No outside funding sources; Global Works is self-funded

The Work They Do: Global Works is an environmental and community-service travel program for high school students aged 14–18 that offers options for language learning and home stays. Examples of past work done by volunteers include an archaeological dig in France; work at wildlife rehab center in the San Juan Islands, Washington; cabin painting at migrant farmworker housing in Skagit County, Washington; assistance with Seeds of Hope in Ireland; environmental work in the Gredos Mountains of Spain; house building in Puerto Rico; construction in Costa Rica and Fiji; work with a kiwi habitat in New Zealand; and work with a daycare center in Ecuador.

Project Location: Projects are available in Spain, France, Ireland, Fiji, New Zealand, Costa Rica, Puerto Rico, Ecuador, Mexico, and the Pacific Northwest of the United States. Accommodations are often rustic, and lodgings include environmental centers, bed-and-breakfasts, and hostels. Bunk-style housing is often used.

With four messy little helpers, a volunteer rolls paint onto a local community building in the Yucatán, Mexico. *Photo courtesy of Global Works*

Time Line: Global Works's three- and four-week programs take place in the summer months, starting in late June and ending in mid-August.

Cost: Program fees run from $3,250 to $4,450 and include room and board. Transportation costs are not included.

Getting Started: Prospective volunteers should visit the Web site listed above. Training is provided as a part of the program.

Needed Skills and Specific Populations: Volunteers must be willing to challenge their typical comfort zones and have a desire to live, work, and travel with others.

Globe Aware

7232 Fisher Road
Dallas, TX 75214
(214) 823-0083; Fax: (214) 823-0084
E-mail: info@globeaware.org
Web site: www.globeaware.org

Project Type: Agriculture; Community Development; Construction; Developmental Disabilities; Economic Development; Historic Preservation; Medical/Health; Museum; Natural Conservation (Land); Natural Conservation (Sea); Orphans; Professional/Technical Assistance; Rural Development; Scientific Research; Trail Building/Maintenance; Women's Issues; Youth

Mission Statement Excerpt: "Globe Aware seeks to promote cultural awareness and sustainability by engaging in locally chosen development projects that are safe, culturally interesting, and genuinely beneficial to a needy community."

Year Founded: 2002

Number of Volunteers Last Year: 400

Funding Sources: Fully funded by donations from individuals.

The Work They Do: Globe Aware's main focus is to carry out work that leads to greater independence and health for local communities. For example, volunteers work with deaf orphans in Peru to teach them a variety of life skills, from first aid and hygiene to employable skills such as sewing and cooking. They also fix playgrounds, paint murals, and give one-on-one attention and care to the orphans. In other programs, volunteers build modified adobe stoves that reduce fuel consumption and dramatically decrease the contraction of upper respiratory disease from smoke inhalation. Globe Aware takes on a broad spectrum of work projects at most sites.

Project Location: Globe Aware currently works in Latin America (Costa Rica, Peru, Brazil, and Cuba) and Asia (Thailand, Nepal, Laos, Cambodia, and Vietnam), and it plans

A volunteer from Los Angeles, California, was placed at an orphanage in Cusco, Peru. Each month the orphanage held a large fiesta to celebrate the birthdays of the orphans. In this photo, an orphan benefits from the artistic talents of the volunteer, who painted a beautiful flower on her face, along with the even more powerful act of giving her his one-on-one, undivided attention. *Photo courtesy of Gregory Jackson, of Globe Aware*

to expand to Africa and Eastern Europe in the near future. Work sites vary tremendously. For example, the Cusco, Peru, work site, where volunteers work with orphans, is a cobblestoned, double courtyarded facility with flushing toilets and hot water. In Thailand, volunteers may teach in clean rural classrooms or build homes in hot and humid (but beautiful) outdoor environments. Food, water, and accommodations are always provided. At project sites in Thailand and Costa Rica there is no hot water, but it is rarely missed due to the warm outside temperatures. In Cusco there are flushing toilets, running hot water, and access to electricity.

Time Line: Each program is offered for at least one week every month, with the exception of the Thailand program, which is available November through May. Most programs last one week, Saturday to Saturday, but about 15 percent of Globe Aware's volunteers extend their service up to one full month.

Cost: Program fees range from approximately $900 to $1,500. Each fee covers the cost of meals, accommodation, on-site travel, emergency medical evacuation, medical insurance, donations to the various community projects, and an orientation package. Airfare is not included in the program fee.

Getting Started: An application is available on the organization's Web site, or Globe Aware can fax, mail, or e-mail the application to prospective volunteers. Orientation materials are sent to volunteers upon registration, and the first day upon arrival is devoted to orientation activities.

Needed Skills and Specific Populations: Volunteers under 16 must fill out a special waiver. Senior volunteers are welcomed. Volunteers with disabilities are welcomed, though there are limitations within each program. For example, the program in Cusco may not suit those who use wheelchairs because the living accommodations and workplace are on cobblestone.

GoXplore

P. O. Box 436, Hillcrest 3650
Kwa-Zulu Natal
South Africa
+270 31 765 1818; Fax: +270 31 765 4781
E-mail: info@goxploreafrica.com
Web site: www.goxploreafrica.com

Project Type: Community Development; Construction; Medical/Health; Natural Conservation (Land); Orphans; Rural Development; Scientific Research

Mission Statement Excerpt: "GoXplore is the leading youth travel organization for opportunities in Africa and around the world."

Year Founded: Four established youth travel organizations combined to form GoXplore in 2004, but each of them had existed for several years before that merger.

Number of Volunteers Last Year: 1,000

Funding Sources: None; self-sustaining

The Work They Do: GoXplore offers volunteer opportunities in both wildlife and community volunteering. Wildlife volunteer opportunities include hands-on work with animals; research; conservation studies; ranger courses; instruction in rehabilitation methods, game farm management, and animal breeding methods; equestrian work; game counts; and work with reptile, primate, or cheetah breeding. Community volunteers may work in children's centers, in community clinics, with community outreach efforts, or in disaster relief. For example, community volunteers have helped build a children's home, renovated an orphanage, helped kids with homework, led field trips, and assisted in vegetable gardens.

Project Location: Most of the wildlife opportunities are located in South Africa (Kruger Park area, Kwa-Zulu Natal, Gauteng, Mpumalunga, or the Greater Limpopo Region), but projects are also located in Zimbabwe and

Kenya. Community projects are in Kwa-Zulu Natal, the Kruger Park area, Gauteng, and Cape Town, as well as in Zambia, Kenya, Senegal, and Tanzania. Accomodations depend on the specific project and range from lodges to campsites. Prospective volunteers should check with GoXplore on lodging details in advance of their commitment to a project. Food is provided and is prepared either by the project leaders or by the volunteers themselves.

Time Line: Projects are available throughout the year, but each has a set start and finish date (there can be some flexibility in regard to these dates). Volunteers make a minimum time commitment of two weeks and a maximum time commitment of one year.

Cost: Calculated in South African Rand, the program fee is R9,000–R25,000. Each program fee includes in-country transportation, airport transfers, accommodation, meals, training, some activities, and a donation to each project. The program fee does not include international or domestic airfare.

Getting Started: Prospective volunteers should contact GoXplore by mail, phone, or e-mail. Volunteers are given an orientation that includes cultural training, wildlife or community information, first aid training, and other additional training.

Needed Skills and Specific Populations: No special skills are required, as needed skills are taught in training. Some specialized skills in construction, medicine, or music may be utilized in the community volunteer programs. Most volunteer programs have a minimum age of 18, though some summer programs accept 16-year-olds. Some programs have upper age limits; all senior volunteers should be aware that most volunteers with GoXplore are 18–30 years old and that the travel is designed for physically fit young people. Prospective volunteers with disabilities should contact GoXplore to examine which specific projects would be appropriate for them.

Greenforce

30 Public Square
Nelsonville, OH 45764
(800) 710-6065
E-mail: info@greenforceusa.org
Web site: www.greenforceusa.org

Project Type: Community Development; Economic Development; Natural Conservation (Land); Natural Conservation (Sea); Rural Development; Scientific Research; Trail Building/Maintenance; Youth

Mission Statement Excerpt: "Implement the requirements of Section 3c of the Rio Earth Summit 1994, to provide environmentally and economically balanced biodiverse regions. Incorporating local requirements utilizing international aid plans."

Year Founded: 1996

Number of Volunteers Last Year: 250–300

Funding Sources: Some funding from private agencies such as the Red Cross or World Wildlife Federation

The Work They Do: Greenforce takes on a number of different projects, all of which are centered around improving the environment and human interactions with it. This mission includes work as diverse as creating a national park or a marine park, undertaking environmentally aware community programs to provide local employability, and implementing sustainable fuel programs to reduce deforestation. A specific example of one of Greenforce's projects is the establishment of a marine park island in Fiji as a World Heritage site to protect the environment. Once this was completed, volunteers trained the local villagers to dive, both to monitor the reef and also to earn an income as dive guides, and to work as boat handlers for visiting scientists. Diving equipment and boats were also donated. The island is now a freestanding, self-monitoring, self-financing reserve.

Discussions with the local community to develop means of protecting and preserving nature are key to Greenforce's work. A volunteer discusses with Maasai Morans (warriors) the possible locations where volunteers will be stationed in order to track and count local elephant and lion populations. *Photo courtesy of Greenforce*

Project Location: Projects are carried out in the Bahamas, Malaysia, Ecuador, Fiji, Nepal, and Tanzania. The first week of each project is spent in the host country's capital for training, during which time volunteers reside either in a hostel or a home. While carrying out a project, volunteers are housed in simple, but clean and safe, local housing, such as a Malay stilt house, a Fijian *bure*, or Maasai *kraal*.

Time Line: Greenforce volunteers depart to work on projects every January, April, July, and October. The minimum time commitment is one month; the maximum is nine months. The average volunteer stays for about three months.

Cost: Greenforce's program fee is £2,300. This covers all meals, accommodations, medical insurance, and language lessons. Volunteers must provide their own international flight to the expedition location.

Getting Started: Prospective volunteers can download an application from Greenforce's Web site or contact the office to request a brochure. Greenforce offers pre-departure orientation packets and an online forum; more extensive training is given once the volunteer arrives on the site.

Needed Skills and Specific Populations: Volunteers must be at least 18 years old. Senior volunteers are welcomed, and Greenforce requests that someone break its record for the oldest volunteer, which is currently held by a 76-year-old.

Habitat for Humanity International's Global Village Work Teams

P.O. Box 369
Americus, GA 31709
(229) 924-6935 x2549; Fax: (229) 924-0577
E-mail: gv@habitat.org
Web site: www.habitat.org/gv

Project Type: Administrative; Community Development; Construction; Economic Development; Human Rights; Professional/Technical Assistance; Rural Development; Social Justice; Youth

Mission Statement Excerpt: "Habitat for Humanity works in partnership with God and people everywhere, from all walks of life, to develop communities with people in need by building and renovating houses, so that there are decent houses in decent communities in which every person can experience God's love and can live and grow into all that God intends."

Year Founded: 1976

Number of Volunteers Last Year: 6,000 in the Global Village Work Teams Program

Funding Sources: Government funds for land and infrastructure

The Work They Do: One of the most well-known volunteer organizations in the United States, Habitat for Humanity International's Global Village Work Teams consist of short-term house-building trips designed to give concerned people a firsthand opportunity to observe and contribute to Habitat's work. Working alongside homeowners and local volunteers, team members assist low-income people in home-building projects. Volunteers are needed for all stages and tasks in these construction projects. Global Village Work Team participants learn about poverty housing, development challenges, and Habitat's ecumenical Christian ministry.

Project Location: Global Village Work Team volunteers work in 100 nations around the world. Most work sites are in rural areas of economically underdeveloped countries, and they tend to be very basic. Team leaders and in-country Habitat hosts make arrangements for volunteers' food, accommodations, and local transportation.

Time Line: Global Village Work Team projects run year-round for 10 to 20 days each.

Cost: Program fees range from $1,000 to $2,200. The program fee includes room and board, in-country transportation, travel insurance, and a donation toward the host community's building program. Airfare to the host country is not included in the cost.

Getting Started: Prospective volunteers can apply online via the Habitat for Humanity International's Global Village Work Teams Web site.

Needed Skills and Specific Populations: Volunteers do not need any prior experience or specific skills, but participants under the age of 18 must either be accompanied by a parent or guardian or be part of a chaperoned school, church, or institution group. Senior volunteers are welcomed. Accommodations for volunteers with disabilities vary by work site and by disability. Individuals and groups of people with diverse backgrounds are encouraged to participate in the Global Village Work Teams Program. Participants must be in good health, as the work assignments often require strenuous manual labor.

Health Volunteers Overseas (HVO)

1900 L Street NW, Suite 310
Washington, DC 20036
(202) 296-0928; Fax: (202) 296-8018
E-mail: info@hvousa.org
Web site: www.hvousa.org

Project Type: Education; Medical/Health; Professional/Technical Assistance

Mission Statement Excerpt: "Health Volunteers Overseas is dedicated to improving the availability and accessibility of health care in developing countries through training and education."

Year Founded: 1986

Number of Volunteers Last Year: 354

Funding Sources: Donations from individuals and foundations, as well as government funding

The Work They Do: HVO provides clinical education and training in various disciplines including anesthesia, burn care management, dentistry, dermatology, hand surgery, internal medicine, nurse anesthesia, nursing, oral and maxillofacial surgery, orthopedics, pediatrics, and physical therapy. HVO also provides needed education-related materials and equipment to program sites to reinforce educational programs. Volunteers are involved in a variety of activities including clinical training, teacher training, curriculum development, student and faculty mentoring, and continuing education workshops. They lecture, serve as clinical instructors, conduct ward rounds, and demonstrate various techniques in classrooms, clinics, and operating rooms.

Project Location: Volunteer assignments with HVO are available in economically developing countries in Africa, Asia, the Caribbean, Latin America, and Eastern Europe. Amenities and the comfortableness of the work sites and accommodations vary by location.

Time Line: HVO's programs are ongoing, and the organization accepts volunteers year-round. Volunteers typically serve for one month, though there may occasionally be options for shorter or longer stints.

Cost: HVO does not charge program fees, but it encourages participants to become members to help provide support for the organization's administrative costs. Volunteers are responsible for covering all of their own costs on the project, including international travel, housing, and living expenses (although free or low-cost housing is often available). The average out-of-pocket cost per volunteer is approximately $2,500 for a one-month assignment.

Getting Started: Prospective volunteers should visit HVO's Web site or call the organization's office. HVO has a pre-departure orientation process that includes communication by phone, e-mail, and fax. All volunteers receive HVO's *Guide to Volunteering Overseas*, a booklet that contains information on international travel, safety and health precautions, and cross-cultural communication skills, as well as teaching and training tips. In addition, volunteers receive an orientation packet that includes a packing list, training and program details, and site-specific information on housing, travel, food, personal needs, and weather.

Needed Skills and Specific Populations: HVO volunteers must be fully trained and licensed health care professionals. In addition, HVO prefers volunteers with three to five years' professional experience, since activities include teaching and training. There is no language requirement for volunteers. The most successful HVO volunteers are well-trained, flexible, adaptable, and open to new experiences. Senior volunteers are welcomed. Qualified volunteers with disabilities are welcomed, though they should work with HVO staff to assess the feasibility of assignments.

Iko Poran

Av. Nilo Peçanha, 50/ 1709
Centro, Rio de Janeiro
RJ CEP: 20.044-900
+ (55-21) 3084-2242; Fax:: + (55-21) 3084-1446
E-mail: rj@ikoporan.org
Web site: www.ikoporan.org

Project Type: Community Development; Economic Development; Youth

Mission Statement Excerpt: "To implement . . . international volunteer programs that make a positive impact on local organizations, promoting intercultural exchanges, and strengthening a constant and growing number of nongovernmental organizations in Brazil."

Funding Sources: Foundation and corporate donors

The Work They Do: Iko Poran partners with Brazilian non-profit human service agencies to provide volunteer placements. The volunteer placements are created and designed according to each volunteer's abilities and interests. This allows volunteers to step in and play a small role within an established organization. Most of the volunteer opportunities have an artistic, creative, cultural, or performance aspect. Examples of past volunteer work include teaching dance with the group AfroReggae; creating a book of poetry and photography portraying the lives of children from low-income communities with Danca pra Galera; interning with OndAzul, an organization that recycles plastic bottles and turns them into furniture as a way to reduce trash and create jobs; and producing theater productions with children who live in poverty.

Project Location: All volunteers work and live in the Brazilian cities of Rio de Janeiro and Salvador. Volunteers are responsible for finding their own accommodations, though Iko Poran will assist with this.

Time Line: Because each volunteer placement is created on an individual basis, all volunteers negotiate the lengths of their projects with Iko Poran and the host organizations prior to their arrival in Brazil. Previous volunteer internships have ranged from three weeks to six months, and volunteers have worked part-time as well as full-time.

Cost: Iko Poran's program fee of R$1,500 (Brazilian real) for the first four weeks and R$200 for each subsequent week covers airport transfers, volunteer placement, local transportation, and a donation to the host agency. Accomodations, food, and international airfare are the volunteer's responsibility.

Getting Started: Prospective volunteers can register with Iko Poran via the organization's Web site.

Needed Skills and Specific Populations: Volunteers must be at least 18 years old. A basic knowledge of Portuguese or Spanish is recommended (but is not mandatory) for most volunteer positions.

Insight Nepal

P.O. Box 489, Zero K.M.
Pokhara, Kaski
Nepal
E-mail: insight@mos.com.np
Web site: www.south-asia.com/insight

Project Type: Community Development; Education

Mission Statement Excerpt: "Insight Nepal was established with a view not only to introduce participants to Nepal's diverse geographical and cultural environment, but also to establish and foster an awareness and understanding of cultural differences through experiential learning."

Year Founded: 1992

The Work They Do: Insight Nepal offers a highly structured, three-phased volunteer experience. Volunteers undergo a thorough one-week training program prior to the volunteer experience, which is followed by a one-week village excursion and elephant tour. Volunteers are partnered with host organizations in accordance with each volunteer's individual interests. Many volunteers teach in Nepali classrooms, while others take on community development projects. During the final leg of the volunteer experience with Insight Nepal, volunteers trek as a group in the Annapurna Mountain Conservation Area, then go on an elephant safari in Chitwan National Park in southern Nepal. Insight Nepal can also organize short-term volunteer experiences for those who do not have the time or the financial resources to undertake the full program.

Project Location: Volunteers work in the cities of Kathmandu and Pokhara in Nepal. Accommodations vary throughout the program: volunteers stay with a host family during orientation, in housing provided by the host organization during the volunteer placement, and in various types of lodging during the travels that end the program. Volunteers receive at least two meals a day throughout the experience.

Time Line: Insight Nepal's programs run for three months each and begin in February, April, August, and October. Insight Nepal accepts no more than 20 volunteers at each placement date.

Cost: Insight Nepal charges a $40 nonrefundable application fee, and the program fee is $800. The program fee includes training, accommodations, food, and the village excursion and elephant safari. Volunteers must pay for their own airfare to Nepal.

Getting Started: Prospective volunteers should contact Insight Nepal via e-mail to request an application form. Applications should reach Insight Nepal at least three months before departure. The orientation and training at the beginning of the program includes information on health care and cultural norms, a city tour, Nepali language instruction, and various lectures.

Needed Skills and Specific Populations: Insight Nepal accepts only volunteers who are 18–65 years old and who have a high school diploma.

International Cultural Adventures (ICA)

81 Jewett Street, #2
Newton, MA 02458
(888) 339-0460
E-mail: info@icadventures.com
Web site: www.icadventures.com

Project Type: Agriculture; Archaeology; Community Development; Construction; Developmental Disabilities; Education; Medical/Health; Natural Conservation (Land); Orphans; Professional/Technical Assistance; Rural Development; Women's Issues; Youth

Mission Statement Excerpt: "The mission of ICA is to enlighten the mind and enrich the spirit of each program participant by providing unique opportunities to acquire new perspectives on their life and gain a greater understanding of our global community through extraordinary cultural, educational, and volunteer service experiences abroad."

Year Founded: 1996

Number of Volunteers Last Year: 46

Funding Sources: None; self-funded

The Work They Do: ICA offers both custom-designed volunteer opportunities and a regularly scheduled volunteer program. Project areas include education, environmental conservation, agriculture, health care and nutrition, child development, care of seniors, small business development, orphanages, and construction. Some specific examples of volunteer work available through ICA include weeding and ox-driven field plowing with local farmers in order to plant potatoes; teaching English to young monks in a rural monastery; constructing beds for an orphanage in order to accommodate street children; repairing windows and painting an inspirational mural for a local secondary school; raising funds and constructing a new computer laboratory at an orphanage; working alongside a local doctor in the oncology department of a modern hospital; teaching art and theater to primary school students; serving meals to street children in a shelter; and collecting toys, books, and games and establishing a game room for the children at an orphanage.

Project Location: The established projects take place in Peru, India, and Nepal, though customized programs can be created in other countries. In the established programs, volunteer opportunities exist in urban, semiurban, and rural locations. Accommodations and work sites are usually clean, comfortable, and basic. Volunteers in customized programs may choose to stay with a host family, in a guesthouse, or in a hotel. Established programs generally house volunteers with host families.

Time Line: Established programs are available either during the summer for six weeks or as 12-week programs beginning in March and September. Customized programs can be arranged at almost any time during the year for any length of time.

Cost: The program fee for a customized volunteer experience is negotiated with the participant. Established summer program fees start at $3,050, and 12-week program fees start at $4,050. Each program fee includes accommodations, transportation to scheduled activities, and most meals. Volunteers must also pay for their domestic and international airfare, visa and passport fees, and airport departure taxes.

Getting Started: Prospective volunteers may contact ICA via the contact information listed above and request program information and an application packet. All volunteers receive extensive in-country orientation. The established six-week programs include two weeks of orientation followed by four weeks of volunteering; the established 12-week programs start with a month of orientation followed by two months of volunteering. Volunteers in customized programs specify the length of their in-country training.

Needed Skills and Specific Populations: Some projects that involve medicine and health care require specific skills of varying levels. Foreign language skills are not necessary to participate in any of ICA's programs, but volunteers in Peru will have more opportunities to serve if they speak Spanish. The suggested minimum age of participants on any of ICA's programs is 18, though younger volunteers may participate with parental consent. In customized group programs, particularly school group programs, participants can be of any age provided that those under age 18 have parental consent. There is no maximum age limit. ICA also welcomes volunteers with disabilities; specific arrangements for accommodations are dependent on each volunteer's disabilities and the program he or she is considering.

International Executive Service Corps (IESC)

901 15th Street NW, Suite 1010
Washington, DC 20005
(202) 589-2600; Fax: (202) 326-0289
E-mail: iesc@iesc.org
Web site: www.iesc.org

Project Type: Agriculture; Community Development; Economic
Development; Legal; Professional/Technical Assistance;
Rural Development; Women's Issues
Mission Statement: "Promoting stability and prosperity
through private enterprise development."
Year Founded: 1964
Number of Volunteers Last Year: More than 350
Funding Sources: A majority of the funding for IESC comes
from the U.S. government, though a modest amount comes
from private donors.
The Work They Do: IESC provides technical and managerial
assistance services to small and medium-sized private businesses and to business support organizations in the developing world and in emerging democracies. IESC pursues its
mission by implementing major development programs
around the world and through the delivery of technical
consultancies by volunteers and professional experts. Volunteer consultants provide technical assistance in virtually
all business sectors, sharing their expertise in training programs, trade development, trade show participation, trade
missions, and quality assurance certification with both private and governmental organizations. IESC volunteers
work very hard—often six days a week—while on a project, and they are usually required to produce a professional "consultant/advisor" report upon completion of an
assignment.
Project Location: IESC works in 55 countries around the
world. Volunteers usually stay in hotels or guesthouses in
or near a major city, though some clients provide an apartment or other housing.

Time Line: Projects are undertaken as requests come in from overseas. Volunteer assignments last from two weeks to three months.

Cost: Executives pay nothing to volunteer with IESC, as their work is carried out under cooperative agreements or contracts with organizations that provide funding. Generally, volunteers receive per diem and housing allowances based on U.S. State Department rates.

Getting Started: Prospective volunteers should register online at the IESC Web site. All volunteers receive briefings before and after their arrival at the host country project site.

Needed Skills and Specific Populations: There is no minimum age to volunteer. Senior volunteers are welcomed, but must have been active in their sector relatively recently. Volunteers with disabilities are welcomed, but it is up to the volunteer to determine the appropriateness of the assignment, as IESC cannot guarantee that accommodations overseas will meet the volunteer's requirements.

International Otter Survival Fund (IOSF)

7 Black Park, Broadford
Isle of Skye, IV49 9DE
Scotland
+ 1471 822 487
E-mail: iosf@otter.org
Web site: www.otter.org

Project Type: Natural Conservation (Land); Natural Conservation (Sea); Scientific Research

Mission Statement Excerpt: "The International Otter Survival Fund (IOSF) was set up to protect and help the 13 species of otter worldwide through a combination of compassion and science."

Year Founded: 1993

Number of Volunteers Last Year: Approximately 50

Funding Sources: Several charitable trusts

The Work They Do: IOSF conducts otter surveys, particularly in the Hebridean Islands; performs otter rescue and rehabilitation; carries out environmental education and scientific research; and funds otter projects worldwide. IOSF volunteers primarily assist with otter surveys, which generally involve walking the coastline to identify otter secondary signs such as feces and tracks. While IOSF always hopes that volunteers will get to see otters in the wild (and the chances of this are good), it cannot promise this. Volunteers walk over rough ground or seaweed-covered shoreline for six to eight miles per day, so a certain level of fitness is required. Some volunteers may help in the otter hospital, but these opportunities are limited, as humans are put in as little contact as possible with the otters to ensure that the animals remain wild.

Project Location: Most projects take place in the Hebrides Islands, off the west coast of Scotland. Accommodations and certain meals are provided.

Time Line: Volunteers are accepted during set dates between May and September, for a minimum of five days and a maximum of seven days.

Cost: Program fees begin at £295, which includes accommodations on a bed-and-breakfast basis in a guesthouse or hotel for five nights, transport during the survey, and any necessary equipment (excluding personal equipment, binoculars, and cameras). Volunteers are responsible for their own travel costs to the venue.

Getting Started: Volunteers can reserve a spot through the IOSF's Web site. On the first day of volunteering, IOSF conducts a training session on how to identify otter signs. The volunteers are then divided into two groups to carry out the survey. An experienced surveyor usually accompanies each group to help.

Needed Skills and Specific Populations: Volunteers should be reasonably fit and have good observation skills, enthusiasm, and a willingness to work in all weather conditions. Volunteers under age 18 must have written parental consent; senior volunteers are welcomed. Volunteers with disabilities are welcomed, though the walking requirements may make it impossible to accommodate volunteers in wheelchairs.

International Volunteer Program (IVP)

678 13th Street, Suite 100
Oakland, CA 94612
(510) 433-0414 or (866) 614-3438; Fax: (510) 433-0419
E-mail: ivpsf@swiftusa.org
Web site: www.ivpsf.org

Project Type: Education; Medical/Health; Museum; Social Justice; Youth

Mission Statement Excerpt: "The International Volunteer Program (IVP) is a nonprofit organization that promotes volunteerism in Europe, the United States, and Latin America. Our volunteer programs are designed to facilitate hands-on service and international exchange opportunities, with the aim of fostering cultural understanding and supporting community development."

Year Founded: 1991

Number of Volunteers Last Year: 35

Funding Sources: No outside funding; IVP is self-supporting

The Work They Do: IVP offers a wide range of projects that include working in a children's hospital, teaching English, working in environmental conservation, working with the elderly or with recovering substance abusers, and working at summer camps for disadvantaged children. Some specific examples of volunteer work include providing companionship and care to AIDS patients at residential facilities near Madrid, Spain; working at a nonalcoholic bar for recovering substance abusers in the Champagne region of France; providing companionship for elderly residents in a facility near Orleans, France; working in charity shops in the French Basque country; serving as counselors at a camp for at-risk youth in northern England; carrying out environmental education and trail maintenance in Northern Ireland; and administering activities for the disabled in Sheffield, England.

Project Location: Projects are carried out in France, Spain, the United Kingdom, and Costa Rica. Volunteers are placed with host agencies on an individual basis to give them maximum exposure to the language and culture of their host countries. Conditions at work sites vary according to the assignment. Some placements in Costa Rica and Northern Ireland involve working outdoors and require volunteers to be physically active. Host agencies arrange room and full board for all volunteers; many volunteers stay in dormitory-style accommodations and eat in cafeterias, while others stay with host families.

Time Line: Project dates are flexible and are available throughout the year. Volunteers must apply at least 90 days before the desired departure date. Volunteer assignments are for a minimum of four weeks and a maximum of twelve weeks, with the average placement lasting six to eight weeks.

Cost: The program fee depends on the length and location of the placement and ranges from $1,450 to $3,330. Each fee covers placement with a host agency; accommodations and full board; health, accident, and repatriation insurance; in-country transportation; orientation materials; and around-the-clock emergency assistance. The fee does not cover the volunteer's airfare to the host country or visas.

Getting Started: Prospective volunteers can download an application from IVP's Web site or request one by e-mail. A $100 registration fee is required at the time of application. IVP provides an orientation in the form of written materials after acceptance into the program, and host agencies provide on-site orientation upon arrival in the host country. Volunteers are responsible for obtaining their own visas.

Needed Skills and Specific Populations: Volunteers must have an intermediate-to-advanced level of fluency in Spanish or French, depending on the country of service. Volunteers in Costa Rica have the opportunity to enroll in Spanish language classes for the first two weeks of their placement. Volunteers must be at least 18 years old, and senior citizens are encouraged to apply. Prospective volunteers with disabilities should contact IVP to discuss the nature of the disability and the possibility of locating an appropriate work site.

Involvement Volunteers Association (IVA)

P.O. Box 218
Port Melbourne, Victoria 3207
Australia
+ 61 3 9646 9392; Fax: + 61 3 9646 5504
E-mail: international@ivvolunteering.org
Web site: www.volunteering.org.au

Project Type: Administrative; Construction; Developmental
Disabilities; Museum; Natural Conservation (Land); Natural Conservation (Sea); Scientific Research; Trail Building/Maintenance; Youth

Mission Statement Excerpt: "The aim of the Involvement Volunteers Association (IVA) is to make volunteering readily available to people who are seeking to assist others while learning from their volunteer experiences, related to social service or the natural environment, anywhere around the world."

Year Founded: 1988

Number of Volunteers Last Year: 189

Funding Sources: None; IVA is self-supporting

The Work They Do: IVA offers customized volunteer experiences to both individuals and groups. Examples of volunteer projects include shearing sheep in Australia, helping to care for orphans in Korea, and helping to restore ruins in Spain.

Project Location: IVA's volunteer projects are carried out in Argentina, Australia, Austria, Bangladesh, Brazil, Cambodia, China, Ecuador, Estonia, Fiji, Finland, France, Ghana, Greece, Guatemala, Guinea-Bissau, India, Israel, Italy, Kenya, Korea, Kosovo, Latvia, Lebanon, Lithuania, Mexico, Mongolia, Nepal, New Zealand, Peru, Philippines, Poland, Malaysia, Samoa, South Africa, Spain, Tanzania, Thailand, Togo, Turkey, United Kingdom, Ukraine, United States, Vietnam, and Zambia. The standards of living vary around the world, and work sites usually reflect the living conditions of the local population. Work sites and accommodations are often basic, but they are clean and safe, and volunteers are always provided descriptions of them in advance.

A disabled girl receives hands-on help from a volunteer as she strives to master mobility. Special education is just one of many areas in which volunteers can serve and make a substantial difference in people's lives. *Photo courtesy of Involvement Volunteers*

Time Line: Some projects are available year-round, while others are offered only during certain times of the year. Programs with specific dates are updated on IVA's Web site. Most programs have a two-week minimum commitment, though programs that work with children or seniors may require a six-week minimum commitment to allow ample time for volunteers to earn the trust of the people they are serving. The maximum length of stay is one year.

Cost: IVA negotiates program fees with volunteers on an individual basis, with fees beginning at $300 plus a $105 placement fee that doubles as a nonrefundable deposit. On average, a four-week placement costs approximately $1,400. Each program fee covers food and accommodations, in-country transportation, and administrative costs. Volunteers must provide their own transportation to the country of service.

Getting Started: Prospective volunteers should send an e-mail to request information on registration. Orientation and training are provided in-country as needed.

Needed Skills and Specific Populations: There is no set minimum age, though most volunteers are at least 17 years old. There is also no maximum age limit, as long as volunteers are "useful, responsible, and productive." Volunteers with disabilities are welcomed, "but they must respectfully agree that the chain is only as good as the weakest link."

Iracambi Atlantic Rainforest Research Center

Fazenda Iracambi, Caixa Postal No. 1
Rosário da Limeira, CEP 36878-000
Minas Gerais, Brazil
+55 32 3721 1436; Fax: +55 32 3721 0545
E-mail: iracambi@iracambi.com
Web site: www.iracambi.com

Project Type: Administrative; Agriculture; Community Development; Economic Development; Legal; Natural Conservation (Land); Professional/Technical Assistance; Rural Development; Scientific Research; Social Justice; Trail Building/Maintenance; Youth

Mission Statement Excerpt: "To make conservation of the rainforest more attractive than its destruction."

Year Founded: Iracambi was started as a working farm in 1989 and became established as a nonprofit organization in 1999.

Number of Volunteers Last Year: 144

Funding Sources: Private sources

The Work They Do: Iracambi carries out four specific projects: land use management, forest restoration, income-generating alternatives, and community understanding and engagement. Volunteers help with these projects by working on information technology; marketing; fundraising; Web site maintenance; trail maintenance; plant nursery management; environmental education and farmer outreach; GIS mapping; plant, animal, and bird identification and surveys; medicinal plant work; house maintenance; promotional material design; legal research and advice; and socioeconomic research.

Project Location: Volunteers work at Fazenda Iracambi and in the surrounding towns and villages. Iracambi has four volunteer houses and is in the process of building five new cabins. The houses are very simple and are built in the same style as local houses. Each volunteer shares a room with someone of the same sex, unless they come as a couple. Volunteers are expected to share cooking and cleaning responsibilities with members of their house.

Time Line: Volunteers are accepted year-round for a minimum of one month and a maximum (because of visa restrictions) of six months.

Cost: The volunteer program fee is $350 for the first month, $330 for the second month, and $310 for each month thereafter. The program fee covers all room and board; volunteers are responsible for all other costs, including airfare to Brazil.

Getting Started: Prospective volunteers should send a cover letter and a CV or resume to the e-mail address listed above. The cover letter should detail the areas of work that are of most interest to the applicant. All volunteers are given an orientation to the project, the farm, and their roles.

Needed Skills and Specific Populations: Given the range of roles that need to be filled at Iracambi, the program can find a use for almost any skill a volunteer may possess. Volunteers must be at least 18 years old, and senior volunteers are welcomed as long as they accept the somewhat basic living conditions. Individuals with disabilities may be able to volunteer with Iracambi, depending on the type of disabilities involved and the type of work they wish to undertake.

i-to-i

190 East 9th Avenue, #350
Denver, CO 80203
(800) 985-4864; Fax: (303) 765-5327
E-mail: usca@i-to-i.com
Web site: www.i-to-i.com

Project Type: Archaeology; Community Development; Construction; Developmental Disabilities; Historic Preservation; Medical/Health; Museum; Natural Conservation (Land); Natural Conservation (Sea); Trail Building/Maintenance; Youth

Mission Statement Excerpt: "To allow travelers from around the world to give something back to the communities they visit by contributing to worthwhile projects during their stay, sharing skills and experiences, and promoting cultural understanding, and to provide local projects in communities worldwide with a consistent supply of trained and committed volunteer workers who will work toward the project's own goals."

Year Founded: 1994

Number of Volunteers Last Year: 2,500

Funding Sources: No outside sources

The Work They Do: i-to-i offers more than 300 projects designed to help disadvantaged communities and ecosystems around the world. Project offerings are quite diverse, and they include protecting endangered Panda in Xian, China; coaching tennis and basketball to young children in India; assisting soccer league coaches in Costa Rica; conserving forests on the island of Zanzibar, Tanzania; building homes for the disadvantaged in Cape Town, South Africa; working in a community health center for early childhood development in Tanzania; protecting endangered lions in South Africa; building homes for families in Costa Rica and Honduras; and care work, such as helping orphaned children or street youth in Brazil or India.

Project Location: i-to-i offers projects in Australia, Bolivia, Brazil, China, Costa Rica, Croatia, the Dominican Republic, Ecuador, Ghana, Guatemala, Honduras, India, Ireland, Kenya, Mexico, Mongolia, Nepal, Peru, South Africa, Sri Lanka, Tanzania, Thailand, and Vietnam. Accommodations depend on the project and range from campsites to apartments to home stays. Volunteers on conservation projects should expect basic conditions, sometimes without electricity or running water.

Time Line: Each project is available year-round, with two start dates per month. Projects last from one week to six months; the average volunteer serves for six to eight weeks.

Cost: Program fees vary by location and length of the project, but a typical four-week placement with i-to-i costs $1,695, which includes accommodations and food, a welcome orientation, and a TEFL (Teaching English as a Foreign Language) course. Volunteers are responsible for providing their own airfare.

Getting Started: Prospective volunteers can call the toll-free number listed above to talk with a travel advisor or visit i-to-i's extensive Web site for details and booking arrangements. Every trip includes a standard orientation session upon arrival in the country. The orientation session lasts two or three days and covers administrative issues, health and safety, code of conduct, expectations during the project, how to succeed as a volunteer, and cultural tips. All of i-to-i's teaching and community development projects require volunteers to take a 40-hour online TEFL course before they leave for their projects. i-to-i also offers additional Spanish language lessons as needed.

Needed Skills and Specific Populations: Most of i-to-i's projects do not require specific knowledge or skills, but some media, marketing, and health projects require volunteers to submit their resumes in advance. Volunteers must be at least 18 years old, and senior volunteers are welcomed. Placement for volunteers with disabilities will be done on an individual basis in order to be 100 percent sure that the programs in which they are interested will be able to support them fully.

Jatun Sacha

Programa de Voluntarios, Fundación Jatun Sacha
Eugenio de Santillan N34-248 y Maurian
Casilla 17-12-867
Quito, Ecuador
(593) 2-243-2173 or (593) 2-243-2246;
Fax: (593) 2-245-3583
E-mail: volunteer@jatunsacha.org
Web site: www.jatunsacha.org

Project Type: Agriculture; Community Development; Construction; Economic Development; Natural Conservation (Land); Natural Conservation (Sea); Rural Development; Scientific Research; Trail Building/Maintenance

Mission Statement Excerpt: "Jatun Sacha is dedicated to promoting the conservation of forest, aquatic, and *páramo* ecosystems of Ecuador through technical training, scientific research, environmental education, community development, sustainable management of natural resources, and the development of leaders with a high participation of ethnic groups and women to improve the quality of life of the community."

Year Founded: 1989

Number of Volunteers Last Year: 800

Funding Sources: Private sources, nonprofit organizations, and USAID

The Work They Do: Jatun Sacha focuses on biological conservation and cultural diversity through private reserves, environmental education, and the development of productive projects and research that improve the lives of the people in its zones of influence and activities. The volunteer program offers opportunities in a variety of activities including data field research, environmental education, community service, plant conservation, agroforestry, and reserve maintenance.

Project Location: Volunteer projects are all in Ecuador, but they can be located on the coast, in the Amazon rainforest, on the Galápagos Islands, or in a cloud forest. Volunteers often take part in strenuous outdoor activities.

Time Line: Volunteers are accepted throughout the year for a minimum of two weeks and a maximum of six months. Jatun Sacha estimates that the average volunteer stays for one month.

Cost: Volunteers pay a $35 application fee ($50 for the Galápagos) and a program fee of $395 per month. The program fee covers lodging and all meals. Volunteers are responsible for transportation and all other costs.

Getting Started: Prospective volunteers should send an application letter that indicates their experience in conservation activities, future interests, reasons for applying, and preferred station and participation dates, along with a CV or resume, a recent health certificate, a police record card, two passport-sized photos, and the application fee. Jatun Sacha provides an orientation before volunteers travel to sites that consists of an overview of the foundation, its reserves, and its respective projects; volunteer activities; and directions to the volunteer's reserve. Once at the reserves, volunteers receive a more in-depth orientation on the activities in which they will participate, and they receive on-the-job training throughout their service.

Needed Skills and Specific Populations: Volunteers must have at least a basic knowledge of Spanish and be at least 18 years old. Senior volunteers who are physically fit are welcomed. Volunteers with disabilities are welcomed, provided that the necessary accommodations can be made.

Joint Assistance Center (JAC)

P.O. Box 6082
San Pablo, CA 94806
(510) 237-8331; Fax: (510) 217-6671
E-mail: jacusa@juno.org
Web site: www.jacusa.org

Project Type: Administrative; Agriculture; Community Development; Construction; Developmental Disabilities; Economic Development; Medical/Health; Natural Conservation (Land); Orphans; Rural Development; Trail Building/Maintenance; Women's Issues; Youth

Mission Statement Excerpt: "The international volunteer programs of the Joint Assistance Center (JAC) are intended to provide opportunities for visiting friends from abroad to see India and learn about its people and their concerns while traveling."

Year Founded: 1990

Number of Volunteers Last Year: 10

Funding Sources: None; self-funded

The Work They Do: JAC offers a variety of volunteer opportunities, all of which focus on human services work; each program is individually created and tailored to the applicant's skills and desired volunteer experience. Examples of work done by volunteers include cooperating with villagers on projects in the areas of sanitation, construction, agriculture, environmental improvement, literacy, women's welfare, and health, including local herbal medicine. Volunteers can also assist in JAC's New Delhi office; prepare for and attend conferences on development, disasters, and environmental issues; and teach English.

Project Location: All of JAC's programs take place in various parts of India, including Delhi, the region of Uttar Pradesh, and the region of Orissa. Volunteers are provided modest accommodations and vegetarian food.

Time Line: Volunteers are accepted year-round for a minimum of three weeks and a maximum of six months.

Cost: JAC's program fee is $150 per month. Accommodations and food are included in this program fee, as are airport transfers. Volunteers must provide their own airfare to India.

Getting Started: Prospective volunteers should e-mail JAC and request an application. JAC offers an orientation by phone.

Needed Skills and Specific Populations: Volunteers must be at least 18 years old, and senior volunteers are welcomed. JAC has not had any experience hosting volunteers with disabilities, but believes that it will be able to accommodate people with a wide range of disabilities.

Just Works

Unitarian Universalist Service Committee
130 Prospect Street
Cambridge, MA 02139
(800) 388-3920 or (617) 868-6600; Fax: (617) 868-7102
E-mail: justworks@uusc.org
Web site: www.uusc.org/info/workcamps.html

Project Type: Community Development; Human Rights; Political Action; Social Justice

Mission Statement Excerpt: "With more than 32,000 members and supporters, the Unitarian Universalist Service Committee (UUSC) is a nonsectarian organization that promotes human rights and social justice worldwide . . . . Our programs are based on Unitarian Universalist principles that affirm the worth, dignity, and human rights of every person."

Year Founded: 1996

Number of Volunteers Last Year: Approximately 250

The Work They Do: Just Works offers short-term work camps that help volunteers examine and understand the causes and damaging effects of injustice. Participants work directly with people in the communities they serve and experience social justice struggles firsthand. While learning about human rights issues and promoting intercultural understanding and reconciliation, volunteers are taught advocacy skills to address issues of poverty, discrimination, and racism. Participants may then make use of these skills in their congregations, campuses, and communities when they return home. Specific examples of Just Works programs include electoral-related skills training in Atlanta, Selma, Montgomery, and Birmingham (which was timed to honor the 40th anniversary of Freedom Summer); a "Defending Democracy" program, held in conjunction with presidential nominating conventions, that trained volunteers to organize, educate, and register voters; and a program for teenagers that focused on human rights issues such as race, sovereignty, and culture among Native Americans in the Pacific Northwest.

Project Location: Just Works programs change every year and may be held anywhere in the United States. Accommodations depend on the project; they have included RVs and dormitories in the past.

Time Line: Most projects are one week long, and they usually take place in July and August.

Cost: The program fee is $300 ($25 discounts are available to UUSC members and to volunteers who register at least eight weeks in advance). The program fee includes all accommodations, food, and local transportation during the project, but it does not include transportation to and from the project site. In general, Just Works volunteers eat locally grown food prepared by local people.

Getting Started: To apply for a Just Works project, prospective volunteers can download an application from the organization's Web site or contact the office via e-mail or phone. Applicants are encouraged to submit their materials at least six to eight weeks before the project's start date.

Needed Skills and Specific Populations: In general, volunteers must be at least 16 years old, though some projects are designed specifically for youth and young adults, and some projects have a minimum age of 18.

Kokee Resource Conservation Program (KRCP)

Hui O Laka/Kokee Natural History Museum
P.O. Box 100
Kekaha, HI 96752
(808) 335-9975; Fax: (808) 335-6131
E-mail: rcp@aloha.net
Web site: www.krcp.org

Project Type: Natural Conservation (Land); Trail Building/Maintenance

Mission Statement Excerpt: "Kokee Resource Conservation Program (KRCP) seeks to involve the public in protecting native ecosystem resources by coordinating volunteers to conduct essential removal of invasive noxious weeds in selected areas."

Year Founded: 1998

Number of Volunteers Last Year: 2,100

Funding Sources: Government and private grants

The Work They Do: KRCP focuses on reforestation projects in Kokee State Park on Kauai Island, Hawaii. Most of its work involves weeding invasive plants from native Hawaiian mountain forests. About 1,000 acres are actively managed, and KRCP removes ginger, guava, privet, and several types of plants. Other work, such as trail maintenance and nursery planting, occasionally takes place. Volunteers join staff members daily to hike and work off-trail, treating specific weeds, in a section of the park. The park has a variety of forest ecosystems and weed problems, so work does not become monotonous.

Project Location: All volunteers work in Kokee State Park, which is 3,000 to 4,000 feet above sea level and is made up of swamp, wet forest, and dry forest. Conditions can be muddy and involve steep terrain; hiking and off-trail bushwhacking are common. Volunteers should be prepared for rain, but they may be comforted to know that there are no snakes. Lodging is in a 1930s bunkhouse, constructed by the Civilian Conservation Corps as a part of the New Deal, that has hot running water and a communal kitchen.

Time Line: Volunteers are accepted year-round for one day to four weeks. The average stay is two weeks.

Cost: There is no cost to volunteer with KRCP, and housing is provided free of charge in the bunkhouse. Volunteers are responsible for purchasing their own food, which is obtained in a town that is 45 minutes away from the site. Transportation to Kokee State Park is difficult, and volunteers should plan on providing their own travel to the work site, such as by renting a car. Volunteers must also have health insurance.

Getting Started: Prospective volunteers should contact KRCP at the address listed above and request an application form. Much of the first day of volunteering is spent in training and orientation, and more training is given daily as needed.

Needed Skills and Specific Populations: Anyone who can handle the strenuous, off-trail work is welcomed, including senior volunteers and volunteers with disabilities. Volunteers are expected to work with mild herbicides and machetes. Volunteers under age 18 should be accompanied by their parents or volunteer as a part of a group, and they are not allowed to use herbicides or machetes.

Landmark Volunteers

P.O. Box 455
Sheffield, MA 01257
(413) 229-0255; Fax: (413) 229-2050
E-mail: landmark@volunteers.com
Web site: www.volunteers.com

Project Type: Community Development; Construction; Natural
Conservation (Land); Trail Building/Maintenance; Youth
Mission Statement Excerpt: "Landmark Volunteers . . . [gives]
high school students the chance to make a real difference in
the world around them. We offer one-week spring and
two-week summer volunteer opportunities with leading
cultural, environmental, historical, and social service organizations across the country."
Year Founded: 1992
Number of Volunteers Last Year: 725
Funding Sources: Individual donars and foundations; volunteer
program fees pay for roughly two-thirds of the program
expenses
The Work They Do: Landmark Volunteers participants primarily do manual work for host organizations, including clearing and building trails, painting, construction, and grounds
maintenance. Volunteers may also work directly with one
of the host organization's target populations, such as disadvantaged youth. Many of Landmark Volunteers's host
organizations determine their specific projects shortly
before volunteers arrive, so volunteers should be prepared
to take on a variety of possible tasks for eight hours per
day. Volunteers, who are all high school students, serve in
teams of up to 13 people under the full-time leadership and
supervision of an adult Landmark Volunteers team leader.
Project Location: Landmark works in 60 locations across the
United States. Lodging is arranged in cooperation with the
host organizations and varies by site. Possibilities range
from cabins to dorms to tents to local churches or schools.

Time Line: Spring projects are available in March and April and run for one week. Two-week summer projects run from mid-June to mid-August.

Cost: Program fees range from $875 to $925. Each fee covers food, lodging, transportation, and adult supervision. Day-off activities are not included in the program fee.

Getting Started: Prospective volunteers can apply via Landmark's Web site.

Needed Skills and Specific Populations: Landmark volunteers must be 14–18 years old. Landmark's nondiscrimination policy states that "we do not discriminate in admissions . . . against any individual on account of that individual's . . . disability."

La Sabranenque

Rue de la Tour de l'Oume
30290 Saint Victor la Coste
France
+ 0033 466 500 505; Fax: + 0033 466 500 077
or
La Sabranenque
c/o Jacqueline Simon
124 Bondcroft Drive
Buffalo, NY 14226
(716) 836-8698
E-mail: info@sabranenque.com
Web site: www.sabranenque.com

Project Type: Historic Preservation; Rural Development

Mission Statement Excerpt: "La Sabranenque works toward the preservation of traditional Mediterranean architecture through work projects aimed at consolidating and rehabilitating sites and through teaching volunteers the construction techniques."

Year Founded: 1969

Number of Volunteers Last Year: 250

Funding Sources: No outside funding; La Sabranenque is self-funded

The Work They Do: La Sabranenque works on consolidating and rebuilding traditional regional architecture in southern France. Projects range from the paving of a village path to the consolidation of a Romanesque chapel to the complete reconstruction of a complex of houses. Volunteers take an active part in the restoration work, including clearing rubble, cutting stone, walling drystone, paving paths, tiling floors or roofs, and plastering walls. The main construction technique used is stone masonry.

Project Location: Volunteers work in Provence, France. Work sites may be houses, chapels, or medieval castle sites, either

For this particular renovation, volunteers from France, Holland, and the United States worked together to rebuild the old medieval rampart of Saint Victor la Coste, located in the beautiful Provence region of France. *Photo courtesy of La Sabranenque*

within a village or on a hilltop. Volunteers are housed, two to a room, in the restored village of Saint Victor la Coste. Food is prepared by a chef and is described as one of the highlights of the experience.

Time Line: Volunteers are accepted from May through October, and they can stay from one week to several months. The average volunteer stay is one to two weeks.

Cost: La Sabranenque's two-week program fee is $710, which includes housing and full board, all activities, and pickup and drop-off at the Avignon train station. The program fee does not include international airfare or train costs to Avignon. La Sabranenque is run by volunteers, so approximately 90 percent of the program fee goes directly toward program costs.

Getting Started: Prospective volunteers should contact La Sabranenque and request a brochure and an enrollment form. All volunteers are trained in the traditional construction techniques used while on the job.

Needed Skills and Specific Populations: No construction skills are needed; La Sabranenque's volunteers rarely have experience in this kind of work. Volunteers must be at least 18 years old; there is no maximum age limit, and La Sabranenque regularly hosts volunteers who are in their sixties. Due to the layout of the village and the access to projects, La Sabranenque may not be able to accommodate people who have difficulty walking.

Madre

121 West 27th Street, #301
New York, NY 10001
(212) 627-0444; Fax: (212) 675-3704
E-mail: volunteers@madre.org
Web site: www.madre.org

Project Type: Administrative; Agriculture; Community Development; Construction; Economic Development; Human Rights; Legal; Medical/Health; Political Action; Professional/Technical Assistance; Rural Development; Social Justice; Women's Issues; Youth

Mission Statement Excerpt: "Madre provides essential support to our partner organizations through our volunteer program, Sisters Without Borders. When requested by our partners, Madre arranges for culturally competent, skilled professionals to work with women and children and to provide assistance to staff and community leaders."

Year Founded: 1983

Number of Volunteers Last Year: 7

Funding Sources: Madre receives support from individual donors, foundations, and religious communities. Madre does not receive government funding.

The Work They Do: Madre is a women's human rights organization whose programs address many issues of global importance. Madre also provides resources and training to sister organizations around the world to help them meet immediate needs in their communities and develop long-term solutions to the crises they face. Examples of Madre volunteer projects include sending volunteer health care professionals to work with the communities of their sister organizations to assist local professionals in combating AIDS, breast cancer, pediatric diseases, and other threats to women and children's health; creating human rights training and popular education workshops on women's human rights, labor rights, the rights of indigenous people, and sexual and reproductive rights; trauma counseling;

agriculture, including organic farming; and budget management and planning.

Project Location: Madre volunteers work in Guatemala, Mexico, Nicaragua, Peru, Kenya, and Palestine. Volunteers sometimes work in rural, underserved communities that lack critical resources such as potable water and electricity. Volunteers usually stay in nearby hotels or hostels or with local families, depending on each volunteer's preference.

Time Line: Volunteers must be able to commit to a minimum of three months; there is no maximum length of time for volunteer projects. Under certain circumstances, volunteer opportunities with a time commitment of one month or less may be arranged for advanced professionals such as physicians and nurses who have necessary language skills and experience working abroad.

Cost: Madre does not charge a program fee, but volunteers are responsible for all of their own costs. Madre will help arrange room and board for volunteers. Depending on the country and placement, volunteer expenses range from approximately $400 to $900 per month, with an average being around $500 to $600 per month; this monthly cost does not include the cost of international airfare.

Getting Started: Prospective volunteers should send a cover letter and resume that states their country or program of interest, relevant skills, background, and level of fluency in appropriate languages for the country of service. Madre's orientations are personalized for each volunteer and generally consist of at least two in-person meetings and background materials on the project and the community in which the volunteer will be working.

Needed Skills and Specific Populations: Volunteers must have experience and professional skills or credentials to work with Madre. Volunteers must be at least 18 years old, and senior volunteers are welcomed. Volunteers with disabilities may be able to join a Madre project, depending on the project location and each volunteer's specific disability.

Mar de Jade

PMB 078-344
827 Union Pacific
Laredo, Texas 78045-9452
(800) 257-0532
E-mail: info@mardejade.org
Web site: www.mardejade.org

Project Type: Community Development; Economic Development; Medical/Health; Rural Development; Youth

Funding Sources: Mar de Jade is a for-profit resort that also offers volunteer opportunities.

The Work They Do: Mar de Jade is an oceanfront resort and retreat center located on Mexico's Pacific coast, north of Puerto Vallarta. As a socially responsible vacation site, Mar de Jade offers its guests volunteer opportunities in a nearby community. Volunteer activities include health care services and an after-school program that offers high-protein meals and cultural activities for children, in which volunteers often provide English, art, computer, or music classes. Volunteers can also help with organic home-gardening projects, and Mar de Jade would like to pursue other projects such as food canning and preserving, ceramics, sewing, embroidery, weaving, and other crafts.

Project Location: Volunteers work in the nearby tropical farming town of Las Varas, Nayarit, near the Pacific coast in Mexico.

Time Line: Volunteers are accepted year-round for three-week programs. Volunteer projects have specific start and end dates.

Cost: Program fees for the three weeks range from $1,400 per person for accommodations in a shared guesthouse to $2,000 per person for a double master suite. Each program fee includes accommodations, daily transportation, and three buffet meals per day, but not transportation to Mexico.

Getting Started: Prospective volunteers can complete a reservation form on Mar de Jade's Web site. Reservations are confirmed when a deposit of 50 percent of the program fee has been received.

Needed Skills and Specific Populations: Volunteers will find it especially helpful to have some level of proficiency in Spanish, but this is not a requirement. Volunteers who wish to work in the clinic must be licensed professionals or enrolled medical students.

Medex International (MEI)

1235 N. Decatur Road
Atlanta, GA 30306
(404) 815-7044; Fax: (404) 892-6672
E-mail: info@medexinternational.org
Web site: www.medexinternational.org

Project Type: Medical/Health

Mission Statement Excerpt: "Medex International . . . provides health care to some of the world's most underserved people and animals. We travel to some extremely remote regions of the world and bring medical care to people in developing countries as well as rural areas of more advanced nations."

Year Founded: 2004

Number of Volunteers Last Year: 63

Funding Sources: Donations from private sources

The Work They Do: MEI provides medical and dental care to individuals and families. The organization also trains local health care providers, neuters dogs and cats, and treats acute illnesses in all animals. This care is provided by physicians, physician assistants, nurse practitioners, nurses, physical therapists, dentists, veterinarians, and other medical professionals. Nonmedical support volunteers may work in triage or in the pharmacy, do very basic lab work, or help with crowd control.

Project Location: MEI currently works in India and Ecuador. Work sites range from thatched roof huts in Ecuador to a newly built medical clinic at a Tibetan settlement in India. Volunteers often, but not always, work in facilities with no electricity or climate control. Living conditions vary, and accommodations might be in an ecolodge, a church, a monastery, or a very basic hotel. Some medical sites require camping in a tent.

Time Line: MEI offers one-week trips to Latin America and two-week trips to Asia throughout the year.

Cost: The program fee runs from $1,500 to $1,945, which includes lodging, most meals, all in-country transportation, medical supplies, guides, interpreters, and one or two days of sightseeing after the work is completed. The program fee does not include international airfare.

Getting Started: Prospective volunteers should fill out the application form found on MEI's Web site. Informational materials are sent to volunteers before their departure, and orientation is held the night before medical work begins.

Needed Skills and Specific Populations: Although several non-medical support volunteers are taken on each trip, volunteers with any medical or veterinary skills are most needed. Licensed medical professionals are required to provide their professional license numbers. Volunteers must be at least 10 years old. Senior volunteers are welcomed, but they must be in good shape, as the trips tend to be somewhat physically challenging. Most of MEI's medical sites are in rural areas of developing countries that do not meet U.S. standards for accommodating physical disabilities; availability of work for volunteers with disabilities depends upon the disability of the potential volunteer. Citizens from other countries are welcome to volunteer with MEI.

Making House Calls Around the World

❖ **By Suzi Battle** ❖

Medex International (MEI)

The author is a banker, author, and frequent MEI participant.

House calls. The term evokes visions of a gray-haired Marcus Welby type, trudging through the snow, carrying his cracked and weathered black medicine bag, or traveling from house to house by horse and buggy. But the mission trip participants of Medical Expeditions International (MEI) are more likely to be seen wearing safari-type zip-off pants tucked into black, knee-high rubber boots.

For this particular house call in the Amazonian rainforest of Ecuador, travel was first by bus, then small plane, then canoe. On the last leg of the journey, there were no telephones, cell or otherwise, no computers, television, or radio. Just the quiet of the water lapping against a canoe and the unmistakable cacophony of sounds from the jungle of the myriad of birds and animals that inhabit this area along with the villagers of the Achuar community—MEI's patients for the week.

The Achuar community has a total population of about 4,500 and comprises 56 villages. On this mission, we aimed to visit three villages in addition to seeing roughly 20 staff members of the Kapawi Ecolodge. The team included two physicians, a dentist, a nutritionist, a pharmacist, and other medical and nonmedical people. These 11 people united with one common goal, experiencing a mission of hope to these underserved communities and creating a lifelong bonding friendship with people from around the world.

We arrived at Kapawi (one of the top ecolodges in the world!) after a day of sightseeing in Quito, the capital of Ecuador, followed by two days of travel into the rainforest. Kapawi is managed and operated jointly by the Canodros company and members of the Achuar community. Long-term ecotourism will protect the community from oil exploration in addition to providing financial support for education and health programs in the area. In 2011 the lodge is slated to be turned over to the Achuar community to run on their own.

At Kapawi we slept in thatched-roof huts erected on stilts over marshy waters, and were awoken at 6:00 A.M. by the resonating, low hum of a hollowed-out bull's horn. After a breakfast of rather exotic food grown locally by the Achuar and prepared by the lodge's chef, we pulled on our heavy rubber boots and headed to the canoes for a two-hour trip upriver.

Our first stop was a village of 117 people. We were welcomed by laughing, barefooted children running along the steep, muddy bank of the river. Upon arriving at each village, the team was ceremoniously escorted by the community's inhabitants to the "clinic" of the day, sometimes a roughhewn, makeshift schoolhouse or a large open-air thatched-roof building with a dirt floor. Crowd control was an issue, as the entire village shows up to be treated or, in many cases, just to watch in wide-eyed wonder.

The medical team saw a variety of illnesses during the three-day mission. The most common were fungal and parasitic skin infections, anemia, parasites, lice, headaches, and toothaches. The patients were treated with albendazole for parasites, and the children and women of childbearing age were provided vitamins.

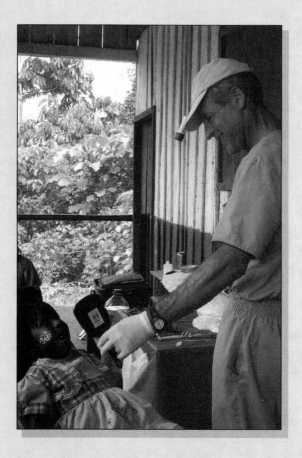

A retired dentist (a worldwide traveler and participant in
multiple volunteer vacations with many organizations) from
Bethesda, Maryland, smiles as one of his young patients
warily peers into a mirror at the dental work she has just
bravely endured. This particular expedition was to an ongoing site in the Achuar federation in southeastern Ecuador.
*Photo courtesy of Suzi Battle, of Medical Expeditions
International*

In Ecuador, two species of malaria parasites are found: *P. Falciparum* and *P. Vivax*. Rapid-test kits that detect *P. Falciparum* with whole blood were used for testing those who had signs and symptoms of malaria. Luckily, there were fewer cases of malaria than usual; only six in total. All malaria patients were treated with mefloquine (Lariam).

Anemia appeared to be prevalent in this area, so hemoglobin levels were tested. Over the course of three days we tested 159 patients and detected 14 cases, almost 9 percent of the villagers who sought medical care. Patients diagnosed as anemic were treated with ferrous sulfate supplements.

In a separate hut nearby, the dentist saw a total of 21 patients and performed a total of 38 extractions. Amazingly, most children came alone to see the dentist and stoically withstood their treatments with the courage of an adult.

Weary and mud-soaked, everyone climbed back into the canoes at the end of each day, exhausted but exhilarated from their experiences and eagerly awaiting the next day's adventures.

Medical Ministry International (MMI)

P.O. Box 1339
Allen, TX 75013
United States: (972) 727-5864; Fax: (972) 727-7810
Canada: (905) 524-3544; Fax: (905) 524-5400
E-mail: mmitx@mmint.org
Web site: www.mmint.org

Project Type: Medical/Health

Mission Statement Excerpt: "Medical Ministry International is an opportunity to serve Jesus Christ by providing spiritual and physical health care in this world of need."

Year Founded: Began with individual efforts in 1968, and originally founded as Medical Group Missions

Number of Volunteers Last Year: 1,554

Funding Sources: Private sources and some faith-based organizations

The Work They Do: MMI sends volunteer teams of health care professionals to serve the world's poor who have little or no access to medical care. The health care MMI offers is usually all that is available to the recipients. Both medical and nonmedical volunteers are accepted, including dentists, primary care and specialty physicians, surgeons, optometrists, nurses, health educators, other health professionals, translators, technicians, handy people, and general helpers. To provide the very best possible care for patients, only qualified professionals participate directly in surgical or dental procedures. Medical and project directors assign each participant a role, matching his or her skills and training to the needs of the project. Days are full, and volunteers work hard as a team to see as many patients as possible during the week.

Project Location: The organization works in 25 countries around the world. Work sites vary; some involve a short-term clinic set up in a school or community center for the duration of a project. Others involve a clinic that is moved by volunteers to different areas every few days. Teams may also work at an existing hospital. Accommodations are usually in a hostel, dorm, or small hotel, all of which have bathroom facilities. MMI uses its own cooks to ensure that volunteers and staff members receive healthful food and water.

Time Line: One- and two-week projects are scheduled year-round, though most are for two weeks. It may be possible to stay longer than two weeks, but volunteers will need to work this out with the hosts on location. Some MMI volunteers add tourist travel to the end of their stay.

Cost: The program fee is $775 for a one-week project and $1,075 for a two-week project. All room and board costs are included in the program fee; volunteers must provide their own airfare to the country of service. Each project has a project director and a medical director who will work with volunteers to coordinate all needed medicines and supplies. More than 90 percent of the program fee goes directly into program services.

Getting Started: Prospective volunteers can apply online, download an application online, or request an application from MMI's office. MMI provides preparatory materials that outline how to plan for the trip and what to expect. Team orientation occurs on the first day in the host country.

Needed Skills and Specific Populations: Doctors, dentists, and surgeons must be currently licensed to practice. Volunteers aged 12 to 14 must be accompanied by a parent; youths 15 to 17 years old must be accompanied by a designated adult and need a notarized letter signed by both parents (or legal guardians) authorizing them to make the trip; volunteers under 18 years of age will not be allowed in operating rooms. People aged 18 and over are welcome to volunteer as adults. Senior volunteers are welcomed, and spouses may accompany medical volunteers. Volunteers with disabilities are welcomed provided they are able to travel in places that are not handicap-accessible; please contact MMI before applying.

Mercy Ships

P.O. Box 2020
Garden Valley, TX 75771
(903) 939-7000
E-mail: jobs@mercyships.org
Web site: www.mercyships.org

Project Type: Administrative; Agriculture; Community Development; Construction; Education; Medical/Health

Mission Statement Excerpt: "Mercy Ships, a global charity, has operated a growing fleet of ships in developing nations since 1978. Following the example of Jesus, Mercy Ships brings hope and healing to the poor, mobilizing people and resources worldwide."

Year Founded: 1978

Number of Volunteers Last Year: Approximately 1,600

Funding Sources: Government, faith-based, and private

The Work They Do: Mercy Ships provides medical care, relief aid, and training for long-term sustainable change in developing nations. A global charity that serves people of all faiths, Mercy Ships is best known for its work in health care services, which are provided to patients free of charge. Mobile medical and dental teams establish field clinics in nearby communities to offer vaccination programs, dental care, and minor operations. Mercy Ships supports the training of national doctors and nurses in the countries it serves, and it provides local people with education in hygiene, nutrition, and basic health care. Mercy Ships teams also help to construct hospitals, clinics, schools, vocational training facilities, homes, and churches; they carry out agricultural projects, teaching communities how to become more productive and efficient in growing food for themselves and for the marketplace; and they test local water sources and train village representatives in how to break the water-borne disease cycle. The teams assist with individual and community latrine construction, and they

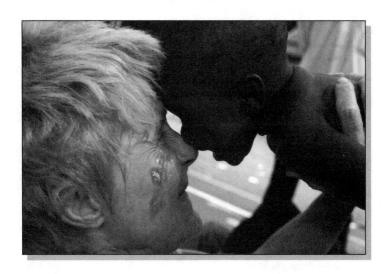

A delighted volunteer nicknamed Super Gran works hard in Western Africa to keep the children entertained during an initial medical screening before surgeries begin aboard a Mercy Ships vessel. *Photo courtesy of Scott Harrison, of Mercy Ships*

drill and rehabilitate wells to provide safe water for consumption and irrigation.

Project Location: Most projects are located in West Africa and Central America or the Caribbean. Most volunteers are fed and housed on a Mercy Ships vessel.

Time Line: Project time lines are available on the Mercy Ships Web site. Volunteers commit to at least two weeks of service, which they can extend for as long as they like, even to the extent of making a career of being a Mercy Ships volunteer or doctor. Volunteers are considered short-term if they work for two weeks to one year. Career volunteers commit to at least two years plus a training period.

Cost: Volunteers on Mercy Ships pay an onboard living fee of $125 per week, which includes all meals and accommodations. Medical volunteers pay an additional medical fee. Volunteers are responsible for paying for their own international travel expenses.

Getting Started: Prospective volunteers can download an application from the Mercy Ships Web site. Volunteers receive training onboard their Mercy Ship vessel, and career volunteers have additional training.

Needed Skills and Specific Populations: Mercy Ships offers both skilled and unskilled volunteer opportunities. Medical volunteers must be fully certified. Volunteers must be at least 18 years old; there is no maximum age limit as long as the volunteer is healthy. Due to the limited confines of the Mercy Ships vessels, the organization cannot accommodate people with disabilities.

Mobility International USA (MIUSA)

P.O. Box 10767
Eugene, OR 97440
(541) 343-1284 (TTY); Fax: (541) 343-6812
E-mail: exchange@miusa.org
Web site: www.miusa.org

Project Type: Community Development; Human Rights; Social
Justice; Women's Issues; Youth

Mission Statement Excerpt: "Empowering people with
disabilities around the world to achieve their human rights
through international exchange and international
development."

Year Founded: 1981

Number of Volunteers Last Year: Approximately 50

Funding Sources: Some funding from private foundations

The Work They Do: MIUSA organizes international exchange
programs for people with and without disabilities that feature volunteer work as a key component. International
exchange trip activities include living with homestay families, leadership seminars, disability rights workshops, cross-
cultural learning, and team-building activities such as river
rafting and challenge courses. Participants develop strategies for making changes both within themselves and in
their communities. MIUSA programs provide a cross-
disability, cross-cultural leadership experience for participants interested in leadership and disability rights. Past
volunteer projects have included working at the Tokyo
Wild Bird Park and visiting schools for deaf and blind children.

Project Location: International exchange programs are held
throughout the year in the United States and abroad. Past
exchange locations include Azerbaijan, Russia, Japan, England, Costa Rica, Mexico, Germany, Uzbekistan, Australia,
and China.

Time Line: MIUSA usually offers two to four exchange programs during each calendar year. Each program typically lasts two to four weeks.

Cost: Program fees vary, and most are subsidized by grants or other funding. An example of a program fee is $850 for a two-week exchange to Japan, which includes round-trip international airfare from San Jose, California, to Tokyo, Japan, accessible lodging, meals, and activities. MIUSA also offers generous partial scholarships to qualified applicants. Prospective volunteers must send in a $15 nonrefundable fee at the time of application.

Getting Started: Prospective applicants can download a four-page application from MIUSA's Web site, which may then be submitted by e-mail or postal mail. Applications also require letters of recommendation. All application materials are available in alternative formats upon request, including large print, Braille, and on diskette. Application deadlines are typically three to four months before the departure date, but late applications will be considered as space permits. Qualified applicants will be interviewed by telephone, TTY, or online via Instant Messenger. Accepted applicants will receive an orientation packet and will be put in contact with an alumnus of a similar MIUSA program in order to communicate about airline travel, accessibility, packing tips, health and safety, and any other questions or concerns the volunteer may have.

Munda Wanga Trust

P.O. Box 38267
Lusaka, Zambia
+ 260-1-278 456; Fax: + 260-1-278 529
E-mail: sanctuary@zamnet.zm
Web site: www.mundawanga.com

Project Type: Natural Conservation (Land); Scientific Research
Mission Statement Excerpt: "Munda Wanga Environmental
Park is a Zambian institution embarking on a rehabilitation program to rejuvenate a neglected botanical garden
and transform an old menagerie-style zoo into a modern-
day wildlife park and sanctuary. As a nonprofit conservation education organization, Munda Wanga Environmental
Park is trying to counteract and prevent further environmental devastation through education and public awareness, wildlife rehabilitation, endangered species breeding
programs, and a threatened plants program."
Year Founded: 1998
Number of Volunteers Last Year: 15
Funding Sources: Private sources, such as companies and zoos
The Work They Do: Munda Wanga Environmental Park is a
small wildlife park that fell into a state of disrepair in the
early 1990s, and for almost 10 years the animals there suf-
fered terribly. In December 1998 new management took
over and decided to revitalize the park. The park and sanctuary now displays more than 40 species of mammals and
birds, including lions, tigers, an African painted dog, a
baby elephant, American black bears, and a large variety of
antelope, primates, and smaller mammals, all in large,
modern, environmentally enriched enclosures. Volunteer
job descriptions depend upon the individual's expertise and
areas of interest, and upon the priorities of the park and
sanctuary at the time of arrival. Specific examples of work
done by volunteers include cleaning animal enclosures,
helping to hand-rear animals, building walls or climbing

apparatuses for primates, assisting local vets in both minor and major medical matters, fund-raising, teaching schoolchildren, and simply spending time with an injured animal. The proximity of the park to Lusaka provides an opportunity for most of the Zambian population to view wildlife, which makes Munda Wanga Environmental Park an ideal place to create an educational program directed toward the conservation of indigenous wildlife.

Project Location: Munda Wanga Environmental Park is nine miles south of Lusaka, Zambia. Accommodations are provided at the park and are fairly basic. Volunteers can cook their own food or obtain it at the local restaurant.

Time Line: Volunteers are accepted year-round for a minimum of three weeks and a maximum of three months.

Cost: The program fee is $750 for three weeks, which includes accommodations and a weekly food allowance. International airfare is not included in the program fee. After the initial three-week period, the Munda Wanga Trust allows volunteers to stay on for no additional cost as long as the volunteers fit in with the staff, are hardworking, and cover all their expenses other than accommodations, which are provided.

Getting Started: Prospective volunteers should e-mail the operations manager for a questionnaire, which is to be submitted with a CV or resume. All needed training is done on-site after arrival.

Needed Skills and Specific Populations: Though previous experience with animals is a plus, it is not required to volunteer with the Munda Wanga Trust. Volunteers must be at least 18 years old; senior volunteers are welcomed as long as they have been cleared by their family doctor. The organization is not currently set up to accept volunteers with disabilities, but it is willing to review such applications on a case-by-case basis.

MunYaWana Leopard Project

c/o School of Biological Sciences
Monash University, Wellington Road
Clayton, VIC, 3800
Australia
+ 1 718-741-8188; Fax: + 1 718-364-4275
E-mail: lhunter@wcs.org
Web site: www.biolsci.monash.edu.au/Honours/
leopards/volunteer.htm

Project Type: Natural Conservation (Land); Scientific Research
Year Founded: 2002
Number of Volunteers Last Year: 24
Funding Sources: Some private sources
The Work They Do: MunYaWana Leopard Project conducts
research on a persecuted population of wild leopards in
South Africa in order to reduce the impacts of threats to
the species and to ensure the conservation of leopards in
the region. Volunteers assist in capturing live, wild leopards
in order to fit the leopards with radio-collars and collect
tissue samples and physical measurements. Volunteers
spend long hours radio tracking and observing leopards.
Volunteers may also monitor other carnivore species such
as lions, cheetahs, and spotted hyenas; conduct intermittent
counts of prey species; and enter data into databases. Volunteers are expected to help cook and clean up along with
the rest of the staff.
Project Location: Volunteers work in Phinda Game Reserve in
northern KwaZulu-Natal Province, South Africa. The
reserve is about 12 miles from the Indian Ocean on the
warm, humid, low-lying Mozambique floodplain. There is
a warm, fairly dry winter from April to mid-September and
a hot, humid summer from mid-September to the end of
March, which includes the rainy period. The hottest, raini-
est months are November to February. Accommodation is
in a large farmhouse within the reserve's boundaries.

Volunteers share one bedroom in the farmhouse, which is very basic but dry and safe. It has electricity and both hot and cold running water.

Time Line: Volunteers are accepted throughout the year. The standard volunteer stint for MunYaWana Leopard Project volunteers is 10 days, but this may be increased for outstanding volunteers.

Cost: The program fee for 10 days is $2,990, which covers in-country flights, accommodations, and food. Volunteers must provide their own airfare to and from South Africa.

Getting Started: Prospective volunteers can begin the application process by visiting the organization's Web site listed above. All training is provided on-site.

Needed Skills and Specific Populations: Volunteers need to be relatively fit; the work is not especially demanding, but it does entail long hours during both the day and night. Volunteers do not need any specialized skills, but they must have a lot of patience and the ability to sit in a vehicle for hours on end watching or waiting for leopards without talking loudly or moving around. Volunteers over 18 years old are welcomed, including senior volunteers. MunYaWana Leopard Project is not equipped to host volunteers with disabilities.

Here Kitty!

❖ By Victoria Mitchell ❖

MunYaWana Leopard Project

I am listening to a leopard feeding somewhere in the dark. It is late at night, I can't see a thing, and the big cat is only about 30 yards from us. Exhilarating, but how did I end up here?

I have always dreamed of seeing big cats in the wild, in "their" world, in the African bush. To realize this dream, I signed on to play assistant to leopard researcher Guy Balme on the MunYaWana Leopard Project—a major research effort designed to halt the decline of a beleaguered leopard population in KwaZulu Natal, South Africa. Historically, leopard conservation has been based mainly on guesswork, but this project aims to change that. By fitting leopards with radio-tracking collars as well as conducting comprehensive camera trapping surveys, the conservation concerns facing the leopard are being scientifically and accurately assessed. So this is how I find myself trying to help catch a leopard.

The adventure began earlier that evening. As dusk set in, we drove into the bush looking for leopards. Spot lighting was one of my duties as a volunteer—suddenly, I'm an expert at finding leopards? I'm more likely to find a needle in a haystack, but I diligently swept the light rapidly from side to side as instructed, looking for the "eye shine" of a big cat. We had been driving for only half an hour when I suddenly picked up twin yellow embers staring straight at us. "What's that?" I whispered. Guy suddenly gasped. Shielding the light with a red filter (most mammals cannot see red light and ignore a filtered spotlight), he homed in on the eye shine. A leopard! In whispers, Guy told us it was probably an adolescent male and not yet radio collared—an ideal animal for the study. One of the main goals is to assess how young animals survive when they are forced to disperse from protected areas into leopard hostile lands. Collaring this young male would reveal some critical information.

We immediately sprung into action, securely wiring bait (the carcass of an impala) to a tree. The bait brings the leopard within range of a dart gun, about 30 meters. Otherwise, we'd never get close. Then we waited, sitting in the dark in our cut-down Land Rover, listening to the African bush and trying not to nod off. Nothing happened, so we backed off and planned to come back in a few hours. As we approached home base, a message came across the radio: "Leopard seen heading in an easterly direction, in the canopy." We giggled at this notion. A tourist vehicle had spotted our leopard, who immediately shot up a tree and made his escape by jumping from tree to tree. If we catch him, we will call him Sinkwe, Zulu for tree walker.

Circling back to the bait, we wait. Sometime after midnight, like a ghost, the big cat suddenly materialized. My heart pounded so loudly in my chest, I was sure it would scare him off. It was my first good look at a wild leopard, an image of breathtaking magnificence that will stay with me for life. This is a critical time when no one can move or make any noise. Leopards sometimes dodge the dart with extraordinary *Matrix*-like gymnastics. I had stopped breathing, waiting for the moment, when THUMP! The dart hit home, sounding more like a fist hitting a pillow than a shot. Briefly spooked, our leopard lurched a few meters into the bush, then settled down to pull out the dart and play with it like a kitten. Gradually the anesthetic took effect and 10 minutes later, we had our cat!

Working quickly, we retrieved the sedated leopard—Sinkwe—from the bush. We placed him in an open clearing, allowing us to keep an eye out for other predators as we worked and to easily monitor his recovery. He was in fantastic condition. His coat glistened in the spotlight. I'll never forget the soft silky fur, without scent, as if he had just been bathed. I could have stroked him for hours, but there was work to be done. We quickly and carefully fit the collar; not too tight and not too loose, just as you would fit a collar on a domestic cat. Fit it too tight and Fluffy will choke; fit it too loosely and Fluffy will just flick it off; fit it just right and Fluffy won't even know it's there! Once the collar was on—the most important task—we took measurements, weighed him, and took a small tissue sample for DNA testing. The DNA profile allows Guy to assess how related the leopards are and work out how young males like Sinkwe disperse into other areas.

An hour after we darted him, we have finished and backed off to monitor his recovery. I'll see Sinkwe again a number of times during my trip, as we track him by his new radio collar. Each day brings a little extra data, hopefully building up enough knowledge to ensure that Sinkwe and his species persist in the area forever. I know that, in one small way, I am now part of that.

National Meditation Center for World Peace (NMCWP)

Route 10, Box 2523
Jacksonville, TX 75766
(903) 589-5706
E-mail: Nmc@nationalmeditation.org
Web site: www.nationalmeditation.org

Project Type: Administrative; Community Development; Economic Development; Orphans; Rural Development; Youth

Mission Statement Excerpt: "Prevent community degradation through direct advocacy."

Year Founded: 1983

Number of Volunteers Last Year: 22

Funding Sources: Private donors

The Work They Do: NMCWP works in advocacy and leadership roles to train personnel at host agencies. They also offer opportunities to volunteer directly with youth and adults. Examples of past projects include operating leadership academies, working with the poor, and helping organizations with strategic planning. Volunteers have been instrumental to the NMCWP's work, helping with tasks such as working with media agencies, handling office jobs, loading equipment, and working with youth.

Project Location: Volunteers can work either at the project site in the Philippines or at NMCWP's headquarters in Jacksonville, Texas. In the Philippines, volunteers work in rural, poverty-stricken areas. Housing, which is arranged by NMCWP, is rustic and offers cold showers.

Time Line: Most volunteer projects in the Philippines run from April through August, though there are occasionally additional opportunities in December. Volunteers must commit to a two-week stay.

Cost: Program fees run from $1,500 to $2,200. The program fee covers lodging, typically in a hotel or motel, and meals for volunteers in Texas, but not in the Philippines. Airfare within the United States is not included in the program fee, but the NMCWP has some grants to cover half of the costs of flying to the Philippines from Los Angeles.

Getting Started: Prospective volunteers should contact the NMCWP by phone or e-mail (if contacting by e-mail, include the phrase "volunteer tour" in the subject line). Volunteers receive an orientation and training in Filipino culture.

Needed Skills and Specific Populations: Volunteers with specialized skills in construction, mechanics, or working with the media are particularly needed. Volunteers aged 16–21 need their parents' consent; senior volunteers are welcomed. Applicants with disabilities may volunteer to work at the Jacksonville, Texas, office. Volunteers staying in the Philippines more than 30 days will need to apply for a visa; NMCWP does not assist non-U.S. citizens with this process.

Naucrates

Via Corbetta, 11
22063 Cantu' (CO)
Italy
+ 39 3334306643; Fax: + 39 031716315
E-mail: naucrates12@hotmail.com
Web site: www.naucrates.org

Project Type: Community Development; Natural Conservation
(Land); Natural Conservation (Sea); Scientific Research
Mission Statement Excerpt: "We work toward conservation of
nature with particular interest in endangered species and
habitats."
Year Founded: 2001
Number of Volunteers Last Year: 40
Funding Sources: Naucrates receives money from some private
sources.
The Work They Do: Naucrates takes on conservation, education, and scientific research projects, specifically in the
areas of sea turtle survival and the protection of mangrove
forests. Volunteers help by walking the beach looking for
sea turtles, taking weather measurements, observing and
feeding captive turtles, participating in fundraisers, educating local schoolchildren, and monitoring turtle nests.
Project Location: Naucrates's work is mainly conducted on an
island off the coast of Thailand. This island was badly
damaged by the December 26, 2004 tsunami, Naucrates is
planning to build a new project site beginning in early
2006. Details on lodging will be available via email.
Time Line: The Thailand project runs between December and
April; volunteers must commit to a minimum of two
weeks. Most volunteers stay for one two-week period.
Cost: The program fee is $760 for two weeks, which covers
three meals a day, accommodations, and training. Travel
expenses and insurance are not included.

Getting Started: Prospective volunteers can download an application from the Naucrates Web site or contact the organization to request one. Training is provided on the first day, and workshops are held throughout the stay.

Needed Skills and Specific Populations: Volunteers must be fit and able to work in a group. The minimum age for volunteers is 18; seniors are welcomed provided they are in good physical health. Naucrates cannot host volunteers with disabilities.

New Era Galápagos Foundation (NEGF)

780 Shotwell Street
San Francisco, CA 94110
(415) 336-4091
E-mail: info@neweragalapagos.org
Web site: www.negf.org

Project Type: Community Development; Natural Conservation
(Land); Natural Conservation (Sea); Youth

Mission Statement Excerpt: "To conserve the Galápagos
Islands by empowering local residents through educational
programs and environmental action projects."

Year Founded: 2000

Number of Volunteers Last Year: 25

Funding Sources: Private donations

The Work They Do: NEGF programs consist of educational
and environmental action projects, including foreign language training and art, communications, and environmental education programs. All of these empower local
residents with the skills and awareness needed for the long-
term conservation of the Galápagos Islands, while simultaneously providing human and social development
opportunities that enable the local population to benefit
from conservation. Specific projects include running a summer camp for children and teens, teaching courses in English as a Foreign Language (EFL), camping with Boy Scouts
and Girl Scouts, teaching teens gardening skills, and helping with coastal cleanups.

Project Location: All of NEGF's projects are located in Puerto
Baquerizo Moreno, San Cristóbal Island, Galápagos,
Ecuador. The building in which EFL and environmental
education courses take place has electricity year-round and
reliable air conditioning in the summer months of December through February. Volunteers can either stay with a
local host family or live in a local hotel or apartment.

Time Line: Projects are available from February through
December, though not all projects are available year-round.

All outdoor volunteer opportunities are offered from May through December. The summer camp requires a minimum of a one-month commitment in the month of February; all other programs require a three-month commitment. Exceptions are rarely made and are based solely on resource needs. Most volunteers stay for three months.

Cost: There is no program fee. Volunteers typically pay $350 to $450 per month to live in the Galápagos, depending on housing and food arrangements. Volunteers must cover all of their own costs, including airfare. NEGF provides all volunteers a waiver for the $100 Galápagos National Park entrance fee.

Getting Started: Prospective volunteers can either fill out the online application form at the Web site listed above or send a resume with a cover letter that specifies area of interest, level of Spanish, and dates available for volunteer work to the e-mail address listed above. Volunteers can decide on housing arrangements after they arrive. NEGF provides a general overview of its programs and basic introductions to the volunteer program. For the summer camp, volunteers arrive a minimum of one week in advance to design and prepare the various programs. All volunteers, regardless of the programs in which they are involved, are encouraged to arrive one week before their programs start.

Needed Skills and Specific Populations: Most volunteers have previous EFL teaching experience, though exceptions are made for proficient English speakers when resources are limited. Proficiency in basic Spanish (at a minimum) is preferred, but is not required, for the EFL program. Volunteers who teach environmental education typically also have a background in this area or in the natural sciences, as well as a moderate level of proficiency in Spanish. All other positions require some level of proficiency in Spanish. NEGF requires all volunteers to be at least 21 years of age. Senior volunteers and volunteers with disabilities are encouraged to participate in NEGF's programs, and it has hosted several volunteers from each of these populations.

Swimming with Sea Lions

By Rachelle Gould

New Era Galápagos Foundation (NEGF)

"*Sigue nadando. Juega con ella*," my companions yell at me from the cove's rocky shore. *Just keep swimming. Play with her.* My head bobs just above the equatorial saltwater as I sputter and gasp for air, recovering from the shock. A sleek, graceful female sea lion has suddenly whizzed past me as I snorkel. She wants, as I am to learn, to play with me. This moment is just one more instance during my work with New Era Galápagos Foundation in which I said to myself: "Take a deep breath, believe that it's actually happening, and live it."

I am held captive in the water by the huge round chestnut eyes of my playmate, who stops her twirling and darting every once in a while to stare intently, teasing and taunting, into the large flat lens of my snorkel mask. Can she see my eyes? According to Joseph Campbell in *The Power of Myth*, many native peoples saw wild animals as wise, knowledgeable beings with a lot to teach us. It takes little more than a few moments' gaze into an animal's engulfing eyes to believe that. It is experiences like this—playtime with a sea lion—that have impressed upon me the incredible nature of the world we live in.

Day to day, when I find myself forgetting how phenomenal the world really is, I need only look back at my time with the New Era Galápagos Foundation, my experience living and volunteering on a remote island 1,000 kilometers from the Ecuadorian coast, to remember. The experience breathed life into my study of environmental science and public policy at Harvard. The depth and complexity radiating from that sea lion's "windows of the soul" reenergized my interests in—and just plain old love of—the world.

But the chance to feel that depth, that connection, is an opportunity I had to create for myself. I had very little international experience in my youth. I knew that there was a world out there full of people who approach life in a way entirely different than the way I'd learned to approach it. I knew how deeply rewarding volunteering my time and energy is; volunteering is an integral part of my life. And I knew that I am lucky enough to live in a society in which I had the chance to apply for funds to volunteer internationally. I wanted to see a tiny speck of the impressiveness of the natural world, and I wanted to experience the richness of another culture. So I applied to volunteer in the Galapagos Islands, and a few months later found myself starting a teenage ecological group there.

Living in the islands, I had the opportunity to learn about the Galápagos, to contemplate the natural oddities found there. The unnervingly tame boobies, whose nests are open and bare on the predator-free island ground. The prehistoric-looking marine iguanas, those meter-long lizard-like creatures that sprawl on the volcanic rocks and then slip into the water to swim and eat seaweed. The enormous land tortoises that lumber ever so slowly, their rough, crude, thick paws crunching down intermittently, their small, flat eyes observing calmly and wisely.

The overall goal of my summer in the Galápagos was to create a local ecological action group: to create a structure that would remain in place for years and allow local teenagers to organize activities in their community. My core group of about 12 children was a tremendously inspiring mix of personalities, of outgoing, boisterous leaders and quiet,

Rachelle Gould accompanies a cohort of tortoises to a new, safer home. The tortoises weighed 200 pounds and more, and each was middle aged (about 50 years old). *Photo courtesy of Rachelle Gould, of New Era Galápagos Foundation*

subtle organizers. Very diverse kids, but with a commonality that made my task of starting the group constantly urgent and, every day, more easily achieved: curiosity. I have never heard conversations punctuated by so many question marks. As we hiked along the beach, picked slowly through iguana bodies, or drove up to a hilltop rainforest, they watched, they listened, they thought, and they asked.

Spend a few days really watching the natural world, and you realize that there certainly is a lot to learn. How could we ever be done? How could we ever forget the kind of wizened, weathered teacher that simply cannot enter a four-walled classroom? How could we ever eliminate from our decision making what she has taught us? That professor's teachings continue years after she gives her lesson; sights, smells, sounds, and textures are not easily erased.

Like periwinkle. The bright periwinkle feet of the blue-footed boobies that waddled down the beach as I walk to work each morning on San Cristóbal Island, Galápagos. I can't, and don't, forget the boobies.

But of course, having experienced these more foreign beautiful scenes only serves to enunciate the beauty of the everyday and the nearby. Like the living translucent blue of my hometown's southern California sky, still (normally) free of the smog enveloping nearby L.A. The light-catching, purple-white-blue of the interior of a mussel's shell—a mussel that could be from the coast of California or the waters off Tierra del Fuego. Or the deep glittery royal blue of the early morning Charles River inexpertly nipped by intramural oars.

At home in Southern California, a morning jog puts me alone on a beach with a baby California sea lion: the very same species as my Galápagos swimming partner. As I approach slowly, she doesn't spook but allows me to see again, but years later and thousands of miles to the north, those shiny bulbous eyes that stare so intently. She sits in the glistening, reflecting trail of a recently receded wave. She is calmly propped on her front flippers and her short hair is bronzed after a few minutes of drying in the windy morning air. She's young enough to have not yet learned to be afraid. She looks at me calmly for a moment, staring with a wise, peaceful curiosity.

As another jogger approaches us rapidly, her eyes dart nervously and she turns to waddle back toward the surf. She clunks along, ungainly on land. But I know that when she's reached the waves big enough to slick over her back, she'll disconnect from the sandy bottom and slickly, beautifully swim away. But perhaps she'll return. If she's like me, she's still got some questions she wants answered.

Oceanic Society

Fort Mason Center, Building E
San Francisco, CA 94123
(800) 326-7491 or (415) 441-1106; Fax: (415) 474-3395
E-mail: info@oceanicsociety.org
Web site: www.oceanicsociety.org

Project Type: Education; Natural Conservation (Land); Natural
Conservation (Sea); Scientific Research

Mission Statement Excerpt: "The mission of the Oceanic Society is to protect marine wildlife and oceanic biodiversity
through an integrated program of scientific research, environmental education, volunteerism, and the establishment
of nature reserves."

Year Founded: 1969

Number of Volunteers Last Year: 258

Funding Sources: Private sources, including individual donors
and foundations

The Work They Do: The Oceanic Society's work is focused on
conservation. It primarily conducts conservation research
that includes geographic information systems to help establish nature reserves. For example, in Belize, research project results reported in a Biosphere Reserve proposal by the
Oceanic Society will be used for an ecologically sustainable
management plan. The society also provides training for
Belizean students on its projects and works closely with
local groups and agencies. In the past, volunteers have collected data on dolphins, manatees, crocodiles, and coral
reefs, and they have helped to map the distribution of various species of wildlife. They have also mapped habitats and
conducted transects to monitor reef health.

Project Location: Most of the Oceanic Society's volunteer projects are located in Belize, Suriname, Midway, Peru, Brazil,
and Guyana. (As of this writing, the Midway program is
inactive, but it may be reactivated by the book's publication date.) Volunteers work in remote areas. They should

be prepared to face obstacles such as heat and insects. All volunteer accommodations include hot water and electricity, and they are usually double-occupancy cabins. Food is primarily of the local cuisine and is prepared locally.

Time Line: Volunteer projects are available year-round for a minimum of seven days and a maximum of three weeks. On average, volunteers stay for eight days.

Cost: The average program fee is $1,600, which covers all costs except airfare to the host country, non-meal refreshments, and tips for local guides.

Getting Started: Prospective volunteers should carefully review the project descriptions on the organization's Web site, complete an application form (which is also available on the Web site), and submit it with a $300 deposit. The Oceanic Society provides all volunteers a detailed research plan listing goals, objectives, and methods. It also sends, in advance of a volunteer's departure date, an outline of specific volunteer tasks and sample data sheets. Tutorials are also sometimes provided on its Web site. Once on-site, formal briefings and training are provided by the researcher prior to beginning the field work. Equipment trials are run before data is collected.

Needed Skills and Specific Populations: Some projects require snorkeling abilities before beginning the volunteer assignment. There are a variety of tasks associated with each project and the Oceanic Society matches each task to the volunteer's abilities and interests. Most projects have a minimum age of 16, though some require volunteers to be at least 18 years old. Some, but not all, projects accept senior volunteers. Volunteers with disabilities are welcomed as locations allow.

Oikos

Via Paolo Renzi 55
00128 Rome
Italy
+ 0039 06 5080280; Fax: + 0039 06 5073233
E-mail: volontariato@oikos.org
Web site: www.oikos.org

Project Type: Agriculture; Community Development; Construction; Natural Conservation (Land); Trail Building/Maintenance; Youth
Year Founded: 1979
Number of Volunteers Last Year: About 250
Funding Sources: None outside of program fees
The Work They Do: Oikos offers volunteers, most of whom are Italians, the opportunity to carry out culturally appropriate technical and environmental projects. Projects are carried out in cooperation with the village or region in which the project is based. Examples of past programs include establishing a sanitation project in Bangladesh, painting traditional houses in Turkey, staffing an arts camp in Armenia, and renovating playgrounds in Germany.
Project Location: Volunteer projects are located in Africa, Asia, South America, and Europe.
Time Line: Projects are offered year-round, for a minimum of 10 days and a maximum of one year.
Cost: Oikos's program fees range from $180 to $300, which covers accommodations and all meals. Volunteers are responsible for providing their own airfare.
Getting Started: Volunteer applications are available on Oikos's Web site; prospective volunteers can also e-mail Oikos directly. Oikos encourages potential volunteers to visit its headquarters for an interview, if possible. Oikos also has an annual post-experience reflection and feedback day.
Needed Skills and Specific Populations: Volunteers must be at least 18 years old.

Operation Crossroads Africa (OCA)

P.O. Box 5570
New York, NY 10027
(212) 289-1949; Fax: (212) 289-2526
E-mail: oca@igc.org
Web site: www.operationcrossroadsafrica.org

Project Type: Agriculture; Community Development; Construction; Economic Development; Education; Medical/Health; Rural Development; Women's Issues

Mission Statement Excerpt: "Make a difference for others, see the difference in yourself."

Year Founded: 1957

Number of Volunteers Last Year: Approximately 250

Funding Sources: None; OCA is self-funded

The Work They Do: Through OCA, groups of eight to ten volunteers of diverse backgrounds work together with local people on community-initiated projects. Projects tend to be physical in nature and fall into one of five categories: community construction and development (such as constructing youth training centers, health centers, and wells); health and medical outreach; agriculture and reforestation (such as clearing land, planting seeds, and digging ditches); education and training (in which volunteers might teach ESL, help with youth recreation events, or give computer lessons); and women's development (primarily income generation and microenterprise projects).

Project Location: As its name indicates, OCA works in Africa. Specific host countries change each year, but in past years OCA has operated projects in 35 African nations including Ethiopia, Ghana, Kenya, Gambia, Lesotho, Malawi, Namibia, South Africa, Tanzania, Uganda, Benin, Mali, Niger, Senegal, and Togo. Volunteers live communally, often in very basic conditions and almost always in rural areas.

Time Line: All of OCA's projects run during the summer. Volunteers spent six weeks working on a volunteer project, followed by one week of travel in the host country, during which local transportation is used.

Cost: OCA's program fee is $3,500. This program fee is remarkably inclusive, in that it takes care of the volunteer's international airfare and all in-country transportation, food, accommodations, visas, and international health insurance during both the volunteer experience and the week of travel afterward.

Getting Started: A program application is available on OCA's Web site; it includes requirements of a two-page autobiographical essay and responses to five questions. Applications are due in February. OCA requires volunteers to complete three days of orientation and training before departure.

Needed Skills and Specific Populations: OCA volunteers must be at least 17 years old. Except for those volunteers who wish to work in the areas of medicine and health, no special skills are required. Racial, gender, ethnic, regional, and educational diversity are primary goals of OCA, and groups are structured to be as inclusive as possible.

Pacific Crest Trail Association (PCTA)

5325 Elkhorn Boulevard PMB 256
Sacramento, CA 95842-2526
(916) 349-2109; Fax: (916) 349-1268
E-mail: info@pcta.org
Web site: www.pcta.org

Project Type: Trail Building/Maintenance

Mission Statement Excerpt: "The mission of the Pacific Crest Trail Association (PCTA) is to protect, preserve, and promote the Pacific Crest National Scenic Trail (PCT) so as to reflect its world-class significance for the enjoyment, education, and adventure of hikers and equestrians."

Year Founded: PCTA was founded in 1977, though precursors of the group date back to the 1930s.

Number of Volunteers Last Year: The number of volunteers is not available, but last year PCTA volunteers donated 30,000 hours of their time.

Funding Sources: PCTA receives funding from both private donations and the federal government.

The Work They Do: PCTA volunteers carry out a wide variety of trail maintenance, construction, and reconstruction projects including brushing, blowdown removal, tread rehab and construction, and the creation of rock and log structures.

Project Location: Volunteers work along the 2,650-mile Pacific Crest Trail, which runs through the coastal ranges of Washington, Oregon, and California all the way from Canada to the United States-Mexico border. Work sites range from low-lying deserts to temperate rainforests, and from wilderness backcountry sites to easily accessible locations. Arrangements are usually made for group meals and cooking. Lodging ranges from campgrounds to backcountry tent sites.

Time Line: Projects are available year-round, though not in all locations due to weather and elevations. Volunteer projects include one-day, weekend, and week-long commitments.

Cost: There is no program fee to volunteer with PCTA. Some projects require a $25 deposit to hold a spot in a work crew, which is refunded upon arrival. Meals are sometimes provided. PCTA volunteers' major expense is their travel to the work site.

Getting Started: Prospective volunteers should start at PCTA's Web site. All crews receive a safety and training orientation before work begins and project-specific training on-site.

Needed Skills and Specific Populations: Volunteers should be capable of traveling through and living in the backcountry, but no prior experience in trail work is needed. There is no minimum age to volunteer, but some tasks are limited to adults. Many of PCTA's most active volunteers are seniors. PCTA welcomes volunteers with disabilities as long as they can carry out the tasks safely.

Passport in Time (PIT)

P.O. Box 31315
Tucson, AZ 85751
(800) 281-9176; Fax: (520) 277-1627
E-mail: pit@sricrm.com
Web site: www.passportintime.com

Project Type: Archaeology; Historic Preservation; Museum; Natural Conservation (Land); Scientific Research

Mission Statement Excerpt: "The goal of Passport in Time (PIT) is to preserve the nation's past with the help of the public."

Year Founded: 1988

Number of Volunteers Last Year: 1,500

Funding Sources: The U.S. Forest Service, an agency within the U.S. Department of Agriculture, sponsors PIT.

The Work They Do: PIT is a volunteer program of the USDA Forest Service. PIT volunteers work with professional Forest Service archaeologists and historians in national forests throughout the country on such diverse activities as archaeological excavation and survey, historic structure restoration, and analysis and curation of artifacts. PIT projects are individually tailored to the specific needs of the resource. PIT volunteers may select from projects that involve all aspects of archaeological and historical research, including (but not limited to) archival research, archaeological survey and excavation, artifact processing and analysis, documentation, site monitoring, historic building restoration, oral history, and interpretation. PIT is unlike many other volunteer archaeology programs in that the projects are not designed solely for the public; they are the daily responsibility of archaeologists within the federal government. Volunteers help with ongoing research and management of archaeological and historical resources on public lands, and they are involved in decisions that affect forest service management of public lands.

Project Location: PIT projects take place in national forests and grasslands across the United States. Some work sites are in towns or communities, but most are in woodland areas. Some projects provide group meals or a camp cook and ask volunteers to contribute to group meals. In most cases, volunteers camp out near the project areas. Facilities range from forest service campgrounds to bunkhouses, guard stations, and primitive campsites. In addition, some projects are located close to towns, making it possible for volunteers to stay in hotels. Project leaders provide prospective volunteers a complete list of facilities, food, and lodging options.

Time Line: Projects take place year-round. Projects vary in length, but most are five days long. Many offer the option of staying for two five-day sessions. A few projects have a minimum time commitment of one day, and a few have longer-term options that span months, but those are exceptions to these general guidelines.

Cost: There are no program fees to volunteer with PIT. Volunteers provide their own transportation to the projects and, usually, their own meals and lodging. Out-of-pocket expenses vary widely depending on the type and length of the project and whether volunteers are camping or staying in local hotels.

Getting Started: PIT's application form is available in the *PIT Traveler,* a free publication issued in March and September that lists all of the PIT projects. The application can be mailed or faxed to the PIT Clearinghouse. Project listings and the application are also available online at the Web site listed above. PIT volunteers receive training on-site from professional archaeologists and historians during the projects.

Needed Skills and Specific Populations: Most projects do not require specific skills; those that do note this in their project descriptions. Volunteers must be at least 18 to participate without an adult, but many PIT projects accept children who are accompanied by an adult. The Forest Service encourages participation by families, and it is pleased with the increasing number of grandparent-grandchild pairs who serve on PIT projects. Senior volunteers are "absolutely" encouraged to work with PIT. Many of PIT's projects are in locations that are fully accessible to volunteers with disabilities, and the toll-free number listed above includes TTY. Volunteers with special needs are encouraged to contact PIT directly to see if the projects they are interested in can accommodate their needs. International volunteers can apply to work with PIT using a tourist visa.

The Best of America: Hopes, Dreams, Stories, and Freedom

❖ By Jane Kersting ❖

Passport in Time (PIT)

This past June, I joined a Passport in Time project. We were based in Boise, Idaho, working on a dig that uncovered the history of Americans and Chinese and mining in the midwest. This PIT experience promised to be very special, as my 10-year-old granddaughter was sharing my tent.

It was close to solstice, an annual time which I take for reflection every year. Prompted by a conversation in a lovely museum in an old Idaho mining town (population 62, where the mayor serves because he loves the community), my thoughts took me back to the days after 9/11. I was profoundly affected by that tragedy on many levels, but mostly because I understood that the world would never be the same for my grandchildren. They lost their innocence, their trust, and their feeling of safety. The price of instant news, instant visuals, instant commentary, and televised war is high. Many tears were shed in a vain attempt to answer an 8-year-old's questions about "the incident" and "that bad man." It must have seemed like a crazy world to a child (and to many adults). Two years later, I was here in Boise, Idaho, with this granddaughter, attempting to reclaim some of what we had before terrorism struck at the heart of America.

For a week, PIT volunteers, Boise archaeologists, visitors, townspeople, and grandchildren were united in a small community doing what we as Americans do best—

sharing hopes, dreams, stories, and the freedom to be together without fear. Eating spaghetti off paper plates at picnic tables in a town square. Watching as the children feed a stray dog. Appreciating PIT organizers who go the extra mile for volunteers. The words "kindred spirits" and "family" were repeated often in a group that had just met. The conversation often touched on the bonding that we felt as a group, our shared worldview, and understanding of our "humanness."

As the week went on, s'mores became more gourmet. Marshmallows were toasted to a perfect bronze or instantly blackened and rated by opposing camps. Laughter was the rule as we talked about favorite candy bars, ice cream, and childhood horror stories. The latest Harry Potter book was the hot topic, not the *Washington Post*. It was an innocent time. The last morning, my 10-year-old granddaughter remarked that she had "never heard adults discuss candy bars with such intensity." Her life lesson was that adults could be so honest and admit that they ate candy at all, much less salivated over it. Adult life lessons included an appreciation for the Chinese culture that co-existed with the Anglos in a common goal to mine precious metals from the earth, while at times teaching the dominant culture a thing or two about mining.

It was such a joy to spend time with people with no hidden agendas—a respite from our busy lives, a counterpoint to life out of balance. We understood our connectedness as human beings—a life lesson worth learning.

Peace Villages Foundation

Lomas de Piedra Canaima, Santa Elena de Guiaren
Estado Bolivar
Venezuela
+0058 414 2456307
E-mail: volunteer.pvf@mipunto.com
Web site: http://mipagina.cantv.net/peacevillages/index.htm

Project Type: Agriculture; Community Development; Construction; Developmental Disabilities; Education; Human Rights; Medical/Health; Natural Conservation (Land); Professional/Technical Assistance; Social Justice; Trail Building/Maintenance; Women's Issues; Youth

Mission Statement Excerpt: "We promote empowerment through challenging community development projects in humanitarian, educational, and environmental fields, and we support and contribute to the psychological, emotional, physical, cultural, social, and vocational development and integration of children who belong to the most underprivileged members of Latin American society."

Year Founded: 2001

Number of Volunteers Last Year: 25

Funding Sources: None outside of program fees

The Work They Do: Peace Villages Foundation carries out several kinds of projects, including integrating underprivileged children, special-needs children, and teenagers into workshops and kindergartens, as well as providing play therapy to the children; constructing an ecologically friendly building; carrying out wildlife conservation, environmental conservation, or historical preservation with local people; and teaching conversational English classes in Santa Elena, Venezuela, schools and private institutes or at the kindergarten and preschool levels.

Project Location: Volunteers work in and around Santa Elena and remote villages in Venezuela. Volunteers live in Peace Villages Foundation's guesthouse or with a host family, or they camp in villages.

Time Line: Volunteers are accepted year-round for a minimum of one week. There is no limit to the amount of time one may volunteer with Peace Villages Foundation.

Cost: Program fees vary with the length of stay and level of accommodations, ranging from $230 for one week in a guesthouse to $2,900 for five months with a host family. The program fee covers accommodations with a private bathroom and airport transfers; for volunteers who choose to stay with a host family, the program fee also covers two meals per day. Volunteers must provide their own airfare to Venezuela. Only 10 percent of Peace Villages' program fee goes toward administrative overhead.

Getting Started: Prospective volunteers can download an application from the Web site listed above and mail it to Peace Villages Foundation. Volunteers are provided a brief, general orientation upon arrival.

Needed Skills and Specific Populations: Volunteers must be at least 18 years old, and senior volunteers are welcomed. Volunteers with certain disabilities may apply, but they will not be able to stay in the village. The ability to speak Spanish is helpful but not essential.

Playing Santa Claus in Venezuela

❖ By Belinda Jordan ❖

Peace Villages Foundation

July 14, 2004

Just over one week has passed of my two-month stay in Santa Elena de Uiarén, Venezuela, volunteering for Peace Villages Foundation. This is my first experience of traveling abroad solely to participate in a volunteer program, as well as my first trip to South America. Despite having traveled extensively around the world, it was still an intense cultural translocation to arrive here last week.

The landscape surrounding the village of Santa Elena is beautiful and expansive, reinforcing the feeling of having "escaped it all." The bus ride from Caracas provides some glimpses of stunning scenery. The indigenous people are charming and kind and, despite the language barrier, I have felt most welcome and comfortable being part of their community. Living with an indigenous family is a great privilege and at times a humbling one, to see how people manage without many of the luxuries we consider essential in our daily lives.

My minimal Spanish has been a barrier that at times has felt overwhelming and isolating, but the patience and persistence of the locals to help me communicate has been a great reassurance. Anyone coming from a fast-paced city will quickly need to adjust to the relaxed and simple pace of life.

For me, it is great to not hear my mobile phone ringing nor be rushing around in traffic, forever watching the clock.

There are so many opportunities here for volunteers to contribute to the development of the community, through working with children and adolescents, teaching English, and sharing other useful skills and trades. I already feel that my time is passing too quickly, and wish I could stay longer. I would recommend this opportunity to anyone wishing to immerse themselves in another culture, to help a community, and to discover new things about themselves in the process.

July 30, 2004

I am now into my fourth week, halfway through my volunteer program here in Santa Elena and really enjoying my time here. The Spanish is improving slowly—poco a poco—and I am feeling more at home here with the local people. I have been doing therapy with several special-needs children and this week I decided to go into a local child care facility to play with the children. Walking past there each day, I had observed a lack of toys. I bought some toys and I truly felt like Santa Claus going in with my bag of goodies—the kids played for hours, and it was such a wonderful feeling to see them learn and explore. Your imagination is really the only limitation to what can be done here; the community is very open to suggestions and assistance, whether it is with children or other activities such as environmental projects. My only concern now is that the next four weeks are going to pass by much too quickly.

August 30, 2004

Well, as I predicted, the last four weeks have flown by and tomorrow I am leaving Santa Elena. This morning I have

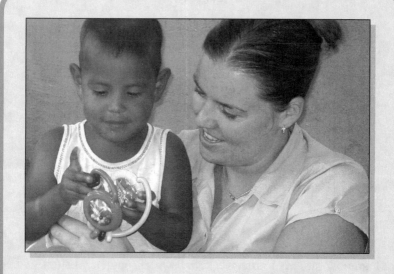

Volunteer Belinda Jordan worked in Venezuela with a kindergarten and day care to integrate both underprivileged and special-needs children back into the regular classroom. *Photo courtesy of Peace Villages Foundation*

my final visit to the nursery to play with the children and say good-bye. I have just returned from a great weekend in La Gran Sabana, seeing some totally amazing landscapes and magnificent waterfalls as well as observing the Pemon culture up close. I have been working with a local lady this last week who is going to continue the work in the nursery by integrating two or three children with special needs. This is an exciting development, as the concept of integration is very new here, and so far the nursery has been very open to giving it a try. Sharing skills with local people is an important part of the program here and ensures that your work or project can continue once you leave. I think the sense of empowerment and an education (provided by sharing your knowledge and skills) are the best gifts one person can give to another, and it has been my privilege to do so here with Peace Villages Foundation.

Peacework

209 Otey Street
Blacksburg, VA 24060
(800) 272-5519; Fax: (540) 953-0300
E-mail: mail@peacework.org
Web site: www.peacework.org

Project Type: Community Development; Construction; Developmental Disabilities; Economic Development; Education; Human Rights; Medical/Health; Natural Conservation (Land); Orphans; Professional/Technical Assistance; Rural Development; Social Justice; Women's Issues

Mission Statement Excerpt: "Peacework is dedicated to meeting humanitarian needs, fostering volunteerism, promoting global understanding, and expanding personal awareness of the world's cultures and people."

Year Founded: 1989

Number of Volunteers Last Year: Approximately 700

Funding Sources: Private donors and project-specific grants

The Work They Do: Peacework arranges and manages global volunteer service projects in collaboration with indigenous community development organizations and educational or service-oriented sponsors around the world. Projects are arranged for groups of volunteers from colleges, civic organizations, professional organizations, and churches. Volunteer assignments include construction projects, teaching, tutoring, providing medical services, providing health education, and a variety of other humanitarian and community development efforts. Almost all of Peacework's project arrangements are tailored for groups of volunteers, such as those from a university or a professional service organization. In some limited cases, projects can be arranged for individual volunteers in special disciplines such as medicine and health care.

Project Location: Volunteer projects are located in Russia, Vietnam, Belize, Honduras, South Africa, Ghana, Dominican Republic, the People's Republic of China, the Czech and Slovak Republics, Guatemala, Nepal, Mexico, Guyana, Bolivia, Ukraine, Cameroon, Gabon, Thailand, India, the U.S., and Kenya. Work sites and accommodations vary depending on the locations, but they are provided by the host community and are consistent with their resources. Accommodations are comfortable, safe, and usually rudimentary.

Time Line: Volunteer projects can take place at any time of year. The minimum length of time for a project is five days; each project's length is mutually agreed upon by the volunteer and the host organization. Typical projects run one to three weeks.

Cost: In general, program fees run from $2,000 to $4,000 per group. Each program fee covers all accommodations and meals, visa expenses, and in-country travel costs, but does not include airfare to the country of service. Average per person costs range from $1,250 to $2,500.

Getting Started: Prospective volunteers should call or e-mail Peacework's office or complete the "Getting Started" form found on its Web site. Volunteers are provided a manual as well as an on-site orientation. More extensive training and orientation is provided as requested by volunteers.

Needed Skills and Specific Populations: In general, the minimum age to volunteer with Peacework is 18, though there are exceptions. Volunteer groups, for example, can include supervised children and young adults who are under age 18. Senior volunteers are welcomed. Peacework can make full accommodations for a volunteer or group of volunteers with disabilities, and it will make recommendations regarding specific project sites, managing travel, and other details to provide for adequate services and accessibility. In some instances, entire delegations of individuals with disabilities have worked on Peacework projects; in other instances, volunteer delegations have worked with agencies and institutions that serve people with disabilities.

Pina Palmera

Apartado Postal 109
70900 Pochutla
Oaxaca, Mexico
+ 00 52 958 58 431 47; Fax: + 00 52 958 58 431 45
E-mail: caippac@yahoo.com.mx
Web site: www.laneta.apc.org/pina

Project Type: Community Development; Developmental Disabilities; Human Rights; Medical/Health; Women's Issues; Youth

Mission Statement Excerpt: "Our mission is to contribute to the improvement of the quality of life for people with disabilities and their families in the southern coast of Oaxaca, helping people with disabilities to accept themselves and integrate into their families, communities, and daily lives, assisting disabled people to be as independent as possible, promoting the development of the abilities of people with disabilities as best as possible, and generating social acceptance in the region toward people with disabilities."

Year Founded: 1984

Number of Volunteers Last Year: 34

Funding Sources: Pina Palmera receives funding from the Mexican government, from national and international organizations, and from private donors.

The Work They Do: The center's efforts focus on changing the way members of the local population regard people with disabilities by promoting awareness and rehabilitation programs for families, schools, and local communities. These programs teach people how to use adaptive equipment and therapeutic techniques, as well as how to take general care of people with disabilities. Pina Palmera organizes various kinds of physical therapy, runs handcraft creation workshops, helps children with disabilities complete their homework, provides full-time care for four children with major disabilities, and organizes vacation camps for children both with and without disabilities. Volunteers can help with any or all of these activities, and Pina Palmera is receptive to volunteer input and ideas for new activities in regard to the people being served. Volunteers are expected to pitch in to help with cleaning and other basic administrative and logistical tasks.

Project Location: Pina Palmera's center is located near a beach and was constructed in 1997. Volunteers live in their own dormitory with a common kitchen and living room. The center is located in a subtropical zone that can be hot, humid, and buggy.

Time Line: Pina Palmera accepts volunteers throughout the year, but requests that applications be filed several months before arrival. Volunteers must commit to at least six months' service; Pina Palmera does not have a stated maximum amount of time for volunteering. Most volunteers stay for six months.

Cost: Volunteers pay $15 per month to help cover the cost of utilities for the center. Accommodations and meals are provided free of charge. Volunteers must provide their own transportation to Oaxaca.

Getting Started: Prospective volunteers should contact Pina Palmera by e-mail. New volunteers are given a one-week introduction to the center, after which the work assignment is decided on by mutual agreement between the volunteer and Pina Palmera's staff.

Needed Skills and Specific Populations: Pina Palmera has a great need for occupational-, language-, and physiotherapists, teachers, nurses, psychologists, sociologists, anthropologists, agronomists, economists, business administrators, electricians, and carpenters. Volunteers must be at least 18 years old, speak Spanish or be willing to learn, and have at least a high school diploma. Senior volunteers are welcomed heartily, since they bring an added dimension of cultural exchange; Pina Palmera's oldest volunteer so far was 70 years old. Because of the nature of its work, Pina Palmera is exceptionally well suited to host volunteers with disabilities.

Programa Restauración de Tortugas Marinas (PRETOMA)

Apdo. 1203-1100
Tibas, San Jose
Costa Rica
+ 506-241-5227; Fax: + 506-236-6017
E-mail: info@tortugamarina.org
Web site: www.tortugamarina.org

Project Type: Community Development; Natural Conservation (Land); Natural Conservation (Sea); Scientific Research; Youth

Mission Statement Excerpt: "PRETOMA's mission is to protect, conserve, and restore the populations of sea turtles and sharks that utilize the marine environment of Costa Rica by preserving the diverse habitats and international waters upon which they depend."

Year Founded: 1997

Number of Volunteers Last Year: 100

Funding Sources: PRETOMA is, for the most part, self-funded, but it receives occasional grants from private organizations such as the National Wildlife Federation, the New England Aquarium, and the People's Trust for Endangered Species.

The Work They Do: PRETOMA focuses its energies on a multifaceted approach to protecting the sea turtles of Costa Rica. Among many other activities, it carries out protection projects for nests and hatchlings, tracks turtles, and has a public education campaign. Volunteers assist project coordinators with these sea turtle conservation activities by walking the beach on a nightly basis looking for nesting sea turtles. When found, turtles are measured, tagged, and checked for general health conditions. Nests are then taken, monitored, and protected in a local hatchery. Turtles lay their nests on the beach after dark, so most of the project work is done during three- to six-hour shifts at night. Participants will be required to walk for the majority of these shifts, with only brief breaks at the end of each sector or when a turtle is found. The turtle nesting season coincides with the rainy season, which means that project participants should be prepared to work in the rain, of which there is a lot. Hatchery duties include monitoring nest temperatures, awaiting the hatching of baby turtles and releasing them into the ocean, and post-hatching nest excavations to determine hatching success rates. Volunteers may also have the opportunity to take part in public education programs or to teach English at a local school.

Project Location: Volunteers work in San Miguel and Punta Banco, two small, isolated coastal communities in Costa Rica. There is electricity, water, and a couple of small markets, but the lifestyle is very simple and basic. There are several options for lodging, including stays at the station house, home stays, or private house rentals.

Time Line: Volunteers are accepted between July 15 and December 20. They can stay as briefly as one week or as long as five months.

Cost: Program fees are $600 to $900 per month, which covers room and board, but not international airfare.

Getting Started: Prospective volunteers should contact PRE-TOMA and request a volunteer information form. Upon arrival at the project site, volunteers are greeted and given a one-hour orientation, during which project details are discussed. They are also provided a project protocol manual upon arrival.

Needed Skills and Specific Populations: Volunteers should be in good enough physical shape to walk the beaches for long periods of time at night, and they should be comfortable living in a rustic environment. There is no minimum or maximum age for applicants. Volunteers with disabilities are welcomed as long as they can perform the job duties described herein. For enrolled students, academic credit may be available for this project.

Find Yourself—Wandering

By Keith Alan Flint

Programa Restauración de Tortugas Marinas (PRETOMA)

I was given *Volunteer Vacations* by my dearest friend. She had listened patiently for years as I talked about my interest in volunteer programs and the potential they offered for travel. I considered a wide range of activities and locations, but when I read the entry for PRETOMA, I knew immediately that I had found my trip. It offered everything I sought—travels beyond my usual means, exposure to another culture, a combination of physical and cerebral activities, and, most importantly, the chance to make an ecological contribution that was both substantial and real.

I arrived at the research station in Punta Banco, Costa Rica, dropped my pack in my room, and headed to dinner. I fell into conversation immediately with the other volunteers. The conversation was lively, the spirits high, and the mood light. Those volunteers who were scheduled to work the early shift finished their meals quickly and went off to patrol their assigned beach sectors. As a new arrival, I was given the night off to settle in and read my packet of information in preparation for work the next day.

My evening of reading was interrupted when one of the local villagers stopped by with news: one of the Olive Ridley nests at the hatchery was showing signs of activity. Quickly, another volunteer and I grabbed flashlights and buckets and hurried across the football field to the hatchery. When we arrived, hatchlings were climbing to the surface of the sandy nest. It was a thrilling sight. The turtles were so small, yet so fierce. Free of the eggs inside of which they had developed over the past 50 days, they had scrambled their way up, clambering over one another in search of freedom. And I was there to see it and to help them get to their ocean home. I have witnessed the birth of numerous animals—piglets, calves, foals, and puppies among them—but this event could be compared to none of those. This experience felt more like participating in the birth of my sons—knowing I was just getting them started—and that what lay ahead would be filled with struggles and perils, along with pleasures and successes. Only a day earlier, I had been thousands of miles to the north, in a bustling city filled with artificial light and excessive noise. Now here I was by this quiet Central American village, in darkness broken only by stars and moonlight, where the principle audible sound was the soft pounding of the surf a few meters away. We collected and counted the hatchlings before packing them in sand-filled buckets to be released during the second shift later that night.

Throughout my time at Punta Banco I had many fine experiences: patrolling the beach; seeing sea turtles crawl out of the surf, dig their flask-shaped nests, and lay the clutches of more than a hundred eggs; tagging turtle flippers; riding on horseback to the Guaymí Indian Reserve; cooling off in the waterfalls behind the station house; sharing stories, reading, and playing guitar with the other volunteers; hiking through the rainforest; and even hearing the excited "*tortuguita!*" cries of village children when they saw their first hatchlings. But that first night—collecting those hatchlings—will stay with me forever.

Travel—the experience and the exploration—is as much about discovering where you have been as where you are going. Immerse yourself—in the environment, the culture, the language, and even the weather. Travel provides much-needed perspective. Ultimately, sometimes one must wander far to find something near.

Projects Abroad

347 West 36th Street, Suite 901
New York, NY 10018
(888) 839-3535; Fax: (212) 244-7236
E-mail: info@projects-abroad.org
Web site: www.projects-abroad.org

Project Type: Agriculture; Archaeology; Community Development; Construction; Developmental Disabilities; Economic Development; Historic Preservation; Legal; Medical/Health; Natural Conservation (Land); Natural Conservation (Sea); Orphans; Rural Development; Scientific Research; Youth

Mission Statement Excerpt: "Projects Abroad sends volunteers to less economically developed countries to do internships and public service projects."

Year Founded: 1992

Number of Volunteers Last Year: 1,800

Funding Sources: No outside funding sources

The Work They Do: As the lengthy list of project types mentioned above indicates, Projects Abroad offers a wide range of volunteer programs including teaching, working in orphanages, building community centers, assisting print and television journalists, doing conservation work, helping in a health clinic or a hospital (including opportunities for premed students), taking care of animals, doing archaeological work, providing business expertise, and coaching sports.

Project Location: Volunteer placements are available in Bolivia, Cambodia, Chile, China, Ghana, India, Mexico, Mongolia, Nepal, Peru, Romania, Russia, Senegal, South Africa, Sri Lanka, Swaziland, and Thailand. In most cases, volunteers stay with host families and have their own rooms, though sometimes the rooms are shared with another volunteer. The host families also provide all meals.

Time Line: Volunteers are accepted throughout the year for one month up to one year. The average volunteer works for three months.

Cost: Program fees vary, but for three-months volunteers pay $3,000. The program fee covers accommodations, food, and travel and medical insurance. Fifty percent of the program fee goes toward administrative costs.

Getting Started: Prospective volunteers can apply online via Projects Abroad's Web site, over the phone, or by requesting a brochure and completing the application form contained therein. Volunteers are sent pre-departure information about what to bring and how to prepare, and they are given a one-day, in-country orientation to the area of service and to the host culture.

Needed Skills and Specific Populations: Volunteers must be at least 16 years old, and senior volunteers are welcomed. Volunteers must be self-dependent, mobile, and able to withstand significant levels of culture shock.

The Funniest and Most Enriching Experience of My Life: Teaching in Bolivia

❖ By Jennifer Way ❖

Projects Abroad

An endlessly rewarding two and a half months awaited me as I stepped off the last plane in a wretchedly sleepless state, armed only with a TOFL handbook and a pitifully random collection of Spanish words, phrases, and abstract rules frantically gathered together in the previous month. This was a potential problem, as the family I stayed with spoke only a little English, but I needn't have worried about language barriers. While at first it was frustrating to keep referring to the disappointingly limited electronic dictionary I had brought with me, I soon developed a huge respect for gestures and the surprising number of similarities in our languages and realized we were always able to make ourselves understood. I was overwhelmed by the love and acceptance I was offered and was immediately made to feel at home and comfortable. Although in a literal sense I couldn't communicate with my "mother," her affection and warmth connected us deeply (and her incredible cooking was always welcoming!).

Clichés aside, teaching conversational English at the San Simon University in Cochabamba, Bolivia, was one of the funniest and most enriching experiences of my life. As soon as I let go of my western notions of punctuality and expectations of full attendance, I began to understand what I could usefully offer. By running on late "Bolivian time," I chatted with the most enthusiastic students about their homes, England, films, and whatever was in the newspapers or books they were reading before starting classes every day. Despite the winter chill and, occasionally, the lack of a classroom, every lesson was energetic and interactive. We played language games ranging from writing plots for movies (which were hysterical!) to giving each other empty plastic bags and asking "Why do you have a monkey/tree/shoe in your bag?" The excuses were really entertaining and a good opportunity to correct errors. The levels of English varied dramatically—I found myself explaining everything from simple sentences to discussing postmodernism and the philosophy of language! The students needed to improve their fluency, which was a great opportunity for me to learn about the history, geography, food, festivals, languages, and religious ideas of the different regions! I was honored when one student, picking up on my keenness to learn about Bolivia, invited me to her house to watch a parade of the different dances and national dresses of the regions. It was a breathtakingly dramatic, rhythmic collection led by small boys in feather headpieces and concluded by men in enormous feathered masks and silver and gold chair-like costumes constructed around them. Another time, I learned how to milk cows and bake bread in an outdoor oven when a student invited me to her farmhouse.

Living in Bolivia, I had the opportunity to participate in some amazing events. I went with some other volunteers and some students on the annual Cochabambian night walk. Originating as a pilgrimage, this eight-hour stroll has become a secular tradition, wherein thousands of people line the streets. We shared sweets, songs, and stories and ate hotcakes from our gloved hands at sunrise.

Cochabamba is a pulsating urban hub in the muscle of the Bolivian mountains. It is located perfectly for exploring the country via bumpy overnight coach rides at terrifying heights leading to infinitely varying landscapes from jungles to salt planes. The intense mixture of color, texture, and scale in the landscape creates an energetic environment for South America's most enchanting, yet widely overlooked country. On weekends, we volunteers set out to explore the surrounding regions. We were struck by the variation in this awe-inspiring country. The hauntingly dramatic carvings and stone totems that the pre-Inca society left in Tiwanaku are not to be missed. The "door of the sun" is astrologically positioned to celebrate the equinox. The jungles of Chapare held climbing, abseiling, and white-water rafting adventures, but the most dazzling landscape was the four-day Toyota ride across the salt planes. Vast stretches of these are literally made out of salt, broken by mountains whose colors are so striking they look as if they've been painted with a children's watercolor set. In places, huge cacti grow, and the piercing colors of the green and red lakes where flamingos wallow are just incredible. If you remain unconvinced, I should probably mention the opportunity for a dip in the hot springs before breakfast. I would highly recommend volunteering with Projects Abroad. And, specifically, I would recommend Bolivia to anyone as a culture thriving on a vitality of music, dancing, and an incredible collection of generous and open people.

> *Bolivia is . . .*
> *Tiny purple flowers*
> *Blessing the ground,*
> *Over trip-up paving stones.*
> *We trod softly,*
> *Feeling our way*
> *Over soft wax prayers*
> *Molded in a flickering cathedral.*

Mates on mountainsides,
Seeping in the vast vision,
Stars which loop
And spin the sky
Into a new, dazzling scale,
With the Milky Way
Like an electric white rainbow.
Salt planes stretching
And tessellating
Into hexagonal infinity
To marble-painted mountains
And bubbling springs.
Spring started to blink,
And I discarded
The morning thick blankets
I'd snuggled in
Against the morning bite
On my blue bench,
When I spoke
In broken language
To centered people.
Octavia and Margarita slush
And expert guidance in salsa
Making me melt.
Tiny beaming amigas
With chicklets and tissues
Stuffed tightly in boxes.
"Los Tiempos" sung
Like a morning mantra.
Melting cake sweetness
Awakening the tiny
Ducts on my tongue,
Eilidh eating tongue
And gagging at the idea.

Language and ideas
Connecting and reflecting.
Spanish sueños.
Lessons in the Lacto Bar,
With the easy-slide juices
And the easy-slide sun.
Overnight buses
Like being tumbled
In a washing machine.
Overnight walking,
Singing and talking,
Eating pastels
Soft cheese melt
With icing sugar
With gloves
At sunrise.
Rising the next day
Blink-bustle
Round the Cancha,
With the thickly textured colors.
Women weaving myths in alpaca,
Huge costume constructions,
Music spinning the streets
Into vivid shape,
And the explosive energy
Of the fiesta.

ProWorld Service Corps (PWSC)

3800 Taylor Avenue
Bellingham, WA 98229
(877) 42WORLD or (406) 245-7348
Fax: (406) 252-3973
E-mail: info@proworldsc.org
Web site: www.proworldsc.org

Project Type: Construction; Education; Medical/Health; Natural Conservation (Land); Women's Issues; Youth

Mission Statement Excerpt: "The mission of the ProWorld Service Corps is to empower communities, promote social and economic development, and cultivate educated compassionate global citizens."

Year Founded: 1998

The Work They Do: PWSC offers internships with nonprofit organizations that are tailored to the individual volunteer's skills and goals for the experience. In general, volunteer projects are available in the areas of health care, education, the environment, microbusiness, appropriate technology, women's rights, construction, journalism, and the fine arts. Examples of specific projects include helping vaccinate children, teaching reading, reforestation, and small-business education.

Project Location: Volunteers work in the Sacred Valley of Peru; on the Caribbean coast and in inland rural communities of Belize; and in Oaxaca, Mexico.

PWSC selects project and program locations based on multiple factors including participant safety, community need, community interest, and quality of participant experience.

Time Line: Volunteers are accepted throughout the year for internships that last one month to one year.

Cost: A four-week internship costs approximately $2,000, with a $300 program fee for each additional week. Room and board with a host family are included in the program fee. Volunteers in Peru also receive intensive Spanish language classes. Volunteers must pay for their own international airfare, as well as for travel within the country of service.

Getting Started: Prospective volunteers can complete an online application, which is available on the PWSC Web site. Volunteers whose applications are received at least three months prior to departure are given priority for project and location placement. The deadline for applications is one month prior to departure. Each volunteer must complete an interview as a part of his or her application.

Needed Skills and Specific Populations: Volunteers must be at least 18 years old and be in good health.

Raleigh International

27 Parsons Green Lane
London SW6 4HZ
United Kingdom
+ 0207 371 8585; Fax: + 0207 371 5852
E-mail: info@raleigh.org.uk or staff@raleigh.org.uk
Web site: www.raleighinternational.org

Project Type: Community Development; Natural Conservation
(Land); Natural Conversation (Sea); Rural Development;
Scientific Research; Youth

Mission Statement Excerpt: "Raleigh International is a youth
development charity that aims to inspire young people
from all nationalities and backgrounds by completing
worthwhile and sustainable environmental and community
projects around the world."

Year Founded: 1984

Number of Volunteers Last Year: Approximately 1,000

Funding Sources: Private donors and the European Union

The Work They Do: Raleigh International runs several expeditions for volunteers aged 17–25. Volunteer groups are large
and diverse, often consisting of about 120 volunteers, and
are guided by 30 to 40 staff members, all of whom are over
age 25 and who are also paying volunteers. Volunteer projects focus on environmental and community activities, and
they include some adventure travel as well. Examples of
volunteer work and adventure travel include diving in
Malaysia as part of an international reef check team, working in remote Namibian communities to help improve sanitation and hygiene, and trekking in the Andes Mountains
in Chile.

Project Location: Raleigh International has projects in Malaysia,
Ghana, Chile, Namibia, and Costa Rica/Nicaragua. Work
sites vary greatly, from the depths of the Malaysian rainforest to the 80-million-year-old Namib Desert in Namibia.
Accomodations vary from tents to community halls.

Time Line: Raleigh International accepts volunteers throughout the year for periods ranging from four to ten weeks.

Cost: Raleigh International's program fees range from £1,500 to £2,995 for volunteers aged 17–25. Volunteer staff members pay a program fee of £1,100. Each program fee covers all food and accommodations, medical insurance, and in-country transportation. Program fees do not cover flights to the country of service.

Getting Started: Prospective volunteers should contact Raleigh International via the "info" e-mail address. Prosepective volunteer staff members should contact Raleigh International via the "staff" e-mail address. Raleigh offers pre-expedition training to both volunteers and staff members.

Needed Skills and Specific Populations: As noted above, volunteers must be aged 17–25, while staff members must be over age 25. Volunteers must be able to swim at least 200 meters (657 feet) and have at least a conversational level of English. Staff positions include medics, project managers, accountants, divers, and mountain leaders. Due to the nature of the work, it may not be possible for volunteers with disabilities to join one of Raleigh International's expeditions.

Reef Check

P.O. Box 1057
17575 Pacific Coast Highway
Pacific Palisades, CA 90272
(310) 230-2371 or (310) 230-2360; Fax: (310) 230-2376
E-mail: rcinfo@reefcheck.org
Web site: www.reefcheck.org

Project Type: Natural Conservation (Sea); Scientific Research
Mission Statement Excerpt: "Reef Check's objectives are: to
educate the public about the coral reef crisis; to create a
global network of volunteer teams trained in Reef Check's
scientific methods who regularly monitor and report on
reef health; to facilitate collaboration that produces ecologically sound and economically sustainable solutions; and to
stimulate local community action to protect remaining
pristine reefs and rehabilitate damaged reefs worldwide."
Year Founded: 1997
Number of Volunteers Last Year: More than 1,000
Funding Sources: Both governmental and private sources
The Work They Do: Reef Check is the only volunteer-based
organization that measures reef health using a standard
method on a global scale. Its programs focus on building a
global community of reef stakeholders and helping them at
the grassroots level to improve reef health. Most volunteers
participate in a coral reef monitoring survey, either by
establishing their own Reef Check team or by joining an
already established team.
Project Location: Reef Check has had teams in more than 70
countries around the world, and there is potential for volunteers wherever there is a coral reef. Conditions vary
depending on the location and the team's setup, but volunteers should expect that their "work site" will be the
ocean, as most Reef Check volunteers spend their days diving and actively looking at reefs.
Time Line: Volunteers can work with Reef Check throughout
the year, depending on weather conditions. Volunteer

assignments are usually for a minimum of one week, but they can vary depending on the monitoring period established by the team.

A volunteer scuba dives in the Indian Ocean, conducting a survey of the invertebrates inhabiting the reef surrounding the Cocos (Keeling) Islands. *Photo courtesy of Robert Thorn, of Reef Check*

Cost: There is no program fee to volunteer with Reef Check, but there may be a small fee for training or other required classes. Volunteers, therefore, are responsible for all of their own costs. Average costs for a volunteer vacation with Reef Check vary depending on location, lodging, length of stay, and dive expenses. Reef Check offers memberships starting at $25 per year, but membership is not a prerequisite to volunteering. All costs are the responsibility of the volunteer unless otherwise arranged with their team.

Getting Started: Prospective volunteers should e-mail Reef Check at the address listed above. Reef Check offers trainings that typically last three days and include both land-based and ocean components.

Needed Skills and Specific Populations: In order to work with Reef Check, volunteers should be certified scuba divers with excellent buoyancy control. Some surveys may be able to be done via snorkel. Additional skills may be required, depending on the team. As long as the diver demonstrates the needed skills and can understand the survey protocol, there are no age or ability limits on who can volunteer with Reef Check.

Rempart

1, Rue des Guillemites
75004 Paris
France
+ 01 42 71 96 55; Fax: + 01 42 71 73 00
E-mail: contact@rempart.com
Web site: www.rempart.com

Project Type: Archaeology; Historic Preservation

Mission Statement Excerpt: "Rempart is a union of 170 nonprofit French organizations that promote heritage preservation."

Year Founded: 1966

Number of Volunteers Last Year: Approximately 3,000

The Work They Do: Rempart's member associations organize more than 200 volunteer work initiatives, known as *chantiers*, every year to carry out archaeological restoration and restoration of historical monuments and sites. Twenty-five percent of Rempart's volunteers come from outside of France. In general, volunteers work in groups of 12, carrying out a wide variety of restoration work and excavations. Volunteers usually work 35 hours per week on restoration activities and have one or two days that are fully devoted to cultural and leisure activities.

Project Location: Rempart's projects are offered at more than 200 sites throughout France. Accommodations range from indoor lodging with hot water and shower facilities to campsites with only cold water available. Most of the time, volunteers organize meals on their own and are responsible for all shopping, cooking, and washing up.

Time Line: Chantiers usually last for two or three weeks, and volunteers are expected to stay for the length of the project.

Cost: While prices vary, volunteers should expect to pay between $5 and $8 per day as a program fee, for a total of $70 to $168 per *chantier*. Prices are available in the Rempart catalog, which is available online. Accommodations and food are included in the program fees, but transportation is not.

Getting Started: Prospective volunteers should download the online catalog, which includes a registration form. Alternatively, prospective volunteers can search for a work camp using a database on Rempart's Web site. There is no closing date to register for a *chantier*; however, after the catalog is released in April, many *chantiers* are quickly booked, especially those that offer volunteer opportunities for minors. Volunteers undergo training on how to use tools and equipment at the beginning of the *chantier*.

Needed Skills and Specific Populations: With some exceptions, volunteers must be at least 18 years old. There is no upper age limit for volunteers, but most Rempart volunteers are 18–25 years old. The exceptions to the minimum age limit are *chantiers* designed specifically for minors and 17-year-olds who successfully petition to participate. French is the primary language spoken on the *chantiers*, so volunteers should have at least rudimentary French language skills before arriving. Volunteers do not need to have other skills or experiences with historical restoration.

Royal Tyrrell Museum

P.O. Box 7500
Drumheller, Alberta T0J 0Y0
Canada
(888) 440-4240
E-mail: tyrrell.info@gov.ab.ca
Web site: www.tyrrellmuseum.com

Project Type: Education; Historic Preservation; Museum; Scientific Research

Mission Statement Excerpt: "To be an internationally recognized public and scientific museum dedicated to the collection, conservation, research, display, and interpretation of the paleontological history, emphasizing Alberta's rich fossil heritage."

Year Founded: 1985

Number of Volunteers Last Year: 85

Funding Sources: Government funds

The Work They Do: The Royal Tyrrell Museum is the only Canadian institution devoted exclusively to the study and exhibition of paleontology. To ensure that the museum remains a world-class institution, five researchers study Alberta's prehistory. This multidisciplinary team ensures that each exhibit and educational program reflects the most up-to-date information available in the ever-changing world of paleontology. Volunteers can participate in many areas of the museum's work, including helping with education programs, doing administrative work, assisting with visitor services, and working in the preparation and collections departments.

Project Location: Volunteer projects are located at the Royal Tyrrell Museum. Volunteers must find their own accommodations in the area.

Time Line: Due to the training offered, the minimum length of time for a volunteer at the Royal Tyrrell Museum is three weeks; there is no limit to the length of the volunteer's stay.

Cost: No program fee is charged, but volunteers are responsible not only for paying for their own food and lodging, but for arranging these as well. Volunteers typically pay somewhere between $300 and $600 for three weeks of food and lodging.

Getting Started: Prospective volunteers should first contact the Royal Tyrrell Museum's volunteer coordinator and request a volunteer application form. A background check may be required as part of the application process. Volunteers are given an overview of the museum's work, then receive on-the-job training for their specific tasks.

Needed Skills and Specific Populations: Volunteers do not need to have any specific skills, but they should have an interest in one of the areas of the museum's work, the visitors to the museum, or post-secondary education in paleontology. Volunteers must be at least 17 years old, and senior volunteers are heartily welcomed. Volunteers with disabilities will find that the museum offers barrier-free access.

Senevolu, the Senegalese Association of United Volunteers

P.O. Box 26, 557 P.A.

Dakar, Senegal

+ 00221 559 67 35; Fax: + 00221 892 44 64

E-mail: senevolu@mypage.org

Web site: www.senevolu.mypage.org

Project Type: Community Development; Medical/Health; Rural Development; Women's Issues; Youth

Mission Statement Excerpt: "Senevolu is dedicated to promoting community tourism by welcoming volunteers and travelers to discover the cultural differences a West African country like Senegal has to offer, while being part of the community."

Year Founded: 2002

Number of Volunteers Last Year: 40

Funding Sources: No outside funding; self-supporting

The Work They Do: Senevolu places volunteers in a variety of settings including private schools, hospitals, nonprofit organizations, the public service sector, health centers, responsible tour operations, centers for the arts, women's associations, and organizations that combat poverty and HIV/AIDS.

Project Location: Volunteers are placed throughout Senegal, mostly in cities. Volunteers stay with host families.

Time Line: Volunteers are accepted year-round, with a minimum commitment of four weeks and a maximum commitment of one year.

Cost: The program fee for four weeks is $525, which covers five days of lodging in a hostel during orientation, transportation costs during orientation, transportation to a host family, and accommodations and all meals with a host family for the duration of the volunteer experience.

Getting Started: Applications can be downloaded from Senevolu's Web site and submitted via fax, e-mail, or postal mail. A five-day orientation starts each volunteer experience, and it includes an introduction to Senegalese culture, French and Wolof language lessons, and excursions into Dakar.

Needed Skills and Specific Populations: Volunteers should have teaching, health care, or administrative and computer skills before arriving in Senegal. Volunteers must be at least 18 years old; there is no maximum age limit, though 90 percent of Senevolu's volunteers are under age 40. Senevolu does not accept volunteers with disabilities.

Sierra Club Outings

85 Second Street, 2nd Floor
San Francisco, CA 94105
(415) 977-5522; Fax: (415) 977-5795
E-mail: national.outings@sierraclub.org
Web site: www.sierraclub.org/outings/national

Project Type: Archaeology; Historic Preservation; Natural Conservation (Land); Natural Conservation (Sea); Scientific Research; Trail Building/Maintenance

Mission Statement Excerpt: "Explore, enjoy, and protect the planet."

Year Founded: The Sierra Club was founded in 1892, and the first Sierra Club Outing was undertaken in 1901.

Number of Volunteers Last Year: Approximately 950

Funding Sources: None; the Sierra Club Outings organization is run entirely on program fees, and it does not receive any funds from outside organizations or from the Sierra Club itself.

The Work They Do: Sierra Club Outings offers a range of volunteer activities focused on the outdoors and environmental work. Volunteer opportunities include but are not limited to archaeological digs, animal and habitat projects, trail work, and invasive plant removal. All service trips include at least one day with no activities scheduled to allow volunteers to explore the surrounding wilderness areas. The leaders of Sierra Club Outings projects are volunteers themselves who scout, propose, plan, and run all of the trips. Sierra Club Outings stresses the importance of building a strong community as a group, so volunteers may feel more of a bond with their fellow participants than volunteers do with other organizations.

Project Location: Outings are offered throughout the United States and in Puerto Rico, the Virgin Islands, and Canada. Work sites vary from national parks and wilderness areas to animal sanctuaries in Maui.

Time Line: Outings are offered almost every month of the year, and most last for one week.

Cost: In general, program fees are between $350 and $600, with a few both above and below this range. Volunteers who are 18 or older must be members of the Sierra Club. The program fees do not cover travel costs to the volunteer sites.

Getting Started: Information and online registration for prospective volunteers are available on the organization's Web site. Training in specific tools and methodologies is provided on-site.

Needed Skills and Specific Populations: Most work sites are "moderately strenuous," but they can be undertaken by anyone in decent physical shape. Usually the minimum age for volunteers is 18, but this can be waived if the project leader agrees and if the minor's parent or guardian also volunteers on the project. The largest demographic group for Sierra Club Outings is people aged 40 to 70 years old, so senior volunteers are very much welcomed. Outings also offers special-interest service trips for multigenerational families, teens, seniors, and women. Specific work sites may be able to accommodate volunteers with disabilities, depending on what disabilities are involved.

Sioux YMCA

P.O. Box 218
1 YMCA Street
Dupree, SD 57623
(605) 365-5232; Fax: (605) 365-5230
E-mail: crandall@siouxymca.org
Web site: www.siouxymca.org

Project Type: Youth

Mission Statement Excerpt: "Our mission is to develop and strengthen the children and families in our Reservation communities so they can fulfill their greatest individual and collective potential, spiritually, mentally, and physically."

Year Founded: Formed in 1872; incorporated in 1972

The Work They Do: The Sioux YMCA is a full-service, multi-program YMCA. Programs offered through the YMCA focus on families and children, and they include an after-school program, a girl's drill team, Girl Scouts, a game room, computer and Internet access, a youth leaders program, and a summer day camp. Most volunteer projects involve a specific work project and youth activities. The majority of Sioux YMCA's volunteers come in groups, but individual volunteers may also be accepted. Groups may have a maximum of 10 participants, including two leaders over the age of 21.

Project Location: All volunteers work at the Sioux YMCA in Dupree, South Dakota, on the Cheyenne River Sioux Reservation. Temperatures on the reservation vary throughout the year from 100°F to -50°F.

Time Line: Volunteers are accepted February through October. All volunteers, whether as part of a group or individually, must arrange the details of their visits prior to arriving and are advised to begin this process well in advance; most groups begin the booking process in the August prior to their arrival. Groups of volunteers come for one to two weeks on average. Individual volunteers should be willing to make a minimum commitment of three months.

Cost: All travel and living expenses are the sole responsibility of the group or individual. The YMCA has limited sleeping space on the floor of the building. There are cooking, shower, and toilet facilities in the public areas of the YMCA.

Getting Started: Groups of volunteers should phone or e-mail Sioux YMCA. An online application is available for individual volunteers.

Needed Skills and Specific Populations: Volunteers must exhibit flexibility, a sense of humor, and a positive attitude. All volunteers, regardless of age, are required to remain tobacco, alcohol, and drug free while at the Sioux YMCA. Women are expected to wear conservative, non-revealing clothing.

Students Partnership Worldwide (SPW)

1401 New York Avenue NW, Suite 500
Washington, DC 20005
(202) 662-0714
E-mail: info@spw-usa.org
Web site: www.spw.org

Project Type: Agriculture; Community Development; Economic Development; Education; Human Rights; Medical/Health; Natural Conservation (Land); Orphans; Professional/Technical Assistance; Rural Development; Social Justice; Women's Issues; Youth

Mission Statement Excerpt: "Students Partnership Worldwide's (SPW) mission is to empower young people to take action to safeguard their own health (in particular their sexual and reproductive health) by delivering interactive, youth-to-youth peer education programs."

Year Founded: 1985

Number of Volunteers Last Year: More than 900

Funding Sources: SPW receives some funding from international governments, private foundations, and individuals.

The Work They Do: SPW is dedicated to making young people central to the development process. Through SPW, young American, European, and Australian volunteers live and work alongside African and Asian volunteers who are recruited by the host country. SPW's emphasis is on training these volunteers (all aged 18–28) to create a sustainable framework for development that responds to the needs of each community. SPW volunteers work in rural communities, where volunteers coordinate with schools and community leaders to identify and resolve key health or environmental issues. Health volunteers accomplish this goal through teaching health classes, providing skills training, and organizing community health workshops. Environmental volunteers introduce and encourage sustainable use of natural resources, waste management, appropriate technologies, and income generation projects.

Project Location: Volunteers work in rural communities in Nepal, India, Tanzania, Uganda, Zambia, Zimbabwe, South Africa, and Sierra Leone. Living conditions are very basic, as volunteers live in the same way that the community members do. Transport around the community is generally by foot. Most villages do not have running water or electricity. Volunteers live in a family's home or in pairs in one house in the village. Accommodations will be arranged in advance by SPW but will be at the discretion of the community, so volunteer lodging may be in a school, an empty house, or a local family's home. Volunteers purchase food from local shops and markets, and they are generally responsible for cooking themselves.

Time Line: Generally, volunteers depart in January, though those in India and Nepal may be able to arrange departure in September or November. The shortest program is six months and the longest is nine months, with the first month devoted to training. Holidays and time off varies by program, but volunteers can expect to have one or two days off each week (though they will generally stay in the village); long-term volunteers receive two to three weeks' midterm holiday.

Cost: The program fee ranges from $5,140 to $6,435 and covers a return flight from London, comprehensive travel and health insurance, a work visa, training, food, accommodations, in-country travel expenses, and pre-departure and in-country support. SPW books volunteers on 12-month return flights, so many volunteers travel independently or in small groups after the program ends. Volunteers are responsible for the cost of travel from the United States to meet with the group flight in London.

Getting Started: SPW's application process is selective and places in programs are limited. SPW recommends applying three to twelve months before departure to maximize choice of programs. Later applications are accepted on a first-come, first-served basis. Prospective volunteers can download an information packet and an application form, or they can contact the office to request that these materials be mailed. All volunteers participate in a pre-departure conference call, which generally lasts two and a half hours and which provides an opportunity for volunteers to talk with returned volunteers and SPW staff. Once in-country, all volunteers will receive three to six weeks of training (depending on the length of the program), which will include program-specific information, training in non-formal education techniques and appropriate rural technologies, participatory rural appraisal skills, and information on language and health and safety.

Needed Skills and Specific Populations: SPW volunteers must have graduated from high school, so most volunteers are at least 18 years old, and the maximum age for volunteers is 28. People with disabilities should contact the SPW office to discuss their specific circumstances. There are no restrictions on citizenship.

Sunseed Desert Technology

Apdo. 9, 04270 Sorbas
Almeria, Spain
+ (34) 950 525 770
E-mail: sunseedspain@arrakis.es
Web site: www.sunseed.org.uk

Project Type: Agriculture; Construction; Education; Natural
Conservation (Land); Rural Development; Scientific
Research
Mission Statement Excerpt: "Sunseed Desert Technology aims
to develop, demonstrate, and communicate accessible low-
tech methods of living sustainably in a semiarid
environment."
Year Founded: 1986
Number of Volunteers Last Year: 250
Funding Sources: The organization receives a few donations
from individuals.
The Work They Do: Sunseed Desert Technology demonstrates
a sustainable lifestyle by using and developing low-tech
methods that have the least detrimental environmental
impact as an appropriate alternative to other often less
accessible technologies and techniques. Program areas
include appropriate technology, construction and maintenance, dryland management, organic growing, and education and publicity. Volunteers can work in all of Sunseed's
departments, both in research as well as in community
activities such as gardening, housework, and building.
Longer-term volunteers may undertake their own individual
projects, choosing an idea from Sunseed's Project Pack or
designing a project themselves in consultation with the
organization. Examples of past such projects include setting up an urban garden, investigating the use of seed pel-
lets, constructing a thermal compost water heater,
producing a study of local ecology, and looking at erosion
control techniques.

Project Location: Sunseed Desert Technology is based in a small rural village located in a valley in the semiarid landscape of southeast Spain. Living and working conditions are basic and shared, but they are comfortable. Sunseed Desert Technology volunteers follow a semi-vegan or vegetarian diet.

Time Line: All of Sunseed's projects are ongoing and accept volunteers throughout the year. Volunteers can participate at two levels: part-time volunteers stay less than four weeks and work four hours per day, six days per week; full-time volunteers stay at least five weeks and work seven hours per day, five days per week.

Cost: Program fees vary by time of year and length of stay, but they range from £35/49 to £188/165. Each program fee covers room and board, but not travel to or from Spain.

Getting Started: Prospective volunteers should download the booking form found on Sunseed's Web site or contact the organization to request that one be mailed. Volunteers receive a two-hour orientation upon arrival. Training is done on the job, and work is supervised as needed.

Needed Skills and Specific Populations: Volunteers under 16 years old must be accompanied by an adult. Volunteers aged 16–18 must provide a written statement from an adult testifying to the volunteer's maturity and ability to volunteer. Senior volunteers are welcomed, but they should recognize the difficulty of the terrain at the center. While Sunseed tries to accommodate as many volunteers as possible, people with restricted mobility may have difficulty navigating the center, as it is not wheelchair accessible.

Swiss Whale Society

Niederwilerstr. 12,
CH-5524 Nesselnbach
Switzerland
+ 41-76-530 91 92; Fax:: + 41-56-426 06 09
E-mail: info@whales.ch
Web site: www.whales.ch

Project Type: Natural Conservation (Sea); Scientific Research
Mission Statement Excerpt: "To promote nonlethal scientific research on marine mammals in their natural habitat, and to collect and publish information on marine mammals, their environment, and their biology."
Year Founded: 2001
Number of Volunteers Last Year: 70
Funding Sources: About 5 percent of the Swiss Whale Society's funding comes from government sources.
The Work They Do: Working from a sailboat, a land base, and two rigid-hulled inflatable boats, the Swiss Whale Society carries out biological research on baleen whales in Canada and Cape Verde. Its research includes studies of bio-acoustics (sound recordings), photo-identification, population genetics (biopsies), contamination, and behavioral studies. Researchers primarily study blue, finback, minke, and humpback whales. On the water, volunteer work includes helping with data collection, such as species identification, using the GPS and range finder, recording the logbook, assisting with sound recordings, videotaping, and helping to navigate. Volunteers in the lab can help with data entry and matching photos of individual whales to those in existing catalogs, and they can help mount the skeletons of seals and toothed and baleen whales.
Project Location: Volunteers work either in Portneuf-sur-Mer, Quebec, Canada, northeast of Quebec City, or in the Cape Verde Islands, west of Africa in the North Atlantic. The land base is in the Canadian location, which can be

extremely cold. Volunteers in Cape Verde live in a tropical climate on sailboats.

Time Line: Volunteers are accepted in Canada from June through September, and in Cape Verde from March through May. Volunteers stay for a minimum of two weeks and a maximum of four months, with the average volunteer staying three weeks.

Cost: A two-week volunteer program in Canada has a program fee of $1,160 (students can receive a discount). Covered in this fee are food, lodging, all excursions at sea, a course booklet, lectures, and a thermo suit. Cape Verde volunteers pay a program fee of $1,600 for two weeks, which covers room and board. Travel expenses are not included in the program fees.

Getting Started: Application forms are available on the Swiss Whale Society's Web site. Training is done during the volunteer experience, and it includes lectures on the use of research equipment, marine mammal biology, navigation, and other pertinent topics, as well as on species recognition and identification of whale behavioral patterns.

Needed Skills and Specific Populations: Volunteers do not need to have specific skills. Swiss Whale Society team members speak English, French, German, and, in Cape Verde, Portuguese. Participants need to be in good enough physical and mental shape to sit in rigid-hulled inflatable boats for several hours at a time and live in a rustic but comfortable camp (Canada) or on a sailboat (Cape Verde). Volunteers with computer, navigation, or photography skills are especially welcomed. Volunteers under 18 years old must have the written permission of their parents. Senior volunteers frequently help with the Canadian research project. Volunteers with disabilities may be able to work with the Swiss Whale Society, depending on the nature and extent of their disabilities. Prospective volunteers should not easily get seasick, and they should not expect to swim with dolphins or dive with whales.

Taita Discovery Centre (TDC)

P.O. Box 48019
00100 Nairobi
Kenya
+254 (0)20 222075 or +254 (0)20 312137
E-mail: info@originsafaris.info
Web site: www.originsafaris.info/community-volunteer.htm

Project Type: Community Development; Economic Development; Education; Natural Conservation (Land); Professional/Technical Assistance; Rural Development; Scientific Research

Mission Statement Excerpt: "The Tsavo Kasigau Wildlife Corridor and Taita Discovery Centre (TDC) are a work in progress. Our plan is to create the largest private conservancy and wildlife corridor in East Africa. Through the investment of human and monetary resources, we work toward four goals: education, conservation, participation, and community service."

Year Founded: 1998

Number of Volunteers Last Year: 80

Funding Sources: Private corporations and individuals, as well as local community leaders and volunteers

The Work They Do: TDC is an environmental education and conservation center. Volunteers can work either on animal-focused scientific programs or in a community-based program. Science volunteers assist with the study and research of elephants and lions, assist with entomology research, and observe animals at a water hole. Community volunteers can teach computer skills, English, or French in local village schools; plant trees; help with school construction projects; gather oral histories; make beehives; dig fishponds; or help create viable and sustainable income-generating projects.

Project Location: Volunteers live and work in the Taita Rukinga Wildlife Sanctuary, near Voi, Taita Taveta District,

Kenya. TDC is set in more than 170,000 acres of woodland. The area lies within the Tsavo ecosystem and adjoins Tsavo East National Park, one of the largest national parks in the world. The area contains many endemic species, has a healthy elephant population, and is home to a large variety of birds and insects. TDC is designed to blend with the environment and, from the air, has the appearance of an African village.

Time Line: TDC recommends that volunteers work at least one month in order to get the most out of the experience.

Cost: Wildlife volunteer projects have a program fee of $2,164 for the first month and $504 per week thereafter. Community volunteers pay a program fee of $1,068 for the first month, followed by a rate of $230 per week. Program fees cover accommodations, but not airfare to Kenya. For wildlife volunteers, the program fee also covers meals; community volunteers purchase and prepare their own food from local shops while living in the village.

Getting Started: Prospective volunteers can contact TDC via mail or e-mail. Volunteers are given on-site orientation and training.

Needed Skills and Specific Populations: TDC does not require any special skills, though volunteers will find computer skills to be useful, and a good command of English is also a distinct advantage. There is no minimum age to volunteer with TDC, and senior volunteers are welcomed. Prospective volunteers with disabilities should discuss their specific situations with TDC before volunteering.

Tethys Research Institute

Viale G.B. Gadio, 2. 20121
Milan, Italy
+ 39 0272001947
E-mail: tethys@tethys.org
Web site: www.tethys.org

Project Type: Natural Conservation (Sea); Scientific Research

Mission Statement Excerpt: "The Tethys Research Institute is dedicated to the preservation of the marine environment. It focuses on marine animals and particularly on cetaceans inhabiting the Mediterranean Sea, and it aims to protect its biodiversity by promoting the adoption of a precautionary approach to the management of natural resources."

Year Founded: 1986

Number of Volunteers Last Year: Approximately 250

Funding Sources: Tethys is funded largely by faith-based and private sources.

The Work They Do: Tethys does scientific research to identify the threats affecting Mediterranean cetaceans, and it proposes solutions to these problems. Projects open to volunteer assistance include cetacean research in the Ligurian Sea Sanctuary and dolphin research in the eastern Ionian Sea. Volunteers actively collaborate in the collection of field data on cetaceans, and they are requested to help in all project activities. These may include recording navigation data, plotting sighting positions on a navigation chart, loading data in the computer, collecting ecological and behavioral data, noting photo-identification data, and helping with the identification of individual whales and dolphins. Volunteers and researchers alike take part in cooking and cleaning shifts.

Project Location: In the Ligurian Sea, Tethys has a 19-meter (62-foot) research ship that normally stays in the harbor of Portosole, San Remo, Italy. Volunteers sleep and live onboard during the research project. The boat is equipped with a full kitchen, two bathrooms, and hot water. The dolphin project is run out of a field station on the island of Kalamos, Greece. This field station is a comfortable house that includes a living room, a kitchen, a bathroom with hot water, and a garden with almond and olive trees.

Time Line: Volunteers are accepted May through October for either six or nine days; volunteers can sign up for more than one project.

Cost: Program fees range from $500 to $830. Each program fee covers all lodging and food, though volunteers must provide for their own travel expenses. Volunteers who stay for multiple projects are offered a discount, as are students under age 26.

Getting Started: Prospective volunteers should call or fax the Milan office during the hours of 9:30 A.M–1:00 P.M. and 2:00–5:00 P.M., Monday through Friday (please remember to adjust for time zones). They will then complete an application form and send the program fee, which will secure the reservation. During each project, researchers give daily lectures on cetaceans and conservation issues. Practical training is also provided during the research project.

Needed Skills and Specific Populations: Volunteers must be able to swim, and they must be at least 18 years old. Volunteers should be able to speak enough English in order to communicate with other project participants and team members. They should be in good physical condition and able to tolerate hot weather, sun, and long periods on a boat. Anyone in good physical condition, including seniors, is welcome to volunteer. Prospective volunteers with disabilities should contact the organization's office and will be considered on a case-by-case basis.

Tolga Bat Hospital

P.O. Box 685
Atherton 4883
Australia
+ 61 (7) 4091 2683
E-mail: jenny.maclean@iig.com.au
Web site: www.athertontablelands.com/bats

Project Type: Community Development; Natural Conservation (Land); Scientific Research

Mission Statement Excerpt: "We are a community group that values education, community partnerships and social participation, volunteering, and capacity building while working specifically for bats and their habitat."

Year Founded: 1996

Number of Volunteers Last Year: 54

Funding Sources: Grants from government and private sources

The Work They Do: Tolga Bat Hospital's main work is to rescue, rehabilitate, and release all species of bats. It also advocates, at all levels of government, for the conservation of bats and their habitats, educates and raises public awareness of issues affecting bats, encourages research into the general ecology of bats and their management, and networks and serves as a resource for local, national, and international bat scientists. Volunteers during the busy season of October through March do lots of hands-on bat work, caring for adults with tick paralysis and the resulting orphans. During the rest of the year, volunteer work consists of captive bat care, building and repair projects, revegetation projects, and garden work. Even during the busy season, Tolga Bat Hospital cannot predict what its workload will be, so volunteers should arrive with possible alternative plans in mind.

Project Location: Most volunteer work occurs at the Tolga Bat Hospital, which is six kilometers (less than four miles) from Atherton, though revegetation projects are at the bat colony about ten kilometers (six miles) from the hospital. The hospital is on a five-acre private residence that is bordered on two sides by a national park. The residence has three separate living areas and all the modern conveniences expected in a rural Australian household. All volunteers can use on-site housing accommodations.

Time Line: Volunteers are accepted throughout the year, but most come during the busy season of October through March. During this busy season, Tolga Bat Hospital requires that volunteers stay for at least one month. During the rest of the year, the minimum stay is just one week.

Cost: Volunteers pay between $A30 and $A50 per day, depending on length of stay. Each program fee covers all accommodations and food, but no travel expenses.

Getting Started: A volunteer questionnaire is available on Tolga Bat Hospital's Web site. All volunteers are given an orientation during the first days following their arrival, and a large library of information on bats is also available.

Needed Skills and Specific Populations: Volunteers are not required to have prior experience with bats, but experience with wildlife, veterinary care, or zoo management is helpful. Volunteers must be at least 21 years old unless accompanied by an adult, and senior volunteers are welcomed. Tolga Bat Hospital's volunteer coordinator is a physical therapist and is happy to try to make accommodations for volunteers with disabilities.

Transformational Journeys

13890 West 127th Street
Olathe, KS 66062
(913) 393-9400; Fax: (913) 764-4692
E-mail: tjourney@sbcglobal.net
Web site: www.tjourneys.com

Project Type: Community Development; Construction; Economic Development; Medical/Health; Natural Conservation (Land); Professional/Technical Assistance; Social Justice; Women's Issues

Mission Statement Excerpt: "To teach people and cultures to love and serve one another."

Year Founded: 1997

Number of Volunteers Last Year: Approximately 125

Funding Sources: Private donors

The Work They Do: Volunteers with Transformational Journeys carry out short-term projects such as building homes, community centers, schools, and churches for economically disadvantaged communities in developing countries. Volunteers lead recreational projects, teach, build, paint, repair, and pour foundations. Some examples of projects include teaching ballet or other dance forms to the children in a community in Brazil; erecting a multipurpose center for a Mayan village in Guatemala; building homes in the Dominican Republic in partnership with local families; and providing for children with HIV/AIDS and other disabilities in Kenya.

Project Location: Volunteers can work on projects in Brazil, the Dominican Republic, Guatemala, and Kenya. Work sites range from very urban environments in Brazil and Kenya to rural Mayan villages in Guatemala's mountains to a Caribbean seaside community in the Dominican Republic. Lodging also varies by country and includes a four-star hotel in Brazil, a three-star hotel in the Dominican Republic, and guesthouses in Guatemala and Kenya.

Time Line: Projects follow set time lines and most take place in the summer, though some are available during winter and spring as well. Contact Transformational Journeys to find out about upcoming dates. Volunteers work for a minimum of nine days and a maximum of fifteen days.

Cost: The program fee and average out-of-pocket expenses total approximately $2,000. The program fee covers airfare from gateway cities and all in-country expenses such as hotels, transportation, meals, travel insurance, translators, and group leaders. Volunteers are responsible for visa fees, which range from $40 to $100 dollars, depending on the country.

Getting Started: Prospective volunteers should e-mail or call Transformational Journeys to request an application. Orientation is required prior to departure, and it includes instructions about culture, language, politics, religion, and sociology of the destination country. Work training is provided on-site.

Needed Skills and Specific Populations: Volunteers must be at least 15 years old or be accompanied by a parent or guardian. Senior volunteers are welcomed. Accommodations can be arranged for volunteers with disabilities.

United Planet

11 Arlington Street
Boston, MA 02116
(800) 292-2316 or (617) 267-7763; Fax: (617) 267-7764
E-mail: quest@unitedplanet.org
Web site: www.unitedplanet.org

Project Type: Community Development; Human Rights; Medical/Health; Rural Development; Social Justice; Women's Issues; Youth

Mission Statement Excerpt: "The mission of United Planet is to unite the world through fostering intercultural understanding and friendship."

Year Founded: United Planet was founded in 2001, but it is the U.S. partner of ICYE, which was formed more than 50 years ago, after World War II.

Number of Volunteers Last Year: More than 2,000

Funding Sources: United Planet receives some donations from individuals.

The Work They Do: United Planet runs many kinds of volunteer programs in more than 50 countries worldwide. Some examples of projects undertaken by United Planet volunteers include helping with conservation efforts at one of the world's largest botanical gardens along the coast of Honduras; assisting in the poorest public school in Kathmandu, Nepal; working at health clinics in Guatemala; and repairing the homes of senior citizens in a small village in northern Iceland. After the volunteer experience, participants are encouraged to share their experience in their schools and communities through the United Planet Cultural Awareness Project and on the Internet via the United Planet online community. This passing on of knowledge is seen as critical to United Planet's mission.

Project Location: Volunteers can work in urban and rural settings around the world. Work sites vary widely from site to site, as do accommodations, which may include home stays, guesthouses, residential accommodations at the project, or hotels.

Time Line: Volunteers can work with United Planet year-round, for one to fifty-one weeks.

Cost: Program fees vary by country, from a low of $495 for two weeks in Iceland up to $7,195 for a year-long program. Each program fee covers all meals, lodging, insurance, orientation, and, in the case of some programs, transportation that includes international airfare. Longer-term commitments carry greater benefits.

Getting Started: Prospective volunteers can download an application from United Planet's Web site or ask for one via e-mail. Orientation is provided and varies according to the length of the volunteer position. The orientation often includes some language training.

Needed Skills and Specific Populations: No specific skills are required to volunteer with United Planet, but if a volunteer has a specialized skill such as medical or dental, computer, educational, or environmental training, the organization will try to place the volunteer in a position that utilizes this skill. United Planet encourages volunteerism by people of all ages, so there is no minimum or maximum age. This philosophy of inclusion extends to volunteers with disabilities, as United Planet does its best to include everyone. United Planet is also open to non-U.S. citizens.

University Research Expeditions Program (UREP)

UC Davis Extension
1333 Research Park Drive
Davis, CA 95616
(530) 752-8811; Fax: (530) 757-8596
E-mail: information@unexmail.ucdavis.edu
Web site: www.extension.ucdavis.edu/urep

Project Type: Archaeology; Community Development; Natural Conservation (Land); Natural Conservation (Sea); Scientific Research

Mission Statement Excerpt: "The mission of UREP is to facilitate a wide variety of domestic and international learning experiences for students and lifelong learners through a unique scientific partnership with university researchers."

Year Founded: 1976

The Work They Do: UREP endeavors to benefit host countries through collaborations with other universities, museums, and institutions. UREP has helped thousands of research teams on expeditions worldwide to investigate critical issues of environmental, human, and economic importance. Examples of UREP volunteer projects include recording traditional mud brick architecture and textile decoration and production techniques in Mali; documenting the life history and movement patterns of the leopard grouper, an exploited marine fish in Mexico; and examining evidence such as rock art from the Neolithic, Copper, and Bronze Ages in southeastern Spain to come to a more holistic understanding of social change during that time.

Project Location: UREP projects are located throughout the world and vary greatly in conditions. Accommodations range from modest hotels to wilderness camps. Some research projects are located in remote areas where facilities are limited.

Time Line: Most UREP trips take place from June to September and typically last about two weeks. A few UREP expeditions may also take place from January through March.

Cost: The $1,400 to $2,500 program fee covers all accommodations and meals, bottled water, restaurant tips, and transportation to the research site from the in-country assembly point and back to the point at the project's end. The program fee does not cover international airfare to the country of service. UREP has a limited number of scholarships available.

Getting Started: An application form is available for download on the UREP Web site, and it must be sent in with a $200 registration fee. If space is not available in the applicant's expedition of choice, UREP will refund this registration fee. Applicants receive notification of acceptance into the program within 10 to 14 days. There is no deadline for applications, which are accepted until the project begins or the available spaces are all filled. UREP volunteers receive full details on the project objectives, field techniques, and site conditions before departure. In addition, UREP offers an orientation session at the research site, as well as ongoing instruction in field methods.

Needed Skills and Specific Populations: UREP welcomes all adults aged 18 or older in good mental and physical health. Youths 16 and 17 years old may participate with approval from the program director and the project leader provided they have a signed parental authorization form.

Visions in Action (VIA)

2710 Ontario Road NW
Washington, DC 20009
(202) 625-7402; Fax: (202) 588-9344
E-mail: visions@visionsinaction.org
Web site: www.visionsinaction.org

Project Type: Agriculture; Developmentally Disabled; Economic
Development; Education; Human Rights; Legal;
Medical/Health; Natural Conservation (Land); Women's
Issues; Youth

Mission Statement Excerpt: "Visions in Action is committed to
achieving social and economic justice in the developing
world through the participation of communities of self-
reliant, grassroots volunteers."

Year Founded: 1988

Funding Sources: VIA programs are funded by program fees,
private contributions, and in-kind donations.

The Work They Do: VIA places volunteers in short-term,
medium-term, and long-term positions with local nonprofit
development organizations, research institutes, health clinics, community and activist groups, and the media. Volunteers can work in one of the following positions: *Project
Manager* (a supervisory position for professionals who
work in the field or office helping to manage rural and
urban development projects); *Program Assistant* (volunteers in this category work with a mentor or supervisor in
an entry-level position); *Community Development* (field-
based positions that entail working with community
groups in low-income neighborhoods or rural areas);
Health Professional (volunteers in this position work in a
health clinic, a medical laboratory, or a hospital as a doctor, nurse, or clinical assistant); *Public Health Educator*
(people in this position perform baseline research, grassroots education, or design health communication materials); *Researcher* (volunteers in this position work as social

science or natural science research assistants); *Journalist* (people in this position work as reporters, photographers, assistant editors, or newsletter editors for newspapers, magazines, book publishers, or nonprofit organizations or as assistant producers for radio or television stations); and *Youth Group Coordinator* (volunteers in this position run an orphanage, counsel runaways, coach, tutor, and lead community service projects for teens and children).

Project Location: VIA places volunteers in work sites in Oaxaca, Mexico; Kampala, Uganda; Arusha and Moshi, Tanzania; and Johannesburg, South Africa. Volunteers usually live together in group housing.

Time Line: VIA usually places volunteers in six- and twelve-month positions, but it also offers three- to seven-week short-term positions in Mexico and Tanzania. Volunteers in Mexico, Tanzania, and South Africa begin in January or July; volunteers in Uganda begin in September or March.

Cost: Program fees for VIA volunteer opportunities range from $2,200 for three weeks in Mexico to $6,700 for the organization's twelve-month programs. Each program fee covers housing, health insurance, orientation, staff support, and program administration. Long-term volunteers also receive a $50-per-month stipend to assist with daily living expenses. Airfare is not included in the program fee.

Getting Started: Prospective volunteers can download an application from VIA's Web site. The application is due three months before the project start date, and it must be submitted along with two letters of recommendation and a nonrefundable $45 application fee. VIA's volunteer programs each begin with several weeks of orientation that include development seminars, language classes, home stays, and travel to areas around the volunteer site.

Needed Skills and Specific Populations: Volunteers must be at least 20 years old and have a college degree or equivalent experience. Volunteers in Mexico must be proficient in Spanish. Health volunteers must have completed at least two years of medical school, have a nursing or physical therapy degree, or have a background in public health.

Abayudaya:
The Jews of Africa

❖ By Emily Chaya Weinstein ❖

Visions in Action (VIA)

It had always been my dream to live and work in Africa. I wanted to take a break from the ethnocentrism, commercialism, and rose-colored idealism of America, and from the routine of my life here. I wanted to understand firsthand what life is like for people living amid a more complex set of unrelenting challenges in the developing world. I also sought to experience the beauty of Africa's culture and natural surroundings. And so it was that I, at the age of 44, found a dynamic organization called Visions in Action that could guide me toward a successful initial experience and provide a wide range of opportunities for service. I left my occupational position, which I had held for 10 years, and the only country I had ever truly known, and boarded a plane for Uganda.

Before going, I did some research and discovered a Jewish community in Uganda called the Abayudaya (translated from the Luganda language as "sons of Judah"). The history of the Abayudaya is a fascinating one. Thousands of Ugandans, under the leadership of one man of faith, became Jews by choice, in a land where no Jews lived, where there were no Jewish texts other than the Bible, and where communication with the world outside Africa was virtually nonexistent. A Christian missionary approached a Muganda general named Semei Kakungulu, giving him a Bible that contained both the Old and New Testament. Upon closer reading, Kakungulu decided to follow the ways of the Israelites. He circumcised himself and his children and encouraged members of the community to do the same. By 1919 a community of more than 3,000 people actively practiced Judaism through observing the Sabbath, celebrating the Jewish festivals, and keeping kosher laws (Kashrut). The community has declined in numbers, largely due to the anti-Semitic acts of terrorism and violence of former dictator Idi Amin. However, in the 1980s, there was a strong community revival. The community is now more than 600 strong and raising its fifth generation.

I visited the Abayudaya during the holiday of Simchat Torah, a celebration held to mark the completion and new beginning of the Torah reading cycle. I was completely moved by seeing men, women, and children in this poor, remote rural area, singing and joyously dancing with their holy Torah in their candlelit synagogue, their eyes sparkling with a deep inner faith. I was impressed not only by the people's faith, but by their ambition. They were intent on making changes in their lives—notably, in education and economic development. Their community was unusual in that there was a primary school and high school that provided some Jewish instruction. Every Abayudaya student was provided with a scholarship, covered by contributions from the Jewish community in America. I later learned that the Abayudaya also provided some community development activities for their non-Jewish neighbors, such as arranging for the low-cost purchase of cows for local women through Heifer International. I wanted to be part of this engaged, dynamic community. I was thrilled when they accepted me as a volunteer.

I lived with the Abayudaya for seven months in the capacity of teacher and consultant, and served them for two additional months from the capital of Uganda, Kampala. I used so many of my occupational therapy, photographic, Judaic, and personal skills I had developed in previous years that I never even realized I had! I taught English, Jewish studies, and Hebrew language. I taught computer, e-mail, and Internet skills. I tutored a college student in research design for his dissertation. I taught English to a high school senior in preparation for her TOEFL exam (Test of English as a Foreign Language). I led life skills, arts and crafts, singing, and games with the younger children. I also consulted about the safety and health needs of the school. And with my camera, I documented this heartfelt, dynamic community.

One of the high points was working with the Abayudaya Women's Association. To combat poverty and build community, the women founded the association in 1993. Before I came, they had already achieved several goals, including provision of cows to 30 women through Heifer International. They also had successfully advocated for educational scholarships for women and expanded a crafts collective that makes crocheted head coverings (*kippot*). While there, I taught the women how to apply for their first grant, which they subsequently received from Aid to Artisans (and have since garnered a second one). The women also established a Sabbath study group. I taught the initial sessions. By the time I left the community, they had learned how to conduct Sabbath mealtime rituals and plan study sessions. Donors from the United States were located to support the study group and computer training, which have since expanded to four congregations.

The weeks passed by, and with them many joyful Sabbaths and holidays. In the spring, a Passover Seder was held at the school. As I sat at the Seder, I reflected upon my experience of the community over the previous seven months. I realized that the longer I had participated in the life of the community, the more my views of the community had changed. At my first Sabbath service, I saw the exotic, the different, the unusual—African garb; the unkempt, dirty torn clothes of kids; the worn benches; the African cloth with the star of David. And now, I saw the beautiful familiar—vibrant dresses, of both African and Western styles; sandals that got a child where she needed to go; gas lamps that were simply gas lamps and not the lack of electricity. I looked around the schoolyard and realized that these were not "African Jews," but Rachel, Naume, and Tziporah, and all the other names of real people I now knew personally, sharing together in the life of the community.

Best of all, what started as an overseas "experience" has now become an integral part of my life. I serve as international volunteer coordinator for Kulanu (www.kulanu.org), an organization that does outreach to lost and dispersed Jewish communities worldwide. My photographs are being used to illustrate articles and books about the Abayudaya. I am returning to work with the Abayudaya for nine weeks in February 2005, sponsored by Kulanu and American Jewish World Service (www.ajws.org), which serves nonsectarian communities worldwide. This time, there will be three other volunteers with me! My focus will be on vocational and economic development, based on my occupational therapy work experience. I will also continue to document the community and work on a photography project with the children.

This experience has brought me many wonderful gifts: closer connection to family and friends, new friends, rewarding work, and finding my passion. I only hope that I am able to give back as much as I have benefited from these opportunities.

Vitalise

Shap Road,
Kendal Cumbria LA9 6NZ
United Kingdom
+ 0845 345 1970; Fax: + 01539 735567
E-mail: admin@vitalise.org.uk
Web site: www.vitalise.org.uk

Project Type: Developmental Disabilities; Medical/Health

Mission Statement Excerpt: "To enable disabled and visually impaired people to exercise choice and to provide vital breaks for careers and inspirational opportunities for volunteers."

Year Founded: 1963

Number of Volunteers Last Year: Approximately 5,000

Funding Sources: Various charitable organizations

The Work They Do: Vitalise works to provide disabled and visually impaired people, who are referred to as guests, opportunities to change directions by starting new careers. Volunteers assist in this work by providing personal and social support to guests and by helping with activities and outings.

Project Location: Vitalise has five centers in the United Kingdom, which are located in Essex, Southampton, Nottingham, Southport, and Cornwall. These centers were built specifically to host Vitalise guests and volunteers. Accommodations are shared.

Time Line: Vitalise accepts volunteers year-round for a minimum of one week and a maximum of one year.

Cost: Vitalise does not charge any program fee and provides room and board free of charge to volunteers. Volunteers are responsible for providing their own transportation to the center.

Getting Started: Prospective volunteers must complete a booking form, provide references, and agree to a background check. Volunteers receive training in health, safety, and moving and handling guests.

Needed Skills and Specific Populations: Volunteers must be reasonably fit and have a good command of the English language. The minimum age for volunteers from the United Kingdom is 16; from other countries it is 18. Senior volunteers are welcomed, and volunteers with disabilities will be considered, depending on their individual circumstances.

Volunteer Africa

P.O. Box 24, Bakewell
Derbyshire DE45 1YP
United Kingdom
E-mail: support@volunteerafrica.org
Web site: www.volunteerafrica.org

Project Type: Community Development; Construction; Rural
   Development
Mission Statement Excerpt: "Volunteer Africa has been established to give people from around the world the opportunity to work on community-initiated projects in developing
   countries."
Year Founded: 2001
Number of Volunteers Last Year: 70
Funding Sources: None; Volunteer Africa is self-funded
The Work They Do: Volunteer Africa recruits volunteers from
   all over the world to work in Tanzania on community
   development projects. Volunteers participate for four,
   seven, or ten weeks on building projects such as school
   classrooms and health dispensaries in rural areas. Volunteers participate in hands-on building work such as rock
   breaking, bricklaying, and carpentry.
Project Location: Volunteers work in the Singida region of
   Tanzania and camp in rural villages with no electricity or
   running water.
Time Line: Volunteers are accepted between May and November for four, seven, or ten weeks.
Cost: Participation for four weeks costs $1,710; seven weeks
   costs $2,400, and the program fee for ten weeks is $3,080.
   Each program fee covers food, accommodation, language
   training, and in-country travel, but does not include insurance or travel to Tanzania. Approximately 60 percent of
   the program fee goes toward direct program costs and is
   therefore invested in the community being served.

Getting Started: Applications are available only online or via e-mail; Volunteer Africa does not maintain a phone or fax line so as to cut down on costs. An interview is required of all prospective volunteers. Volunteers receive an extensive guide for pre-departure arrangements.

Needed Skills and Specific Populations: Volunteers must be at least 18 years old, and senior volunteers are welcomed. Applications from volunteers with disabilities will be screened for appropriate placements, just as any volunteer would be.

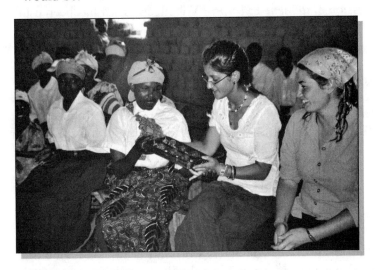

Two volunteers appreciate the music at a welcome ceremony held by villagers in Mampando, located in the Singida region of Tanzania. The volunteers are from Germany and the United Kingdom. *Photo courtesy of Annie O'Connor, of Volunteer Africa*

Volunteers for Outdoor Colorado (VOC)

600 South Marion Parkway
Denver, CO 80209
(800) 925-2220 or (303) 715-1010; Fax: (303) 715-1212
E-mail: voc@voc.org
Web site: www.voc.org

Project Type: Natural Conservation (Land); Trail
Building/Maintenance
Mission Statement Excerpt: "Volunteers for Outdoor Colorado's (VOC's) mission is to motivate and enable citizens to be active stewards of Colorado's public lands."
Year Founded: 1984
Number of Volunteers Last Year: Approximately 4,000
Funding Sources: Government and private sources
The Work They Do: Each year VOC carries out more than 20 projects that involve trail building, trail maintenance, habitat restoration, wetlands restoration, light construction, and nonnative invasive plant control. Volunteers cut and move dirt, move rocks, cut and move brush and tree branches, dig out plants, and plant seedlings. Repeat or experienced volunteers may elect to participate in training programs to take on leadership roles and become involved in the project planning and operation process.
Project Location: VOC projects take place throughout Colorado, from urban areas to plains to high mountains. Work sites may be urban parks, open-space areas, or forested mountain areas. Weather conditions are highly variable in Colorado, and volunteers should be prepared for weather conditions that range from hot and sunny to snow showers. Some sites are open with little shade and others are in heavily forested areas. Though some sites allow for RV or pop-up camper use, most volunteers camp in tents, and food is provided by VOC.

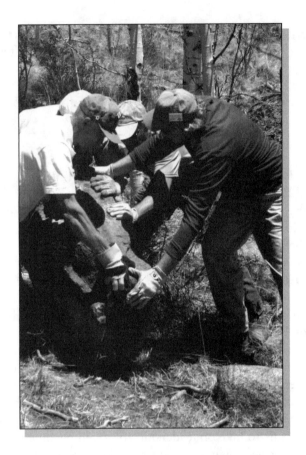

A group of volunteers attempts to move a rock to serve as one of a series of steps in a section of the Davis Meadow Trail in Buena Vista, Colorado. In one weekend more than 100 volunteers came together to construct more than 2,000 feet of new trail in addition to closing unsafe trails and planting vegetation in other areas to combat erosion.
Photo courtesy of Volunteers for Outdoor Colorado

Time Line: VOC typically runs two or three volunteer programs per month from March or April through October. Most of the VOC volunteer opportunities are weekend projects; volunteers arrive early Saturday morning, make lunch, split into work crews of 10 to 12, and work until about 4:00 P.M., with lunch and rest breaks. Everyone then gathers for dinner, which is cooked by a volunteer team, followed by social activities and entertainment. Sunday starts with a hot breakfast, and work continues until the project closes at 4:00 to 5:00 P.M. VOC occasionally offers single-day volunteer opportunities, as well as a five-day event each summer.

Cost: There is no program fee to volunteer with VOC, and most of the food is provided by the organization. Volunteers must provide their own transportation to the work site, tents and sleeping bags, and any personal food needs.

Getting Started: Prospective volunteers should apply via VOC's Web site or call the office. Volunteers must register beforehand, preferably at least two weeks prior to the project's starting date. Any needed training is done on-site during the project.

Needed Skills and Specific Populations: Volunteer crew members do not need to have prior experience or skills. VOC's minimum age for volunteers depends on the project, but it ranges from 8 to 16 years old. Senior volunteers are welcomed. Volunteers with disabilities are welcomed as long as they can perform moderate to hard physical work at altitudes as high as 12,000 feet. Some projects may require applicants to file a brief application or verification of physical health.

Volunteers for Peace (VFP)

1034 Tiffany Road
Belmont, VT 05730
(802) 259-2759; Fax: (802) 259-2922
E-mail: vfp@vfp.org
Web site: www.vfp.org

Project Type: Archaeology; Community Development; Construction; Historic Preservation; Human Rights; Natural Conservation (Land); Orphans; Social Justice; Trail Building/Maintenance

Mission Statement Excerpt: "Volunteers for Peace (VFP) . . . provides programs where people from diverse backgrounds can work together to help overcome the need, violence, and environmental decay facing our planet."

Year Founded: 1982

Number of Volunteers Last Year: 1,030

Funding Sources: VFP receives a few small donations from individuals.

The Work They Do: VFP provides placements for two- to three-week service programs by recruiting volunteers and linking them with programs. They help organize work camp programs in the United States and internationally, partnering with organizations in more than 90 other countries. In the last 22 years, VFP has exchanged more than 22,000 volunteers in international work camps worldwide. In previous years more than 2,500 projects have been listed annually. A typical work camp finds 10 to 15 volunteers from 5 or more countries working together for 30–40 hours per week. VFP's programs have a stated goal of fostering international education, voluntary service, and friendship. An example of a work camp project recently took place in Kenya, about four hours outside of Nairobi. There, volunteers assisted the Amkeni Women's Group with tree planting, farm work, weaving, terracing, and brick making.

Project Location: Volunteers can work in one of 90 countries around the world. Work sites vary widely and range from developed cities to very rural communities; some locations are much more rustic than others. Accommodations are usually in a house, a community center, a school, or tents. Volunteers share cooking and cleaning responsibilities as a group. Unless otherwise specified, volunteers must bring a sleeping bag.

Time Line: Most of VFP's projects take place May through September, although some are offered year-round. A list of the majority of projects is published annually in late March. Most programs last two to three weeks, though some medium-term projects are available for one to six months, and VFP offers a few long-term, six-month to two-year projects.

Cost: VFP's basic fee is $250, which covers lodging, food, and work materials. Programs in developing countries charge an additional fee upon arrival that averages $150, which is kept by the host organization. However, VFP refunds $50 to volunteers who have to pay an extra fee if the volunteer writes a work camp report. Volunteers must pay their own transportation costs.

Getting Started: Prospective volunteers usually become VFP members for an annual fee of $20, then apply via a two-page registration form, which is faxed to VFP's office. Once the volunteer is placed in a work project, VFP will e-mail him or her an acceptance letter and information sheet that details how to get to the project and what to bring. VFP volunteers are responsible for educating them-selves about their destination country, though a basic ori-entation is provided upon arrival in the first days of all projects.

Needed Skills and Specific Populations: No special skills are required, though VFP stresses that volunteers need to be motivated, cooperative, flexible, and culturally sensitive. Though some projects for teens exist in France, Germany, and a handful of other countries, most programs require volunteers to be at least 18 years old. Senior volunteers are welcomed, though they should be aware that the large majority of VFP's volunteers are in the 18–25 age group, and some programs have maximum age limits. Volunteers with disabilities are encouraged to apply, as work camps are designed to provide everyone with an opportunity to help; VFP will make reasonable accommodations. VFP primarily places U.S. and Canadian citizens, but it will also place citizens of countries in which it does not have a partner organization.

Volunteers in Asia (VIA)

Haas Center for Public Service, 3rd Floor
P. O. Box 20266
Stanford, CA 94309
(650) 723-3228; Fax: (650) 725-1805
E-mail: info@viaprograms.org
Web site: www.viaprograms.org

Project Type: Community Development; Developmental Disabilities; Education

Mission Statement Excerpt: "Volunteers in Asia (VIA) is dedicated to increasing understanding between the United States and Asia."

Year Founded: 1963

Number of Volunteers Last Year: 20–30

Funding Sources: VIA is a part of Stanford University's Haas Center for Public Service.

The Work They Do: VIA operates a variety of programs, which can be differentiated into two main categories. First, VIA offers two summer volunteer programs for undergraduate students. Second, VIA also offers college graduates one- and two-year positions teaching English or serving as English resources for nonprofit organizations. Summer volunteers travel to either Vietnam or Indonesia. In Vietnam, four to six volunteers teach a summer course on American culture for students at the University of Hue. Six to eight volunteers in Indonesia combine academic and community service components, taking courses on "Socio-Cultural Change in Bali" and in the local language, followed by hands-on work in local schools and nonprofit organizations. Examples of volunteer projects in Indonesia include a community environmental education and recycling program, a job training center for people with disabilities, an HIV/AIDS health awareness organization, an organization dedicated to community environmental issues, and a school for the blind.

Project Location: Summer programs are located in Vietnam and Indonesia; long-term projects are located in these two countries and in China.

Time Line: The summer programs run for five and a half weeks in Vietnam and eight weeks in Indonesia. The long-term programs are for one or two years.

Cost: VIA's Vietnam summer program fee is $1,500; the Indonesia summer program fee is $1,975. One-year volunteers pay a program fee of $2,500, and two-year volunteers pay a program fee of $1,500. VIA is committed to making this experience open to all students; traditionally, 40 percent of volunteers have received scholarship money from VIA. The short-term program fee covers two weekends of pre-departure training; visa; emergency medical and evacuation insurance; roundtrip airfare; local ground transportation; and hotel and dormitory accommodations. Long-term program fees cover all of the short-term benefits plus two weeks of teacher training in Thailand, an annual conference, a living stipend, and language training.

Getting Started: Prospective volunteers can access application materials and scholarship information from the VIA Web site or by contacting the office. The application deadline is in late February. Applicants must interview in person at VIA's office in California during the month of March. VIA emphasizes training and preparation before departure.

Needed Skills and Specific Populations: Volunteers must speak English with native fluency and attend all training sessions. It is recommended that volunteers also prepare by studying TEFL methodology and the local language. The summer programs are open only to undergraduate students, and the long-term programs are only open to college graduates.

Wilderness Foundation
47-49 Main Road
Broomfield, Chelmsford, Essex
United Kingdom CM1 7BU
+44 (0)1245 443073; Fax: +44 (0)1245 445035
E-mail: info@wildernessfoundation.org.uk
Web site: www.wildernessfoundation.org.uk

Project Type: Administration; Community Development; Natural Conservation (Land); Trail Building/Maintenance

Mission Statement Excerpt: "To preserve and promote wilderness worldwide, through direct personal experience and understanding."

Year Founded: 1976

Number of Volunteers Last Year: 6

Funding Sources: Private donors

The Work They Do: Wilderness Foundation provides volunteers opportunities to work directly in wilderness areas in an attempt to help those volunteers acquire essential life skills and a greater feeling of responsibility toward their environment. Volunteers help with general maintenance of tourism facilities, bookkeeping and administration, path clearance, fence inspection, game counts, and marketing.

Project Location: Volunteer projects are located in Norway, Kenya, and South Africa. Specific work sites range from a small island in the Arctic Circle to deep river valleys in Africa. Accomodations vary and include guesthouses, a small farm, and a tourist camp.

Time Line: Volunteers can work in Africa at any time of the year; the length of the volunteer experience is mutually agreed to by both parties. Volunteers in Norway are limited to three weeks in the end of July and early August.

Cost: Program fees vary by length of stay and location. In Africa, volunteers typically pay about £21 per day, and in Norway volunteers typically pay about £27 per day. Program fees cover housing and food, but not travel expenses.

Getting Started: Prospective volunteers should contact Wilderness Foundation by e-mail. No training or orientation is provided, but the organization provides support both before and after the volunteer experience.

Needed Skills and Specific Populations: Volunteers must bring some skill set to the project that can be used on-site. Skills can range from marketing to conservation to construction skills. Volunteers must have a track record of self-reliance and a strong motivation to participate. The minimum age for volunteers is 20, and there is no maximium age limit. The organization has not yet worked with a volunteer with disabilities, but it would be willing to accommodate needs as best it can, most likely in the South Africa program.

Wildlands Studies

3 Mosswood Circle
Cazadero, CA 95421
(707) 632-5665
E-mail: wildlands@sonic.net
Web site: www.wildlandsstudies.com

Project Type: Natural Conservation (Land); Natural Conservation (Sea); Scientific Research

Mission Statement Excerpt: "To provide undergraduate college students academic field study opportunities."

Year Founded: 1979

Number of Volunteers Last Year: 250

Funding Sources: None; Wildlands Studies is self-funded

The Work They Do: Wildlands Studies provides environmental field study opportunities for undergraduate students, who earn academic credit for their work. Students attend programs searching for answers to conservation challenges facing wildlife populations and wildlands worldwide. For example, the Yellowstone Endangered Species Project focuses on grey wolf, grizzly bear, and mountain goat management policies. Team activities focus on the ecology of the study species, wildlife sign identification, and management alternatives that would insure wildlife survival in Yellowstone National Park.

Project Location: Projects are available in the United States, Thailand, China, Costa Rica, Belize, Nepal, India, New Zealand, and Chile. Students perform work in the field and camp either in base camps or while backpacking, though there is no technical climbing.

Time Line: Projects are available year-round and last from two to ten weeks.

Cost: The program fee for international projects is $1,995; for programs in the continental United States, the program fee is $625; Hawaii's program fee is $1,040; and Alaska's is $1,600. The program fee covers program administration and tuition; all other costs, including transportation, lodging, and food, are left to the volunteer.

Getting Started: Prospective volunteers should contact Wildlands Studies via phone or e-mail. An orientation is provided on-site.

Needed Skills and Specific Populations: No prior research skills are needed. Volunteers must be at least 18 years old. Almost all of the Wildlands Studies volunteers are enrolled in undergraduate college courses; while senior citizens are welcome to volunteer, they should be aware of the organization's target population. Wildlands Studies cannot provide accommodations for volunteers with disabilities.

Winant and Clayton Volunteers

109 East 50th Street
New York, NY 10022
(212) 378-0271
E-mail: info@winantclaytonvolunteer.org
Web site: www.winantclaytonvolunteer.org

Project Type: Community Development; Youth

Mission Statement Excerpt: "Winant and Clayton Volunteers
are an energetic, caring team of volunteers who provide
community service in the United Kingdom and in the
United States, and in the process enhance their personal
development while experiencing both cultures from the
'inside.' "

Year Founded: 1948

The Work They Do: Winant and Clayton Volunteers fulfill the
vision of the late John G. Winant, U.S. Ambassador to
Great Britain during World War II, and the late Reverend
Philip "Tubby" Clayton, vicar of All Hallows Church in
London and private chaplain to the Queen Mother. Following World War II, these two men envisioned teams of
volunteers comprised of people from the United Kingdom,
known as Claytons, and from the United States, known as
Winants, who would travel to the each other's countries to
volunteer and learn about life there. Winant volunteers
from the United States are placed in full-time volunteer
positions on projects dealing with people of all ages with a
variety of needs. Specific examples of volunteer work sites
include community settlement clubs for the elderly, children, immigrants, teenagers at risk; drop-in service centers
for people with HIV/AIDS; psychiatric rehabilitation centers; and summer day care programs for inner-city children. Placements range from structured to self-structured,
but all require energy, enthusiasm, initiative, and flexibility.
Volunteers may be placed alone or with another Winant
volunteer.

Project Location: Winant volunteers serve in Great Britain, primarily in the East End of London. Housing is provided to volunteers in the form of host-family accomodations, flats, or dormitory rooms.

Time Line: Winant volunteers work full time, five days per week, for seven weeks. This volunteer experience is then followed by two weeks of independent travel. The program begins in mid-June and ends in late August.

Cost: Winant and Clayton does not charge a program fee to participate, but volunteers must pay for their own airfare to and from London, which is arranged through Winant and Clayton. Volunteers must travel as a group from New York City. Housing is provided to volunteers at no charge. A volunteer who stays with a host family will be fed by that family; all other volunteers are provided a small stipend of approximately $70 a week for food. If a volunteer is required to use public transportation to travel to and from a work site, those travel costs will be covered. A small amount of financial aid is available.

Getting Started: Prospective volunteers can download an application from the organization's Web site or write or call the office for information and an application. Applicants must submit applications, three references, and a nonrefundable $35 application fee by the deadline in late January. Each applicant will be interviewed, either in New York City or by a former Winant volunteer who lives near the applicant. Accepted volunteers must submit a $100 nonrefundable deposit by mid-April, with the balance due by the end of that month.

Needed Skills and Specific Populations: Winant volunteers must be at least 18 years old and be U.S. citizens.

World Challenge Expeditions (WCE)

945 Concord Street
Framingham, MA 01701
(617) 916-1904; Fax: (508) 879-0698
E-mail: info@wcexpeditions.com
Web site: www.wcexpeditions.com

Project Type: Agriculture; Developmental Disabilities; Education; Medical/Health; Natural Conservation (Land); Orphans; Youth

Mission Statement Excerpt: "Students who participate in a WCE expedition, either in the United Kingdom or overseas, will embark on an amazing journey of both mind and body to learn more about themselves and the world around them."

Year Founded: 1988

The Work They Do: WCE offers European-style gap-year opportunities that focus on volunteer work in either economically developed or economically developing countries. Volunteers travel as part of a group, and most volunteers are placed in pairs. Volunteers can also request a "double placement," such as three months of teaching followed by three months of conservation work. Placements are offered in the areas of agriculture, natural conservation, social work, medicine, education, veterinary medicine, and youth development. Specific examples of volunteer positions include working in Ecuador with orphans who have physical disabilities, tracking animals in South Africa, and assisting on a children's ward in a hospital in Malaysia.

Project Location: WCE places volunteers in Australia, New Zealand, Costa Rica, Ecuador, Malaysia, Mexico, Peru, South Africa, India, Canada, and Madagascar.

Time Line: Volunteers are accepted for either two-week First Challenge programs or for two- to nine-month Gap Challenge programs.

Cost: WCE's program fee ranges from £1,700 to £2,750, depending on the country of service. Each program fee covers transportation to the work site and a 12-month return-air ticket, which allows the volunteer to travel after the project is completed. The program fee does not cover accommodations or food.

Getting Started: Prospective volunteers should complete and submit an inquiry form, available on WCE's Web site, which will then prompt WCE to send an information pack and application form. Following application, prospective volunteers must attend a two-day selection course, which provides an introduction to the Gap Challenge and ensures that the volunteers and their chosen placements are compatible. Accepted volunteers are then sent regular newsletters, a country handbook, and a placement information pack. New volunteers also take part in a two- or three-day skills training course designed to give them the basic training they need for their placements, including detailed country information and tips on independent travel. During the skills training course, volunteers meet the rest of their expedition group and talk with Gap Challengers who have recently returned from their placements.

Needed Skills and Specific Populations: WCE accepts volunteers aged 17–24 only.

World Horizons

P.O. Box 662
Bethlehem, CT 06751
(800) 262-5874 or (203) 266-5874; Fax: (203) 266-6227
E-mail: worldhorizons.att.net
Web site: www.world-horizons.com

Project Type: Construction; Natural Conservation (Land); Natural Conservation (Sea); Trail Building/Maintenance; Youth

Mission Statement Excerpt: "World Horizons facilitates community service projects, promotes cross-cultural learning, and facilitates language immersion in particular locations."

Year Founded: 1987

Number of Volunteers Last Year: Approximately 55

Funding Sources: None; World Horizons is self-supporting

The Work They Do: World Horizons offers high school students the opportunity to participate in short-term international and domestic volunteer projects. Project areas may include working with seniors or children or working in the areas of agriculture, the environment, construction, or painting. Examples of past projects include building an addition onto a community hall and teaching classes in Fiji; painting murals at a daycare center, working with orphans and helping in health clinics in Dominica; running a day camp for underprivileged children and painting a school in Costa Rica; training and helping with abandoned animals in Utah; and maintaining trails in Zion National Park.

Project Location: World Horizons offers international projects in Bulgaria, Fiji, Costa Rica, the United Kingdom, Mexico, the Eastern Caribbean, Canada, and Iceland, and domestic projects in Utah and Boston. In general, accommodations tend to be basic. Students and leaders live in rented houses, community halls, or schools. Volunteers often sleep on the floor in a sleeping bag. Volunteer groups cook for themselves and live as a family unit.

Time Line: Project start dates begin in early June and run through early August. Most projects last four weeks.

Cost: The organization's all-inclusive program fees range from $4,500 to $5,200 and cover all transportation, food, accommodations, and sightseeing. Personal expenses, such as money spent on souvenirs and snacks, are the only expenses not included in the program fee.

Getting Started: Students who are interested in volunteering with World Horizons should visit the organization's Web site and download an application. Orientation is given the night before the trip begins.

Needed Skills and Specific Populations: World Horizons volunteers must be 14–18 years old. The only required skill is at least one year of appropriate language training if the project takes place in a country in which English is not spoken. Volunteers with disabilities would probably find World Horizons projects to be "difficult." World Horizons accepts volunteers from all over the world; volunteers do not have to be U.S. citizens.

WorldTeach

Center for International Development, Harvard University
79 John F. Kennedy Street
Cambridge, MA 02138
(617) 495-5527 or (800) 4-TEACH-0; Fax: (617) 495-1599
E-mail: info@worldteach.org
Web site: www.worldteach.org

Project Type: Community Development; Economic Development; Education; Youth

Mission Statement Excerpt: "WorldTeach . . . provides opportunities for individuals to make a meaningful contribution to international education by living and working as volunteer teachers in developing countries."

Year Founded: 1986

Number of Volunteers Last Year: 300

Funding Sources: Some funding from private donors

The Work They Do: Volunteers teach English to students of a wide age range depending on the needs of the country and host institution. In some countries, volunteers may also teach math, science, computer skills, nature guide training, and HIV/AIDS awareness. Volunteers work as full-time teachers and are employed by their host schools or sponsoring institutions in their placement countries. Most volunteers live with host families or on the school campus, and they participate fully in the lives of their host communities.

Project Location: Volunteers can work in Chile, China, Costa Rica, Ecuador, Guyana, the Marshall Islands, Namibia, Poland, and South Africa. Host institutions may be public or private primary or secondary schools, public or private universities, vocational schools and institutions, community resource centers, local organizations, or government agencies. Placement depends on the needs of the host communities and the location in which volunteers can be of most use to their host countries. Educational resources available to volunteers depend on placement and vary widely from country to country. Volunteers may live with local families, share houses with other local or foreign teachers, or, in some cases, have their own apartments. Volunteers in some countries live in traditional houses without running water or electricity; others have apartments with many modern amenities. Wherever volunteers are placed, they are likely to have their own furnished bedroom and access to a bathroom and kitchen or cafeteria.

Time Line: WorldTeach offers short-term, eight-week summer programs that depart in June; long-term, ten- to twelve-month programs with varying departure dates throughout the year.

Cost: Program fees vary by location and range from $1,000 to $5,990, with the exception of the Marshall Islands year program, which has no program fee and is fully funded. Each program fee covers international roundtrip airfare from a gateway city within the United States to the country of service, room and board, health insurance, emergency evacuation, visa and pre-departure materials, and in-country orientation and training. Long-term teaching volunteers receive a small monthly living stipend that is usually equivalent to what local teachers earn.

Getting Started: Prospective volunteers can download an application from WorldTeach's Web site or call and request that one be sent via postal mail. All candidates must submit two letters of recommendation, and applicants for nature guide training and long-term teaching programs are required to interview with a WorldTeach volunteer who has completed a stint. Admission to some of WorldTeach's programs, especially the fully funded Marshall Islands program, can be competitive. Admissions decisions are made on a rolling basis within two to three weeks of the receipt of a completed application, and final application deadlines are typically three months before the program departure date. WorldTeach provides intensive in-country orientation for every program: seven to ten days for summer programs and three to four weeks for long-term programs. Orientation includes training in the host country's language, instruction on teaching English as a foreign language, a teaching practicum, discussions of the host country's history and culture, informational sessions on health and safety issues, exploration of the region, and group building and social activities. Orientation is led by the in-country field director as well as by orientation assistants, who are usually current volunteers who have already begun their work.

Needed Skills and Specific Populations: Volunteers for the long-term programs must be college graduates; volunteers for the summer programs must be at least 18 years old; and fluency in the English language is required of volunteers in all programs except those in China and Chile, where volunteers must be native English speakers. Volunteers must also be responsible, caring, self-motivated individuals with a strong interest in cultural exchange and teaching. Volunteers do not have to have previous teaching experience or training. WorldTeach welcomes senior volunteers. Because WorldTeach places volunteers in challenging circumstances in developing countries and with local host families, it may not be able to accommodate volunteers with certain disabilities or serious health limitations, or those who require specialized housing arrangements.

World-Wide Opportunities on Organic Farms (WWOOF): United Kingdom and Independent

P.O. Box 2675
Lewes East Sussex, BN7 1RB
United Kingdom
+44 (0) 1273 478286
E-mail: hello@wwoof.org
Web site: www.wwoof.org; www.wwoof.org.uk

Project Type: Agriculture

Mission Statement Excerpt: "To get into the countryside; to help the organic movement; to get firsthand experience of organic farming and growing; to make contact with other people in the organic movement."

Year Founded: 1971

Number of Volunteers Last Year: WWOOF does not keep statistics on the number of volunteers, but the U.K. branch had 1,736 members last year.

Funding Sources: None; WWOOF is self-funded

The Work They Do: WWOOF's premise is simple: volunteers help organic growers in exchange for food and accommodations. WWOOF helps link volunteers to growers, and it leaves the details for the individuals to work out for themselves. Therefore, each volunteer experience with WWOOF is unique, but volunteers can expect that they could be involved with any growing or farming-related activity on an organic farm.

Project Location: WWOOF growers are located all over the world. Living situations vary widely, as each grower provides accommodations to the WWOOF volunteer.

Time Line: With so many opportunities around the world, there is always a WWOOF grower in need of help. The start and end date, as well as the minimum and maximum amount of time the volunteer spends with the grower, are up to the volunteer and the grower to negotiate.

Cost: There is no cost to volunteer. WWOOF's membership fee is £15, for which members receive access to listings of grower hosts and six newsletters per year. Volunteers pay their own travel costs.

Getting Started: Applications are available on WWOOF's Web site, or prospective volunteers may contact the office listed above and request one. Growers are responsible for providing training and orientation to volunteers.

Needed Skills and Specific Populations: WWOOF volunteers must be at least 18 years old; senior volunteers are welcome to work with WWOOF. Volunteers with disabilities must work with individual growers to determine the feasibility of working on specific farms.

Eating and Farming Our Way Through Scotland

By Ruth Dalton

World-Wide Opportunities on Organic Farms (WWOOF): United Kingdom and Independent

The footprints were broad and clearly marked in the damp sand—a purposeful track leading from the scrubby pasture of the shore straight into the sea, and divided where the otter's tail had traced a faint furrow. Our first evening on this small Scottish island and we had watched the maker of the prints tramp, unconcerned, toward his dinner as we strolled along the beach looking at the darkening Isle of Rum.

We saw otters almost every night of our week-long stay at this, our first WWOOF destination of the summer. Scotland is well known for its wildlife, but this west coast island, free of foxes and home to only a scattering of human communities, was a true haven. Staying on a working croft, one of only four on the island still actively farmed, our main task was putting a new tin roof onto our host's workshop. A croft is the name given to a small farm in Scotland, which were formerly worked by very poor peasant tenants. We slithered around on the steep slope wielding cordless drill, tape measure, string, and a fistful of bolts as the sun shone with uncharacteristic vigor. A truly wonderful introduction to self-sufficiency in Scotland, and we left our hosts feeling well-fed, fitter, and with a renewed enthusiasm for WWOOFing.

Next stop was a tiny village on the northwest coast, set in a landscape of hummocky rock and bizarrely shaped

Ruth Dalton and a friend volunteered at three different small farms (called crofts) in Scotland and participated in all aspects of farming, including bringing the cows home for milking. *Photo courtesy of Ruth Dalton, of World-Wide Opportunities on Organic Farms (WWOOF): United Kingdom and Independent*

mountains bounded by green sea and white sandy beaches. Much of the land was crofted, and our hosts farmed a traditional mix of hill sheep, rabbits, hens, ducks and geese, vegetables and even bees. Milk was provided by Molly, a Jersey cow with eyelashes to die for, and we slept in the most beautiful bothy (one-roomed shelter) renovated from an old stone-built byre (cow shed). Our work was varied and included bringing the sheep in for shearing, hoeing the veggie patches, feeding animals, splicing rope, and slotting a foundation of wax into wooden frames for the beehives. There was a definite feeling of community here. Favors were freely traded, offsetting the harshness and remoteness of living in such a place, creating a truly welcoming atmosphere.

Traveling inland, we bumped up miles of forestry track into the Affric Mountains and our final WWOOF farm of the summer—a beautiful croft with a river meandering through the middle. Beautiful, but problematic, as forestry upstream had washed tons of silt and gravel into the river, which was deposited on the croft, creating significant problems with drainage. We were taught to use the tools of the ditching trade and set to work creating drainage runs from the waterlogged fields. We looked increasingly like manic miners as we tried to brush away tiny, annoying flies with our peat-blackened fingers, but we succeeded in making a few respectable ditches.

I return home brimming with ideas and am already marking my WWOOF book with the next places I'd like to visit—Scotland is a fantastic country to experience wilderness, wildlife, and weather in all its forms (the latter often in a single day!), but it is also in the unique position of retaining its crofting laws and traditions. Our travels taught us not only that the principles of hospitality, good food, and organic methods are alive and well, but that it is the diversity between crofting communities that makes this very remote region of Scotland such an exciting place to learn.

World-Wide Opportunities on Organic Farms (WWOOF)-USA

P.O. Box 510
Felton, CA 95018
(831) 425- FARM
E-mail: info@wwoofusa.org
Web site: www.wwoofusa.org

Project Type: Agriculture; Construction; Natural Conservation (Land)

Mission Statement Excerpt: "WWOOF-USA is part of a world-wide effort to link volunteers with organic farmers, promote an educational exchange, and build a global community conscious of ecological farming practices."

Year Founded: 2001

Number of Volunteers Last Year: Approximately 1,500

Funding Sources: None; self-funded

The Work They Do: WWOOF-USA provides a network of organic farms willing to host volunteers who wish to learn about sustainable agriculture through hands-on experience on the farms. Volunteers may help in the farms or gardens by planting, weeding, harvesting, and providing animal care. Other opportunities on farms may include tending medicinal plants, construction, green and alternative building, permaculture, and solar energy projects. WWOOF-USA does not provide actual placements, but rather a directory of potential host farms that volunteers can contact directly.

Project Location: WWOOF-USA lists more than 400 host farms in 38 U.S. states, including Alaska, Hawaii, and the U.S. Virgin Islands. Accommodations vary by host farm.

Time Line: Volunteers are accepted throughout the year. The length of the volunteer experience is directly negotiated between the volunteer and the host farm. Some host farms request that volunteers make multi-month commitments, while others accept weekend volunteers. Most participants volunteer for four to six hours per day.

Cost: The membership fee to join WWOOF-USA is $20 for one person or $30 for two people who plan to travel together. Volunteers receive free room and board from their hosts, but they are responsible for their own travel to the farms.

Getting Started: Prospective volunteers should join WWOOF-USA and obtain the host farm directory. Volunteers can join either through the organization's Web site or by downloading, completing, and mailing in an application with a check. Any orientation or training is left up to the individual host farm.

Needed Skills and Specific Populations: Individual volunteers must be at least 18 years old. Some host farms will accept volunteers under that age, as long as they are volunteering with a parent. Senior volunteers are welcomed. Some host farms may be able to accommodate volunteers with disabilities. In general, no previous experience or skills are needed, though some individual host farms may have their own requirements.

Wyoming Dinosaur Center (WDC)

110 Carter Ranch Road
P.O. Box 868
Thermopolis, WY 82443
(800) 455-DINO or (307) 864-2997; Fax: (307) 864-5762
E-mail: wdinoc@wyodino.org
Web site: www.wyodino.org

Project Type: Archaeology; Museum; Scientific Research
Year Founded: 1993
The Work They Do: WDC offers Dig-for-a-Day programs, which allow volunteers to help discover, collect, and document Jurassic Period dinosaur fossils. Excavation work at the WDC's two main quarries has yielded well-preserved bones of Camarasaurus and Diplodocus dinosaurs. All activities assist in current scientific research projects, which provide valuable information concerning the environment that existed in the area more than 140 million years ago.
Project Location: The dig sites are located 15 minutes from the WDC on Warm Springs Ranch at the northern end of Wind River Canyon in Wyoming.
Time Line: As the project name indicates, this is a one-day volunteer program. When the weather allows, WDC runs the Dig-for-a-Day program from late spring through early fall, Monday through Friday. The day begins at 8:00 A.M., ends by 5:00 P.M., and includes a 30-minute lunch break. If needed, volunteers return to the WDC on one of the hourly tour buses earlier than 5:00 P.M.
Cost: The program fee for Dig-for-a-Day volunteers is $125 per person or $300 per three-member family, which must include at least one child. WDC requires a $25 deposit, which is refunded if the dig is canceled because of inclement weather. Volunteers who cancel a reservation at least 30 days before the project date will receive a full refund. The program fee includes lunch, but volunteers are responsible for all other expenses, including travel, accommodations, and other meals.

Getting Started: Prospective volunteers must call the WDC at the number listed above to register in advance. Volunteers undergo a one-hour orientation at the start of the day that discusses the geology and paleontology of the work site as well as digging and data-collection procedures.

Needed Skills and Specific Populations: Individual volunteers must be at least 18 years old, but children younger than that age may volunteer if accompanied by an adult. Because the work can be physically challenging and strenuous, and because fossil collection is a serious scientific endeavor requiring care and precision, families should carefully consider whether their children are well suited for this activity. The WDC also offers a Kid's Dig program on select days throughout the summer. Volunteers who successfully master the basic skills of fieldwork may join the WDC in more delicate and critical work, and they are not charged for such participation. Dig-for-a-Day programs are limited to six volunteers per day.

YMCA Go Global

5 West 63rd Street, 2nd Floor
New York, NY 10023
(888) 477-9622 or (212) 727-8800, ext. 4303
E-mail: jblock@ymcanyc.org
Web site: www.ymcagoglobal.org

Project Type: Community Development; Youth

Mission Statement Excerpt: "The YMCA Go Global program sends young adults from various parts of the United States to overseas YMCAs and other educational and human service organizations, where they work in a wide variety of cultural and community services."

The Work They Do: YMCA Go Global volunteers partner with YMCAs in other countries to assist those organizations in their work. Work done by volunteers may include teen leadership, health care, education, social work, community development, and many other fields. Specific examples of volunteer opportunities with YMCA Go Global include serving as camp counselors in Australia and the Bahamas, helping with social work and HIV/AIDS awareness projects in sub-Saharan Africa, and helping with public and cultural relations campaigns in Thailand.

Project Location: YMCA Go Global currently has volunteer programs in Australia, the Bahamas, China, Ecuador, Gambia, Ghana, Hong Kong, Italy, Malta, Peru, Scotland, South Korea, Thailand, and Trinidad. Applicants may provide YMCA Go Global a list of three preferred countries, but the organization's staff members make the final decision on volunteer placement. Housing varies by host country, but volunteers typically stay in cabins, apartments, with a host family, or in other similar accommodations.

Time Line: YMCA Go Global offers two- to twelve-month placements. Placements are available throughout the year.

Cost: YMCA Go Global charges a $500 application fee. Food, accommodations, and, in some countries, a small stipend are provided to the volunteer by their host YMCAs. Volunteers must provide their own international airfare.

Getting Started: Prospective volunteers can download an application from the YMCA Go Global Web site. Application deadlines are typically in the season before departure; for example, volunteers who wish to depart in the summer will have an application deadline in the spring. Volunteers may need to attend a pre-departure orientation in New York City. YMCA Go Global also offers an in-country briefing and orientation session upon arrival in the host country, and language lessons as necessary.

Needed Skills and Specific Populations: Volunteers must be at least 18 years old and residents of the United States or Canada. There is no language requirement for YMCA Go Global's placements, with the exception of volunteer sites in Latin America, which ask that volunteers have at least a moderate proficiency in Spanish.

Young Power in Social Action (YPSA)

House #F10(P), Road #13, Block #B
Chandgaon R/Area, Chittagong—4212
Bangladesh
+ 88-031-672857
E-mail: info@ypsa.org
Web site: www.ypsa.org

Project Type: Community Development; Developmental Disabilities; Economic Development; Education; Human Rights; Medical/Health; Rural Development; Social Justice; Women's Issues; Youth

Mission Statement Excerpt: "Young Power in Social Action (YPSA) exists to participate with the poor and vulnerable population with all commitment to bring about their own and society's sustainable development."

Year Founded: 1985

Number of Volunteers Last Year: 4 international volunteers and more than 300 Bangladeshi volunteers

Funding Sources: Government and private donors

The Work They Do: YPSA offers volunteer opportunities in HIV/AIDS prevention, water and sanitation, microlending, labor organizing and advocacy, urban development, information technology education, health and nutrition, and education. Specific examples of volunteer work include teaching English, computer training for disadvantaged youth, and Web site editing.

Project Location: Volunteers work in Bangladesh in the areas of Sitakund and Mirsarai Upazilla and in the city of Chittagong. Volunteers in rural areas should not expect to have electricity or access to phones or the Internet. Volunteers may stay in a guesthouse or in an apartment.

Time Line: Volunteers are welcomed throughout the year for a minimum of three months and a maximum of two years.

Cost: Volunteers pay a program fee of $250 per month, which covers accommodations, local transportation, and food.

Getting Started: Prospective volunteers should send an e-mail, with a resume attached, detailing the type of work the volunteer wishes to do and the time line for the proposed project. YPSA provides an orientation that includes language training, a tour of YPSA's projects, sightseeing, and an introduction to Bangladeshi culture.

Needed Skills and Specific Populations: Volunteers must be at least 18 years old; YPSA welcomes senior volunteers, though the average YPSA volunteer is 25 years old. Persons with disabilities may be able to volunteer with YPSA, depending on the type of disabilities involved and the kind of work each volunteer wishes to undertake.

Youth International

232 Wright Avenue
Toronto, Ontario M6R 1L3
Canada
(416) 538-0152; Fax: (416) 538-7189
E-mail: info@youthinternational.org
Web site: www.youthinternational.org

Project Type: Agriculture; Community Development; Construction; Medical/Health; Natural Conservation (Land); Orphans; Rural Development; Trail Building/Maintenance; Women's Issues

Mission Statement Excerpt: "Youth International opens the doors for young people to actively explore and discover a broader perspective on the world while developing a deeper understanding of who they are and what their place is within that world."

Year Founded: 1997

Number of Volunteers Last Year: 95

Funding Sources: Mostly self-funded, with a few private donors

The Work They Do: Youth International sponsors projects that include, for the most part, physically challenging manual labor, though some teaching positions are also available. Specific examples of Youth International's projects include renovating orphanages and schools, teaching English, carrying out conservation projects in the rainforest, and helping the poor in Mother Teresa's clinics.

Project Location: Youth International has an Asia program with projects located in Thailand, India, and Vietnam, as well as a South America program with projects located in Bolivia, Peru, and Ecuador. About half of the accommodations are in home stays, with the rest in hostels.

Time Line: Youth International places volunteers from September through December and February through May. Volunteer programs last fifteen weeks.

Cost: Youth International's program fee is $7,500, which covers virtually all of the volunteer's costs, including all flights, visas, all overland transportation, and food and accommodations.

Getting Started: Applications for Youth International's programs are available on its Web site. Orientation begins in the United States and is completed in-country, and it lasts three to five days.

Needed Skills and Specific Populations: Volunteers must have a high school diploma. Senior volunteers can work with Youth International, but the organization's efforts are focused on people aged 18–25. Volunteers with disabilities are welcomed, with the caveat that some program areas cannot adequately accommodate all disabilities.

Introduction to Long-Term Volunteer Opportunities

Ready to go to (or at least think about) the next level?

So now you've tried a volunteer vacation, or at least you've busied yourself for many hours dreaming about one. You've chosen where in the world you want to go and what skills you want to use, squirreled away some funds, and had a wonderful adventure. A short adventure, but a wonderful adventure nonetheless.

And you want more.

That's not surprising. Many, many people who go on a volunteer vacation say that it was the single best thing that they've done, that it changed how they viewed themselves and the world, and that they made friends and discovered new passions and talents. How could you not want more?

These reactions, which we have heard time and time again from volunteers, form the basis for the following short section on long-term volunteer opportunities. Note that we don't use the term "vacation" here, and that's on purpose. You can expect that these organizations will request at least a year of your time if not longer. This is especially true of the overseas volunteer agencies, which usually ask for at least two years. Though we know of two couples that joined the Peace Corps within weeks of getting married and jokingly referred to their time abroad as "our two-year honeymoon," the experiences you'll have with these organizations are not just a break from your daily life: they become your daily life.

Of course, if you have done a volunteer vacation, you've also found out that it can be incredibly challenging, and that challenge is even more present in long-term volunteer experiences. Not being fluent in the local language or culture, being far from family and friends, tasting different foods, and facing the problems that others live with on a daily basis in the United States and around the world can be incredibly difficult. Everyone knows the Peace Corps' slogan, "It's the Toughest Job You'll Ever Love." It is a great slogan, and it could be applied to almost any long-term volunteer organization. But there is a temptation, as we think about these programs, to focus on, "I'm going to love my job," and forget that "this will be the toughest job I'll ever have."

So why do it, then? Why leave the comfort of your home, your family, the safety of all that you know and love, for a volunteer assignment across the country or on another continent, for what will seem like a very long amount of time?

Because it is worth it. Almost serendipitously, it is worth it. Surveys of volunteers who complete full-time, long-term volunteer experiences show that the vast majority—over 90 percent—are glad they did it and would do so again. Here are some of the main reasons that you can expect to feel the same way after your experience:

You'll get a much more in-depth knowledge of the problems people face around the world, and have a much better opportunity to help people solve their problems. Their problems become your problems, and you will become a committed activist for change both during the volunteer experience and afterward.

You'll have the opportunity to make great friends who will remain with you for the rest of your life.

You'll learn skills that will benefit you for many, many years to come. As one employer told us, "I love to hire returned overseas volunteers. They're problem solvers, dedicated, flexible, often bilingual, can work independently, and have demonstrated that they really care about the world. Who wouldn't want to hire a person like that?"

You are needed. AmeriCorps has positions that go unfilled every year. Peace Corps can't find nearly enough French speakers to send to West Africa. You have real skills, and you can make a tangible difference in the lives of others.

And in case you hadn't guessed by now, the people you help will make a difference in your life, too. We promise you this: a long-term volunteer experience will change who you are as a person. It can't help but do so. How could you uproot yourself and go somewhere completely new, take on a new job helping others, learn a new language or culture, and come back the same person? You will see the world and yourself in a different light, have different priorities, and have new doors open for you.

We know. We served as rural community development volunteers in the Peace Corps for two years in the village of Ligolio, in central Suriname. (Go ahead, look it up on a map—we didn't know where it was, either. Here's a hint: start with South America.) Anne pursued her graduate degree, a Master's in Public Health, based on her experiences in Ligolio. One of our daughters is named after the old woman who lived across the mango tree from us. And our work in the Peace Corps led to our current jobs, which led Doug to write a magazine article, which led directly to being hired to write the book you're holding in your hands.

We should mention one other benefit that long-term volunteering has over volunteer vacations: by and large, you don't have to pay for the experience. There are other people, including the government, faith-based organizations, and private donors, who think that you going off and doing this is such a great idea that they'll pay for you to do it. You're not going to make any money by being a long-term volunteer, but it probably won't cost you any money, either.

To be clear, we don't want to knock volunteer vacations—we've written this book about them, and we believe in them as firmly as a person can. But the difference between a volunteer vacation and a long-term volunteer experience is similar to the difference between going to London for a week and studying there for a full semester. Both are wonderful things to do, but a semester's worth of study is going to be a much more in-depth experience, and you come home with a very different perspective on the place.

A book could (and should) be written on the organizations that offer fully funded, long-term volunteer opportunities, but we have chosen here to just whet your appetite with descriptions of five of these organizations. We know volunteers who have participated in all of them, and we feel strongly that these organizations offer phenomenal opportunities and take good care of their volunteers. Two are international (Peace Corps and Voluntary Service Overseas); two are domestic (AmeriCorps and Teach for America), and one offers both domestic and international placements (Jesuit Volunteer Corps). As for primary funding sources, some of these programs receive money from the government (Peace Corps and AmeriCorps), one from faith-based groups (Jesuit Volunteer Corps), and two from private donors (Teach for America and Voluntary Service Overseas).

We've kept the same formatting for these organizations that was used for the volunteer vacation organizations, since by this point in the book you've probably become used to it.

We've never met someone who regretted his or her decision to take a year or two and dedicate themselves to full-time volunteer work. Who could take on a challenge like this, and say at the end, "No, that wasn't worth it. I wish I hadn't met those people, learned those skills, helped out, and grown in new and different ways that I never could have dreamed of."

Note that we didn't say "take a year or two *off*" in the last paragraph. It's not time off. It's not a long detour from your pre-programmed road of life that eventually just returns you to the same spot in the road. After this experience, you'll be different.

And it will be worth it.

Good luck. And send us a postcard.

Doug Cutchins and Anne Geissinger

AmeriCorps

1201 New York Avenue, NW
Washington, DC 20525
(202) 606-5000; TTY (202) 565-2799
E-mail: questions@americorps.org
Web site: www.americorps.org

Project Type: Community Development; Construction; Developmental Disabilities; Historic Preservation; Medical/Health; Natural Conservation (Land); Natural Conservation (Sea); Rural Development; Trail Building/Maintenance; Women's Issues; Youth

Mission Statement Excerpt: "To provide opportunities for Americans of all ages and backgrounds to engage in service that addresses the nation's educational, public safety, environmental, and other human needs to achieve direct and demonstrable results and to encourage all Americans to engage in such service."

Year Founded: 1993

Number of Volunteers Last Year: 40,000

Funding Sources: AmeriCorps is funded by the federal government and has an annual budget of more than $400 million.

The Work They Do: AmeriCorps is a national network of hundreds of programs throughout the United States. AmeriCorps comprises three very different programs:

AmeriCorps*VISTA (Volunteers in Service to America) volunteers work to bring individuals and communities out of poverty. VISTA volunteers serve full-time for a year in nonprofits, public agencies, and faith-based groups throughout the country, working to fight illiteracy, improve health services, create businesses, increase housing opportunities, or bridge the digital divide.

AmeriCorps*NCCC (National Civilian Community Corps) volunteers commit to a ten-month, full-time residential program, serving in teams of 10 to 15 members. NCCC volunteers work on projects in the areas of public safety, public health, and disaster relief. Teams are based at one of five campuses across the country but are sent to work on short-term projects in neighboring states.

The third group of programs comes under the general heading of AmeriCorps. These programs are found in local and national organizations throughout the United States such as the American Red Cross, Habitat for Humanity, Boys and Girls Clubs, and local community centers and places of worship.

Project Location: AmeriCorps partners with 1,000 local and national groups across the United States to offer 50,000 positions in many cities and towns. Volunteers are usually responsible for locating their own housing, with the exception of NCCC volunteers, who live as a group, often on decommissioned military bases.

Timeline: AmeriCorps volunteers typically commit to ten months to one year of service. Most assignments are full-time, but there are some part-time service opportunities available.

Cost: For all AmeriCorps programs, members receive a modest living allowance, and some programs provide housing. Most members find the living allowance to be adequate to cover their needs, though it is not generous. AmeriCorps volunteers may also receive an education award, which can be used to pay education costs at qualified institutions of higher education or training, or to repay qualified student loans. The award currently is $4,725 for a year of full-time service, with correspondingly lesser awards for part-time and reduced part-time service.

Getting Started: Prospective volunteers can complete an application on the AmeriCorps Web site. All volunteers receive training at the beginning of their service and project-specific training during their service.

Needed Skills and Specific Populations: Volunteers must be U.S. citizens or legal permanent resident aliens of the United States, and at least 17 years old (some require volunteers to be 18). There is no maximum age limit for most positions. Some programs have specific skill requests in certain areas, and others look for a bachelor's degree or a few years of related volunteer or work experience.

Jesuit Volunteer Corps (JVC)

801 St. Paul Street
Baltimore, MD 21202-2345
(410) 244-1744
E-mail:
jvceast@jesuitvolunteers.org (for domestic programs);
jvi@jesuitvolunteers.org (for international programs)
Web site: www.jesuitvolunteers.org

Project Type: Community Development; Developmental Disabilities; Economic Development; Education; Human Rights; Legal; Medical/Health; Political Action; Social Justice; Women's Issues; Youth

Mission Statement Excerpt: "The Jesuit Volunteer Corps (JVC) offers women and men an opportunity to work full-time for justice and peace."

Year Founded: 1956

Number of Volunteers Last Year: 350 domestic and 60 international

Funding Sources: Most of JVC's funding comes from individuals, foundations, and the society of Jesus.

The Work They Do: JVC is built on four pillars: social justice, simple lifestyles, community, and spirituality. JVC volunteers live in group households with other JVC volunteers, where they put these ideals into action. During the day, volunteers go to full-time work positions. Hundreds of grassroots organizations across the country count on JVC volunteers to provide essential services to low-income people and those who live on the fringes of our society. Volunteers serve the homeless, the unemployed, refugees, people with HIV/AIDS, the elderly, street youth, abused women and children, the mentally ill, and the developmentally disabled. JVC has become the largest Catholic lay volunteer program in the country. Examples of JVC work placements include a case manager at a homeless shelter in Hartford,

Connecticut; a CPR and first aid instructor in Alaska; a Learning Center counselor in San Francisco; and an English teacher in Nepal.

Project Location: JVC has houses throughout the United States, and volunteers apply to serve in a specific region of the country. International placements are available in Belize, Bolivia, Nicaragua, Peru, Chile, South Africa, Tanzania, Nepal, Micronesia, and the Marshall Islands.

Timeline: Domestic JVC volunteers begin in the first week of August and serve for one year. International JVC volunteers begin in July and serve for two years. Training and orientation classes are offered at the beginning of volunteer service.

Cost: Domestic volunteers pay their way to the orientation site in the region where they will serve. JVC provides travel from the orientation site to the city in which the volunteer will work, transportation to and from retreats during the year, and transportation home at the end of the year. Placement sites pay for the volunteer's housing, utilities, a food stipend, transportation to and from work (in the form of providing the volunteer a bus pass or a bicycle, for the most part), and medical insurance. Volunteers receive a small personal stipend—about $75 a month—to spend on whatever they wish. International volunteers receive transportation to orientation and to the country of placement. International volunteers are asked to undertake fund-raising efforts before they leave, but acceptance into the program is in no way conditional on this fund-raising.

Getting Started: Prospective volunteers can download an application from JVC's Web site or apply online. The deadline for international applications is February 1. Domestic applications are accepted on a rolling basis, with priority given to those received before March 1.

Needed Skills and Specific Populations: Some job placements require specific credentials or licenses, but most JVC jobs can be done by people who have a general educational background and a willingness to learn new skills. Most of JVC's volunteers are recent college graduates.

Peace Corps

1111 20th Street NW
Washington, DC 20526
(800) 424-8580
E-mail: volunteer@peacecorps.gov
Web site: www.peacecorps.gov

Project Type: Agriculture; Community Development; Construction; Economic Development; Education; Medical/Health; Natural Conservation (Land); Natural Conservation (Sea); Professional/Technical Assistance; Rural Development; Women's Issues; Youth

Mission Statement Excerpt: "Three simple goals comprise the Peace Corps' mission: helping the people of interested countries in meeting their needs for trained men and women; helping promote a better understanding of Americans on the part of the peoples served; helping promote a better understanding of other peoples on the part of all Americans."

Year Founded: 1961

Number of Volunteers Last Year: Approximately 7,700 at any given time

Funding Sources: Peace Corps is an independent agency of the United States government and has a budget of more than $300 million.

The Work They Do: Peace Corps volunteers offer expertise and training to people in economically developing nations around the world. The range of opportunities available in the Peace Corps is vast, from traditional international volunteer positions in teaching, health, and agriculture to opportunities for addressing more modern challenges such as HIV/AIDS, information technology, and business development in urban areas. All volunteers work in one of six sectors: education, youth outreach, and community development; business development; environment; agriculture; health and HIV/AIDS; and information technology. Specific examples of volunteer work include training high school teachers; working in an urban planning office; conducting community-based conservation programs such as sustainable use of forest or marine resources, apiculture, and honey production; teaching basic nutrition courses; and implementing computer networks for government offices.

Project Location: Peace Corps volunteers work in more than 70 countries around the world. While applicants can state a preference for placement in a specific region of the world, Peace Corps makes the final decisions regarding what work the volunteer will do and where the volunteer will be placed. As the populations of economically developing countries have shifted to urban areas in the last few decades, so too have more and more Peace Corps volunteers been placed in cities. Accommodations for volunteers vary greatly, from apartments in cities to small huts in very rural areas.

Timeline: After they have completed their eight to twelve weeks of training, Peace Corps volunteers serve for two years. Applications are processed on a rolling basis, and there are no deadlines. Applicants are well advised to apply nine to twelve months before the desired departure date.

Cost: There is no program fee to be a Peace Corps volunteer, and Peace Corps is among the most generous agencies of its type. All of the volunteer's expenses, including international airfare, medical, and dental care, are paid. Volunteers receive a living allowance to pay for accommodations and food, which allows them to live at the same standard as the local people in their community. Volunteers also receive a small vacation stipend and just over $6,000 in a readjustment allowance for completing the 27 months of service. Volunteers with Perkins loans are eligible for a deduction of 15 percent of their outstanding balance for each year of Peace Corps service.

Getting Started: Prospective volunteers should complete an online application. The application itself is quite extensive and includes two essays. Applicants must also complete a one-hour interview with a recruiter and pass stringent medical and legal checks before being cleared to volunteer.

Needed Skills and Specific Populations: Peace Corps volunteers must be at least 18 years old. There is no maximum age for volunteers, and 6 percent of Peace Corps volunteers are more than 50 years old; currently, the oldest volunteer is 82. While a college degree is not required for all positions, 96 percent of Peace Corps volunteers have graduated from a four-year institution. Each volunteer position has both educational and experiential qualifications that an applicant must meet; some positions require that volunteers have taken one or two years of college-level French or Spanish. Only married applicants will be considered for placement together. Volunteers with disabilities should not be discouraged from applying to the Peace Corps.

Snapshots from Paraguay

❖ By Sarah Gossett ❖

Peace Corps

The following are excerpts from the volunteer's e-mails to family and friends during her first three months in Peace Corps Paraguay.

9/26/2004

Hello everyone! Well, as of 5:30 A.M. tomorrow, I'm off to Miami for two days of getting shots and visas, and then I head to Paraguay.

10/2/2004

E-mail seems to be working now. I must hurry because there are 35 volunteers waiting for three very slow computers. My host family is wonderful. I have three sisters ages 15, 17, and 19, and a 22-year-old brother. My mother is very loving and is always giving me hugs, and my dad makes jokes I cannot understand. My Spanish has taken a serious beating. I bathe from a bucket and use an outhouse. We do not have running water but get it from trash cans filled with water, but we do have electricity. I am sorry about the choppy writing. This computer does not have normal punctuation and I cannot find apostrophes or other such indicators of normal English grammar. I think my favorite possession at this time is my mosquito net. The bugs here are very big. The cat eats them for dinner. All throughout the day and night I hear a pounce and then happy crunching.

10/19/2004

Like any small town, everyone knows what everyone else is doing, and it's even worse for Peace Corps volunteers, since we are new. I got the runs (*chivivi*) one day and my dad made me some herbal tea, which really helped, but even later on in the day people I had never met before said, "I heard you had *chivivi* and your dad made you some tea with such and such herbs. Feel better now?" And another trainee had quite the opposite problem, and she had people saying, "Have you pooped yet? Have you pooped yet?" So my pride about bodily functions, if I ever had any in the first place, has officially left the campo.

More about my host family—I think I'm closest with my youngest sister Karina (15), because I can understand her the best. That's probably because she likes talking about cute boys, and that's pretty much at my level in terms of language. So she tells me all of her secrets and I help her learn English phrases so that she can impress her boyfriend. She also tells me how to dress for certain things, because I never know. Soccer games, unless you are playing, are huge social events, so you don't wear a grubby T-shirt. I also tried to get away with not shaving, but she called me out on that, saying, "Yeah, you really need to shave." "Why? It's annoying." "Because it is ugly and people will stare at you." Then Javier walked by and said that I looked like a goat. So I shaved. Once again, pride . . . gone.

Random update on my life: my backyard has banana, papaya, and lime trees, and we also have some grapevines but they won't be ripe for another month or so. Every day we make fresh-squeezed juice to drink and it is SO good.

10/31/2004

Although my Spanish and Guarani are improving, I still have the self-deprecating sense to share one of the winners I have said throughout my first month here: I referred to the compost pile as the "lawyer" for a week until I figured out I was using the wrong word. Put the orange peels in the lawyer. The lawyer needs to be turned over, etc. My family loved that one.

But the worst one by far was the fact that until three days ago, I had been saying things are "mono." It means monkey, but in Mexican Spanish it also is "cute." So every time I thought I was telling one of my sisters she was "so cute," I was really saying, "How monkey! You are so monkey!" Let's just say I said this a lot, and no one ever told me. One night I was sitting up with my mom talking and I asked her that if I ever did anything that wasn't correct in Paraguayan culture that she would tell me. She said of course she would. Then I looked down at the cat, which was cradled in my arms, and I said, "You are such a monkey cat!" AND SHE STILL DIDN'T SAY ANYTHING!

12/6/2004

Well, I just got back from visiting the village I will be placed in, Jerovia. It has made me realize that there are even more levels of "poor" than I realized. Although my host family in Pindoty is one of the poorest compared to the other host families, they seem very well off compared to my new community. Also, only three people speak some Spanish in the whole community, which means I'm going to have to learn Guarani even more quickly if I'm to get anything done. One thing that is the same is that all the people are very nice. I'm going to be living with an old toothless woman who laughs a lot because she is the only one with an extra room for me.

Other random stories from my new site:

- There is a chicken at my house that sat on the wrong eggs and now has ducklings for babies. After it rained the ducklings were happy as can be, splashing around in the puddles, and as far as chicken facial expressions go, it looked very confused.
- I met with my women's group. They specifically requested a female volunteer to work with them. We made homemade conditioner that smelled like apples.

12/26/04

I'm at my site, in my new village. I've been helping out in the fields . . . thinning sesame, harvesting mandioca, making mandioca flour, picking peanuts, etc.

I'm picking up Guarani a little faster now, since I'm surrounded by it daily. But when I don't understand something, I just smile and say one of my key phrases. "I am happy in Paraguay." "How old are you?" "I like cats." "I know how to use a hoe." Sometimes I wonder what they think I actually know, though. Yesterday one of my brothers asked me if I knew how to peel a banana.

Random facts time: my family eats a lot of cow hooves (I just eat the beans). It is really freaking hot. I am attacked daily by small children wanting hugs and kisses. I like going next door and hanging out with an old couple, not talking, just sitting in comfortable silence in the shade.

I wonder what the next 20 months of Peace Corps service will bring?

Love, Sarah

Teach For America (TFA)

315 West 36th Street
New York, NY 10018
(800) 832-1230; Fax (212) 279-2081
E-mail: admissions@teachforamerica.org
Web site: www.teachforamerica.org

Project Type: Community Development; Education; Rural
Development; Social Justice; Youth

Mission Statement Excerpt: "One day, all children in this
nation will have the opportunity to attain an excellent
education."

Year Founded: 1990

Number of Volunteers Last Year: Approximately 3,000

Funding Sources: TFA receives support from public and private
donors, including individuals, foundations, businesses, and
local, state, and federal governments.

The Work They Do: TFA corps members commit to teaching
for two years in one of the low-income rural or urban communities that the organization serves throughout the
United States. TFA expects that corps members will remain
lifelong advocates for educational equality long after their
teaching experience.

Project Location: Corps members teach in one of (as of this
writing) 26 regional sites, which tend to be either very
urban or very rural. Sites currently include Atlanta, Baltimore, the Bay Area (California), Charlotte, Chicago, eastern North Carolina, greater New Orleans, Houston, Las
Vegas, Los Angeles, Miami and Dade County, the Missis-
sippi Delta, New Jersey, Newark, New Mexico, New York
City, Philadelphia, Phoenix, the Rio Grande Valley, South
Dakota, south Louisiana, St. Louis, and Washington, DC.
(Please note that TFA expands this list regularly.) Applicants state their preferences for regions, and 99 percent of
corps members end up in a region for which they indicated
a preference. Corps members find their own housing, often
with other corps members, but they are given advice on

doing so by TFA. Housing during the summer training is in dormitories.

Timeline: Typically, TFA has two deadlines for applications each year, in October and February, with final notification regarding acceptance in December or April. Regardless of application deadline, all new corps members begin training in the summer and are in the classroom at the start of the school year.

Cost: TFA corps members are hired as regular, first-year teachers by their host school districts and are paid the same salary as other first-year teachers. Because of the wide range of locations and salaries, TFA corps members earn somewhere between $22,000 and $41,000 annually, with the higher salaries in the most expensive cities. TFA corps members are also eligible for need-based transitional grants and no-interest loans to help bridge the gap between the end of college and the beginning of teaching, or for moving expenses. TFA is also a member of AmeriCorps, so corps members can receive forbearance on any college loans and the AmeriCorps $4,725 education award for each of the two years of service.

Getting Started: TFA's written application process is done entirely online through its Web site. The most promising applicants are invited for a day-long interview, which includes teaching a sample lesson and participating in a group interview, an individual interview, and written exercises. Admission to TFA is highly selective; fewer than one in five applicants are given the opportunity to become a corps member. All accepted corps members complete a very intensive, five-week training institute the summer before they begin teaching, as well as a regional orientation, and they have ongoing support throughout the TFA experience.

Needed Skills and Specific Populations: TFA applicants do not need to have a background in education or a teaching certificate. Instead, TFA seeks out people who have demonstrated leadership, can motivate others, possess strong critical thinking and organizational skills, take personal

responsibility, have an understanding of cultural differences, and are deeply committed to improving underserved
communities. Applicants must have or be in the process of
completing an undergraduate degree with a minimum GPA
of 2.5; the average corps member's GPA is 3.5, and 93
percent of corps members held a leadership role on their
campus. TFA also specifically recruits people of color,
math and science majors, and Spanish speakers. Applicants
must be U.S. citizens. Though there is no age limit to join
TFA, corps members are overwhelmingly recent college
graduates.

Voluntary Service Overseas (VSO)

806-151 Slater Street
Ottawa, ON K1P 5H3
Canada
(888) 876-2911 or (613) 234-1364; Fax (613) 234-1444
E-mail: inquiry@vsocan.org
Web site: www.vsocan.org

Project Type: Administration; Economic Development; Education; Medical/Health

Mission Statement Excerpt: "Voluntary Service Overseas (VSO) is an international development agency that works through volunteers. We promote volunteering as a way to fight global poverty by supporting people to share their skills, creativity, and learning with people and communities around the world."

Year Founded: 1958

Number of Volunteers Last Year: 1,500

Funding Sources: Private donors and organizations

The Work They Do: VSO recruits volunteers to work full-time with overseas partner organizations. VSO's work is focused on six development goal areas: education, HIV/AIDS, disability, health and social well being, secure livelihoods, and participation and governance. In general, volunteers can work as hands-on service providers; work alongside colleagues to share skills; strengthen organizations' systems, planning, and management; or develop organizations' abilities to network and influence policy at the local, national, and international level. VSO's partners include a wide range of organizations, from government ministries to community-level groups, and from small enterprises to local, national, and international nonprofit agencies. Specific examples of volunteer work through VSO include working as a radiology assistant in Tanzania, working as an advocacy and research advisor in Rwanda, and training teachers in Kenya.

Project Location: VSO places volunteers in more than 30 countries throughout Africa, Asia, Eastern Europe, the Caribbean, and the Pacific; everywhere from Bangladesh to Zambia. VSO places volunteers based on their skill sets, so volunteers must be flexible regarding placement location. Types of accommodations vary from mud-floored rooms to urban apartments, but volunteers have their own bedrooms, as well as basic furnishings such as a bed and mattress, storage space, a table and chairs, and cooking facilities.

Timeline: Most of VSO's opportunities are for two-year stints. Applications are accepted throughout the year, and applicants should plan on at least a four-month placement time span between application and departure.

Cost: VSO covers most costs of volunteering, including travel for pre-departure training courses; training course fees, food, and accommodations; the costs of required medical examinations and immunizations; roundtrip airfare to the volunteer's country of service; a pre-departure grant of up to $1,000 for the purchase of supplies and equipment; health insurance; an in-service grant and end-of-service grant; support for ongoing language training; and quarterly payments. Volunteers are encouraged to assist in fund-raising, with a suggested goal of $2,000.

Getting Started: Prospective volunteers can complete an application online. Qualified applicants are invited to an assessment day in Ottawa or Vancouver, for which VSO will provide funding for travel expenses. Applicants are told whether or not they have been accepted into VSO within 10 days of the assessment. In general, VSO seeks volunteers who are adaptable, sensitive to the needs of others, and interested in immersing themselves in a culture that may be very different from what they are used to. VSO also looks for a certain degree of self-assurance, natural problem-solving abilities, and an aptitude for teamwork.

Needed Skills and Specific Populations: Most VSO positions require a college degree plus at least two years of professional experience. VSO offers pre-departure and in-country training, including a three-day "Preparing for Change" course. Language training and a cultural orientation are provided when volunteers and interns arrive in the country of their placement. VSO welcomes applications from people with disabilities and seeks to enable these volunteers to fully participate in VSO's volunteer assessment process.

Index by Project Cost

$2,000– $2,999

$3,000 or More

Index by Project Length

Less than One Week

One Week

Three or Four Weeks

One or Two Months

Six or More Months

Index by Project Location

Royal Tyrrell Museum, 302
Sierra Club Outings, 306
Swiss Whale Society, 315
World Challenge Expeditions (WCE), 353
World Horizons, 357

Caribbean

Ambassadors for Children (AFC), 11
American Jewish World Service (AJWS), 19
Amigos de las Americas, 24
Amizade, 27
Asociacion ANAI, 37
Bimini Biological Field Station, 52
Caribbean Conservation Corporation (CCC), 69
Caribbean Volunteer Expeditions (CVE), 72
Catholic Medical Mission Board (CMMB), 79
Explorations in Travel (ET), 137
Global Routes, 171
Global Volunteer Network (GVN), 175
Global Volunteers (GV), 178
Global Works, 181
Globe Aware, 183
Greenforce, 188
Health Volunteers Overseas (HVO), 193
i-to-i, 213
Jesuit Volunteer Corps (JVC), 381
Medex International (MEI), 232
Mercy Ships, 240
Peacework, 279
Sierra Club Outings, 306
Transformational Journeys, 323
Voluntary Service Overseas (VSO), 393
World Horizons, 355
YMCA Go Global, 369

Central America

ACDI/VOCA, 1
Alliance Abroad (AA), 7
Ambassadors for Children (AFC), 11
American Jewish World Service (AJWS), 19
AmeriSpan, 21
Amigos de las Americas, 24
Amizade, 27
Caribbean Conservation Corporation (CCC), 69
Catholic Medical Mission Board (CMMB), 79
Cross-Cultural Solutions (CCS), 109
El Porvenir, 135
Explorations in Travel (ET), 137
Foundation for Sustainable Development (FSD), 141
Frontier, 154
Global Citizens Network (GCN), 161
Global Crossroad, 166
Global Routes, 171
Global Volunteers (GV), 178
Global Works, 181
Globe Aware, 183
Health Volunteers Overseas (HVO), 193
International Volunteer Program (IVP), 206
i-to-i, 213
Jesuit Volunteer Corps (JVC), 381
Madre, 228
Mercy Ships, 240
Mobility International USA (MIUSA), 243
Peacework, 279
Programa Restauracion de Tortugas Marinas (PRETOMA), 283
ProWorld Service Corps (PWSC), 294
Raleigh International, 296
Transformational Journeys, 323
Wildlands Studies, 349

Wyoming Dinosaur Center (WDC), 367

Worldwide

Index by Project Season

Fall (September–November)

Year-Round

Index by Project Type

Administration

Alliance Abroad (AA), 7
AmeriSpan, 21
Amizade, 27
AVIVA, 43
Catalina Island Conservancy, 76
Cheyenne River Youth Project, 83
Farm Sanctuary, 139
Foundation for Sustainable
    Development (FSD), 141
Habitat for Humanity International's
    Global Village Work Teams, 191
Involvement Volunteers Association
    (IVA), 208
Iracambi Atlantic Rainforest
    Research Center, 211
Joint Assistance Center (JAC), 217
Madre, 228
Mercy Ships, 240
National Meditation Center for
    World Peace (NMCWP), 252
Voluntary Service Overseas (VSO),
    393
Wilderness Foundation, 347

Agriculture

ACDI/VOCA, 1
American Jewish World Service
    (AJWS), 19
Amizade, 27
Asociacion ANAI, 37
AVIVA, 43
Azafady, 46
Bangladesh Work Camps Association
    (BWCA), 48
Bike-Aid, 50

Citizens Network for Foreign Affairs
    (CNFA), 92
Cultural Restoration Tourism Project
    (CRTP), 116
Eco-Center Caput Insulae—Beli
    (ECCIB), 131
Farm Sanctuary, 139
Foundation for Sustainable
    Development (FSD), 141
Global Crossroad, 166
Global Eco-Spiritual Tours (GEST),
    169
Global Service Corps (GSC), 173
Global Volunteer Network (GVN),
    175
Global Works, 181
International Cultural Adventures
    (ICA), 199
International Executive Service
    Corps (IESC), 202
Iracambi Atlantic Rainforest
    Research Center, 211
Jatun Sacha, 215
Joint Assistance Center (JAC),
    217
Madre, 228
Mercy Ships, 240
Oikos, 264
Operation Crossroads Africa (OCA),
    265
Peace Corps, 383
Peace Villages Foundation, 274
Projects Abroad, 287
Students Partnership Worldwide
    (SPW), 310
Sunseed Desert Technology, 313
Visions in Action (VIA), 329

Construction

Developmental Disabilities

Economic Development

Education

Passport in Time (PIT), 269
Royal Tyrrell Museum, 302
Wyoming Dinosaur Center (WDC), 367

Natural Conservation (Land)

ACDI/VOCA, 1
African Conservation Experience (ACE), 3
African Conservation Trust (ACT), 5
Alliance Abroad (AA), 7
American Hiking Society (AHS), 15
AmeriCorps, 379
AmeriSpan, 21
Amizade, 27
Appalachian Trail Conservancy (ATC), 32
ARCHELON, The Sea Turtle Protection Society of Greece, 35
Asociacion ANAI, 37
Asociacion de Rescate de Fauna (ARFA), 39
Australian Tropical Research Foundation (ATRF), 41
AVIVA, 43
Azafady, 46
Bangladesh Work Camps Association (BWCA), 48
Bike-Aid, 50
Biosphere Expeditions, 54
Blue Ventures, 57
BTCV, 61
Caribbean Conservation Corporation (CCC), 69
Catalina Island Conservancy, 76
Cholsey and Wallingford Railway, 87
The Colorado Trail Foundation (CTF), 98
Conservation Volunteers Australia (CVA), 102
Coral Cay Conservation (CCC), 105

Cultural Restoration Tourism Project (CRTP), 116
Dolphin Research Center (DRC), 123
Earthwatch Institute, 125
Eco-Center Caput Insulae—Beli (ECCIB), 131
Ecovolunteer Program, 133
Explorations in Travel (ET), 137
Foundation for Sustainable Development (FSD), 141
Friends of the Cumbres and Toltec Scenic Railroad, 144
Friends of the Great Baikal Trail (FGBT), 146
Frontier, 154
Gibbon Conservation Center (GCC), 156
Global Crossroad, 166
Global Eco-Spiritual Tours (GEST), 169
Global Routes, 171
Global Volunteer Network (GVN), 175
Global Volunteers (GV), 178
Global Works, 181
Globe Aware, 183
GoXplore, 186
Greenforce, 188
International Cultural Adventures (ICA), 199
International Otter Survival Fund (IOSF), 204
Involvement Volunteers Association (IVA), 208
Iracambi Atlantic Rainforest Research Center, 211
i-to-i, 213
Jatun Sacha, 215
Joint Assistance Center (JAC), 217
Kokee Resource Conservation Program (KRCP), 221
Landmark Volunteers, 223
Munda Wanga Trust, 245

Natural Conservation (Sea)

University Research Expeditions
    Program (UREP), 327
Wildlands Studies, 349
World Horizons, 355

Orphans

Alliance Abroad (AA), 7
Ambassadors for Children (AFC), 11
American Jewish World Service
    (AJWS), 19
AmeriSpan, 21
Amizade, 27
AVIVA, 43
Bangladesh Work Camps Association
    (BWCA), 48
Cross-Cultural Solutions (CCS), 109
Cultural Destination Nepal (CDN),
    114
Foundation for Sustainable
    Development (FSD), 141
Global Crossroad, 166
Global Routes, 171
Global Service Corps (GSC), 173
Global Volunteer Network (GVN),
    175
Global Volunteers (GV), 178
Globe Aware, 183
GoXplore, 186
International Cultural Adventures
    (ICA), 199
Joint Assistance Center (JAC), 217
National Meditation Center for
    World Peace (NMCWP), 252
Peacework, 279
Projects Abroad, 287
Students Partnership Worldwide
    (SPW), 310
Volunteers for Peace (VFP), 342
World Challenge Expeditions (WCE),
    353
Youth International, 373

Political Action

Bike-Aid, 50

Christian Peacemaker Teams (CPT),
    88
Farm Sanctuary, 139
Jesuit Volunteer Corps (JVC), 383
Just Works, 219
Madre, 228

Professional/Technical Assistance

ACDI/VOCA, 1
American Jewish World Service
    (AJWS), 19
Citizens Network for Foreign Affairs
    (CNFA), 92
Foundation for Sustainable
    Development (FSD), 141
Global Service Corps (GSC), 173
Global Volunteers (GV), 178
Globe Aware, 183
Habitat for Humanity International's
    Global Village Work Teams, 191
Health Volunteers Overseas (HVO),
    193
International Cultural Adventures
    (ICA), 199
International Executive Service
    Corps (IESC), 202
Iracambi Atlantic Rainforest
    Research Center, 211
Madre, 228
Peace Corps, 383
Peace Villages Foundation, 274
Peacework, 279
Students Partnership Worldwide
    (SPW), 310
Taita Discovery Centre (TDC), 317
Transformational Journeys, 323

Rural Development

ACDI/VOCA, 1
American Jewish World Service
    (AJWS), 19
AmeriCorps, 379

Scientific Research

Social Justice